Institutionalizing East Asia

T0300290

Institutional activities have remarkably transformed East Asia, a region once known for the absence of regionalism and regime-building efforts. Yet the dynamics of this Asian institutionalization have remained an understudied area of research. This book offers one of the first scholarly attempts to clarify what constitutes institutionalization in East Asia and to systematically trace the origins, discern the features, and analyze the prospects of ongoing institutionalization processes in one of the world's most dynamic regions.

Institutionalizing East Asia comprises eight chapters, grouped thematically into three sections. Part I considers East and Southeast Asia as focal points of inter-state exchanges and traces the institutionalization of inter-state cooperation first among the Southeast Asian states and then among those of the wider East Asia. Part II examines the institutionalization of regional collaboration in four domains: economy, security, natural disaster relief, and ethnic conflict management. Part III discusses the institutionalization dynamics at the sub-regional and inter-regional levels.

The chapters in this book offer a useful source of reference for scholars and researchers specializing in East Asia, regional architecture, and institution-building in international relations. They will also be of interest to postgraduate and research students interested in ASEAN, the drivers and limits of international cooperation, as well as the role of regional multilateralism in the Asia-Pacific region.

Alice D. Ba is Associate Professor in the Department of Political Science and International Relations, University of Delaware, USA.

Cheng-Chwee Kuik is Associate Professor in the Strategic Studies and International Relations Program at the National University of Malaysia (UKM).

Sueo Sudo is Professor at the Department of Policy Studies, Nanzan University, Nagoya, Japan.

Politics in Asia

Institutionalizing East Asia

Mapping and reconfiguring
regional cooperation

Edited by
Alice D. Ba, Cheng-Chwee Kuik and
Sueo Sudo

Routledge
Taylor & Francis Group

LONDON AND NEW YORK

First published 2016 by Routledge

2 Park Square, Milton Park, Abingdon, Oxfordshire OX14 4RN

711 Third Avenue, New York, NY 10017

Routledge is an imprint of the Taylor & Francis Group, an informa business

First issued in paperback 2017

British Library Cataloguing in Publication Data
A catalogue record for this book is available from the British Library

Library of Congress Cataloging in Publication Data
Names: Ba, Alice D., editor. | Kuik, Cheng-Chwee, editor. | Sudâo, Sueo,
editor.
   Title: Institutionalizing East Asia : mapping and reconfiguring regional
cooperation / edited by Alice D. Ba, Cheng-Chwee Kuik and Sueo Sudo.
   Description: New York : Routledge, 2016. | Series: Politics in Asia |
Includes bibliographical references and index.
   Identifiers: LCCN 2015030615| ISBN 9781138892491 (hardback : alk.
paper) | ISBN 9781315709130 (e-book : alk. paper)
   Subjects: LCSH: Regionalism–Southeast Asia. | Institution building–
Southeast Asia. | Southeast Asia–Politics and government. | ASEAN.
   Classification: LCC JQ750.A38 R435 2016 | DDC 303.48/259–dc23
   LC record available at http://lccn.loc.gov/2015030615

ISBN: 978-1-138-89249-1 (hbk)
ISBN: 978-0-8153-6877-9 (pbk)

Typeset in Galliard
by Taylor & Francis Books

Contents

List of illustrations

Figures

Tables

Boxes

List of contributors

Alice D. Ba is Associate Professor of Political Science and International Relations at the University of Delaware. Her research focuses on the politics of regionalism in East Asia, especially ASEAN; Southeast Asia's relations with China, the United States, and Japan; and comparative questions of regime building and change. The author of *(Re)Negotiating East and Southeast Asia: Region, Regionalism, and the Association of Southeast Asian Nations* (Stanford 2009), she has also published in *Asian Survey, Contemporary Southeast Asia, International Relations of the Asia Pacific, Pacific Review*, and many edited volumes. Recent and forthcoming publications address Asia's mixed security logics, China as a leading power in East Asia, and constructivist international relations theory and global governance. A research associate at American University's ASEAN Studies Center, she also serves on the editorial boards of the *Australian Journal of International Affairs, Journal of Current Southeast Asian Affairs*, and Routledge Studies on Comparative Asian Politics series.

Yulius P. Hermawan is a Lecturer in the Department of International Relations, Parahyangan Catholic University, Indonesia. He holds a Bachelor's degree in International Relations from Gadjah Mada University, Yogyakarta, an MA in Politics with a concentration in East Asian Studies from Monash University, Australia and a PhD from Leeds University, UK. His major research interests are Indonesia and the G-20 process, global governance, and ASEAN integration. His current research is about the South–South and Triangular Cooperation Model and the role of Indonesia as an emerging partner in international development cooperation. Dr. Hermawan's most recent publications include *Indonesia's Accountability to the G20* (Jakarta, Ministry of Finance, 2013) and *Indonesia in International Institutions: Living Up to Ideals* (National Security College Issue Brief, Canberra: ANU, May 2014).

Tavida Kamolvej is Associate Dean for Academic Affairs at the Faculty of Political Science, Thammasat University, Thailand. She received her PhD from the Graduate School of Public and International Affairs at the University of Pittsburgh. Her research interests include Disaster Management, Social Network Analysis, Research Methodology, and Public Policy Analysis. Currently, Dr. Kamolvej serves as a Chief Technical Advisor to the Department of Disaster

Prevention and Mitigation, Thailand, under the Technical Assistance program of the United Nations Development Program. She has served as Disaster and Emergency Management advisor to the National Disaster Warning Center in developing an end-to-end disaster warning system. She also joined the sub-committee on Disaster and Risk Communication of the National Committee of Broadcasting, Televising, and Telecommunication, to develop communication regulations and a framework for action. Dr. Kamolvej used to be communication and coordination instructor for the US State Department's Senior Crisis Management Seminar Program in collaboration with American University. She also served as Disaster Management Consultant to the Pacific Disaster Center and to UNESCO/IOC in their Community Resilience and Education for Disaster and Risk Management Program.

Cheng-Chwee Kuik is an associate professor in the Strategic Studies and International Relations Program at the National University of Malaysia (UKM) and an associate member of the Institute of China Studies at the University of Malaya (UM). From September 2013 until July 2014, Dr. Kuik was a post-doctoral research associate in the Princeton-Harvard China and the World Program at Princeton University. Cheng-Chwee has researched and published on China–Southeast Asia relations, regional multilateralism, weaker states' alignment choices, and East Asian security. He holds a PhD from the Johns Hopkins University and an MLitt from the University of St. Andrews. He has held visiting fellowships at the Chinese Academy of Social Sciences, Shanghai Institutes for International Studies, Lee Kong Chian Reference Library (Singapore), American University's ASEAN Studies Center, the Centre for Strategic and International Studies (Jakarta), and the Oxford University. He can be contacted at cckuik@gmail.com.

Md Nasrudin Md Akhir is an Associate Professor and has been Executive Director of the Asia-Europe Institute, University of Malaya since May 2010. He was Deputy Dean (Research and Development) of the Faculty of Arts and Social Sciences from 2009 to 2010; Head of the Department of East Asian Studies from 2004 to 2009; and Coordinator for the Japan Studies Program from 1994 to 2000. As Coordinator, he was responsible for developing the Japan Studies Program in the University of Malaya which was established in 1993. From 1998 to 2012, he was Secretary General of the Malaysian Association of Japanese Studies (MAJAS) and from 2012 he has been advisor to MAJAS. He has been a member in the Steering Committee of the Japanese Studies Association in ASEAN representing Malaysia since 2006. His main research interests include Japan's foreign policy, Malaysia–Korea Relations and East Asian international relations. He is the author and editor of 10 books and numerous academic articles published locally and internationally.

Pinn Siraprapasiri graduated from the University of Oxford and is now a lecturer in International Relations at Thammasat University, Thailand. Her research interests include international negotiation, the Mekong subregion, the Asia-Pacific security landscape, and ASEAN regionalization. She recently concluded a research project and co-authored a book (forthcoming 2015) with Chanintira na Thalang on ASEAN regional identity.

Sueo Sudo is a Professor at Nanzan University, Nagoya, Japan. He received his PhD from the Department of Political Science at the University of Michigan in 1987. Before taking his current position, he was a research fellow at Chulalongkorn University in Bangkok, a fellow at the Institute of Southeast Asian Studies in Singapore and a professor at Saga University in Saga Prefecture, Japan. His research interests are ASEAN and Japan–ASEAN relations. He has published various books in English and Japanese, including *The Fukuda Doctrine and ASEAN* (1992), *The Structure of Southeast Asian International Relations* (1996), *International Relations of Japan and South East Asia* (2002), *Evolution of ASEAN-Japan Relations* (2005), *External Behavior of the State* (2007), and *Japan's ASEAN Policy* (2015).

Chanintira na Thalang obtained her PhD from the University of Bristol, UK and is currently Assistant Professor of International Relations at Thammasat University, Thailand. Dr. na Thalang has authored articles on national politics, ethnic conflicts, and ethno-nationalism with a special focus on Indonesia and Thailand. Her later research interests include ASEAN regional identity.

Tham Siew Yean is Deputy Director and a Professor of International Trade at the Institute of Malaysian and International Studies (IKMAS), National University of Malaysia. She has served as a consultant to several national and international agencies. Professor Tham has published a number of books, numerous chapters in books and academic articles on foreign direct investment, trade policies, industrial development, and trade in services in Malaysia, focusing on the higher education sector. She has a PhD in economics from the University of Rochester.

Nguyen Quoc Viet is Dean of Faculty of Development Economics at VNU University of Economics and Business. He has received an MA in Law at Vietnam National University Hanoi. He obtained a PhD in Economics from the University of Kassel, Germany. Dr. Viet has taught for more than 10 years at the School of Law at Vietnam National University Hanoi. Since 2008, he has been a lecturer at the University of Economics and Business, Vietnam National University Hanoi (VNU-UEB). He researches and lectures in the field of institutional economics, public choice, law and economics, and business law. Dr. Viet's current research projects focus on institutional quality/environment and economic development, local governance and decentralization, regional economic integration and policy reform, business ethics, social enterprises and rural economic development.

Foreword

In Southeast Asia today, spaces of economic and political activity are seen to be the predominant and determinative sites of regional integration. Less heralded is the role of pedagogical materials, scholars, and academic institutions in creating the knowledge and understanding required for effective and informed regionally oriented actors. Bringing together scholars from Brunei, Cambodia, China, Indonesia, Japan, Laos, Philippines, Malaysia, Myanmar, Singapore, South Korea, Thailand, and Vietnam (the "Association of South East Asian Nations Plus Three" or APT countries), the Community of East Asian Scholars project focuses on the potential of academic practice to promote an emergent and responsible regional consciousness.

Supported initially by Thammasat University in Bangkok and later by the first higher education grant awarded to an ASEAN-based project by the ASEAN Plus Three Fund, CEAS' aim was two-fold. The first goal was to commission papers by leading scholars from the ASEAN and APT community. They were asked to analyze, from their viewpoint of being in their respective countries and in the region, the key promises, issues, and challenges faced by ASEAN and APT. The results of their work will appear in three edited volumes. This book, *Institutionalizing East Asia: Mapping and Reconfiguring Regional Cooperation*, was preceded by another volume, *Advancing the Regional Commons in the New East Asia*. A third volume, *Regional Community Building in East Asia: Countries in Focus*, is forthcoming. In providing rigorous and expert perspectives on the history, politics, and institutional processes of Southeast and East Asia, CEAS hopes to encourage mutual understanding among and of APT countries.

The second aim of the project was to stimulate collaboration, as well as long-standing connections among scholars and academic institutions in APT countries. Indeed, one of the highlights of the project has been the process through which the three volumes were developed. In biannual workshops over the past three years, CEAS authors have shared, debated, and modified chapter outlines and drafts. All three volumes reflect the collegial spirit of these workshops.

As our efforts become realized in print, CEAS would like to thank the ASEAN Plus Three Fund for its generous support. Special thanks also go to the Ministry of Foreign Affairs of Thailand, particularly the ASEAN Department and the Permanant Mission of Thailand to the ASEAN Secretariat, for its continuous efforts and coordination, without which the project would not have successfully achieved its goals. The editors recognize and express their great appreciation for the invaluable assistance of Malavika Reddy and Miyo Hanazawa who kept the project on track with their efficient management of tasks and timely reminders. Finally, this volume, as well as the two other volumes, is the product of a long-term commitment by participant authors and editors for which CEAS would like to express its deep gratitude.

Community of East Asian Scholars
Thammasat University
Bangkok, Thailand
April, 2015

Preface

When does a region come to see itself as such? In 1997, at the height of the Asian Financial Crisis, ASEAN member states and East Asian countries came to see ourselves as more economically integrated than we had previously thought. We recognized that we had to work together in order to survive and thrive together. The West, remaining aloof from our plight, called the crisis an Asian problem and suggested Asians solve it. The help that the West did offer by way of the IMF was harsh and conditional. In this context, the aid package that came to be known as the New Miyazawa Plan, although not offering a large monetary sum, was an important symbol of the moment. Spearheaded by Japan, directed towards helping its regional neighbors, supported by China and pragmatically liberal in its terms, the New Miyazawa Plan, at the very least, ensured that debt financing was not for us. We would not borrow into the future to pay for the now. And, our experience of the pains of economic recovery gave us a strong sense of community.

This was a defining moment of regional awareness. Learning from the Miyazawa Plan that we can mobilize on our own behalves, we set up a new uniquely Asian initiative – a common fund of US$240 billion. ASEAN is committed to contributing 20%, both China's and Japan's share is 30%, and Korea will put in 20%. This fund is a first line of defense for Asian economies. The symbolic promise of the Miyazawa Plan was met in this concrete regional rampart. Even if the financial crisis had not been an Asian problem, as some had mistaken it, we Asians *could* work together to ameliorate, if not solve, it and to formalize an architecture to support ourselves through future trials.

I reflect on this history of the *coming into* of regional awareness because a common South East and East Asian regional identity has never been a foregone conclusion. Yet, as explored in the chapters of this volume, a common region *is* coming into being. These chapters suggest that, as our regional mechanisms become increasingly institutionalized, the question for us Southeast and East Asians is no longer "when does a region come to see itself as such?" Rather, the question becomes, "how can our region become a fulcrum in a redefined global architecture?"

Surin Pitsuwan
Former Sectretary-General of ASEAN
(2008–2012)

Abbreviations

AADMER	ASEAN Agreement on Disaster Management and Emergency Response
AADMERWP	ASEAN Agreement on Disaster Management and Emergency Response Work Program
ABMI	Asian Bond Market Initiative
ACD	Asia Cooperation Dialogue
ACDM	ASEAN Committee on Disaster Management
ACFTA	ASEAN-China Free Trade Area
ACMECS	Ayeyawady, Chao Phraya, Mekong Economic Cooperation Strategy
ADB	Asian Development Bank
ADMM	ASEAN Defense Ministers' Meeting
ADMM-Plus	ASEAN Defense Ministers' Meeting-Plus
ADRC	Asian Disaster Reduction Center
AEBF	Asia-Europe Business Forum
AEC	ASEAN Economic Community
AEGDM	ASEAN Experts Group on Disaster Management
AEPF	Asia-Europe People's Forum
AFTA	ASEAN Free Trade Agreement
AHA Centre	ASEAN Coordinating Centre for Humanitarian Assistance on Disaster Management
AICHR	ASEAN Inter-governmental Commission on Human Rights
AIPR	ASEAN Institute for Peace and Reconciliation
AMBDC	ASEAN-Mekong Basin Development Cooperation
AMDA	Anglo-Malayan Defense Agreement
AMEICC	AEM-MITI Economic and Industrial Cooperation Committee
AMF	Asian Monetary Fund
AMM	Aceh Monitoring Mission
AMM	ASEAN Ministerial Meeting
AMMTC	ASEAN Ministerial Meeting on Transnational Crime
AMRO	ASEAN Plus Three Macroeconomic Research Office

AMTA	Agency Coordinating Mekong Tourism Activities
APCN	ASEAN Peacekeeping Centers Network
APEC	Asia-Pacific Economic Cooperation
APG	The AADMER Partnership Group
APSC	ASEAN Political-Security Community
APT	ASEAN Plus Three
APTERR	ASEAN Plus Three Emergency Rice Reserve
ARDEX	ASEAN Regional Disaster Emergency Response Simulation Exercises
ARF	ASEAN Regional Forum
ARF-DOD	ARF Defense Officials' Dialogue
ASA	Association of Southeast Asia
ASEAN	Association of Southeast Asian Nations
ASEAN-CPR	ASEAN Committee of Permanent Representatives
ASEAN-ERAT	ASEAN Emergency Rapid Assessment Team
ASEAN-ISIS	ASEAN Institutes of Security and International Studies
ASEAN-PMC	ASEAN Post-Ministerial Conference
ASEIC	ASEM Small and Medium Enterprises Eco-Innovation Center
ASEM	Asia-Europe Meeting
ASEP	Asia-Europe Parliamentary Partnership
ASPC	ARF Security Policy Conferences
BNPP	National Patani Liberation Front
BRN	Barisan Revolusi National
BRN-C	Barisan Revolusi National Melayu Patani Coordinate
Caricom	Caribbean Community and Common Market
CBDRM	Community-Based Disaster Risk Management
CBDRR	Community-Based Disaster Risk Reduction
CBMs	Confidence-Building Measures
CBTA	Agreement on Cross-Border Transportation
CEP	Core Environment Program
CEPT	Common Effectiev Preferential Tariff
CLMV	Cambodia, Laos, Myanmar, and Vietnam
CMI	Chiang Mai Initiative
CMI	Crisis Management Initiative
CMIM	Chiang Mai Initiative Multilateralization
COP	Conference of the Parties
CPM	Civilian-Military-Police
CSCAP	Council for Security Cooperation in the Asia-Pacific
CSCE	Conference for Security and Cooperation in Europe
CSO	Civil Society Organization
DiREX	Disaster Relief Exercises
DPP	Dewan Pimpinan Party
DPRK	Democratic People's Republic of Korea
DRR	Disaster Risk Reduction

EAC	East Asian Community
EAEC	East Asian Economic Caucus
EAEG	East Asian Economic Group
EALAF	East Asia-Latin America Forum
EAMF	Expanded ASEAN Maritime Forum
EAS	East Asia Summit
EASG	East Asian Study Group
EAVG	East Asia Vision Group
EMEAP	Executives' Meeting of East Asia Pacific Central Banks
ENVforum	Asia-Europe Environment Forum
ERAT	ASEAN Emergency Rapid Assessment Team
EU	European Union
EVSL	Early Voluntary Sectoral Liberalization
EWEC	East-West Economic Corridor
FEALAC	Forum for East Asia-Latin America Cooperation
FMM	Foreign Ministers' Meeting
FPDA	Five-Power Defence Arrangements
FTA	Free Trade Agreement
GAM	Free Aceh Movement
GMIP	Pattani Islamic Mujahideen Movement
GMS	Greater Mekong Sub-region
GMS-BF	Greater Mekong Sub-region Business Forum
GMS-ECP	Greater Mekong Sub-region Economic Cooperation Program
GMS-SF	Greater Mekong Sub-region Agreement on Strategic Framework
HADR	Humanitarian Assistance and Disaster Relief
HDC	Henri Dunant Centre
HFA1	Hyogo Framework for Action 1
IISS	International Institute for Strategic Studies
IMF	International Monetary Fund
IO	International Organisation
ISGs	Inter-Sessional Support Groups
ISMs	Inter-Sessional Meetings
IUCN	International Union for Conservation of Nature
JICA	Japan International Cooperation Agency
JIMs	Jakarta Informal Meetings
JSC	Joint Security Committee
LCS	Littoral Combat Ships
LEMA	Local Emergency Management Agency
MAPHILINDO	Malaysia-Philippines-Indonesia
MDGs	Millennium Development Goals
Mercosur	Mercado Comun del Sur (Common Market of the South)
MGC	Mekong-Ganga Cooperation
MILF	Moro Islamic Liberation Front

MMAEC	Mekong-Menam-Irrawady Economic Cooperation
MOU	Memorandum of Understanding
MRC	Mekong River Commission
MTCO	Mekong Tourism Coordination
NAFTA	North American Free Trade Agreement
NEAT	Network of East Asian Think-tanks
NGOs	Non Governmental Organizations
NSC	National Security Council
NSEC	North-South Economic Corridor
OAS	Organization of American States
OSCE	Organisation for Security and Cooperation in Europe
PAS	Pan Malaysian Islamic Party
PD	Preventive Diplomacy
PGPO	Perdana Global Peace Organisation
PMC	Post Ministerial Conferences
POA	Plan of Action
PPP	Phnom Penh Plan for Development Management
PTA	Preferential Trade Agreement
PULO	Patani United Liberation Organisation
RCEP	Regional Comprehensive Economic Partnership
REI	Regional Economic Integration
ROK	Republic of Korea
SASOP	Standby Arrangement for Disaster Relief and Emergency Response
SBPAC	Southern Border Provinces Administrative Centre
SDGs	Sustainable Development Goals
SEATO	Southeast Asia Treaty Organization
SEC	Southern Economic Corridor
SETIS	Sub-regional Environmental Training and Institutional Strengthening
SFA-TFI	Strategic Framework for Action on Trade Facilitation and Investment
SIWG	Sub-regional Investors Working Group
SLD	Shangri-La Dialogue
SOM	Senior Officials' Meeting
SOPs	Standard Operating Procedures
STF	Sub-regional Transport Forum
TAC	Treaty of Amity and Cooperation
TCS	Trilateral Cooperation Secretariat
TFWG	Trade Facilitation Working Group
TOR	Terms of Reference
TPP	Trans-Pacific Partnership
TSSS	Transport Sector Strategy Study
UMNO	United Malays National Organisation
UN	United Nations

UNDP	United Nations Development Program
UNEP	United Nations Environment Programme
UNESCAP	United Nations Economic and Social Commission for Asia and the Pacific
UNESCO	United Nations Educational, Scientific, and Cultural Organization
UNHCR	United Nations High Commissioner for Refugees
UNISDR	United Nations International Strategy for Disaster Reduction
UNOCHA	UN Office of the Coordination of Humanitarian Affairs
USAID	United States Agency for International Development
USTDA	United States Trade and Development Agency
WFP	UN World Food Program
WGE	Working Group on Environment
WTO	World Trade Organization
WWF	World Wildlife Fund
ZOPFAN	Zone of Peace, Freedom, and Neutrality

Introduction

Alice D. Ba, Cheng-Chwee Kuik and Sueo Sudo

This book is about the institutionalization of the multi-sector, multi-level cooperation among the East Asian countries, namely the 10 member countries of the Association of Southeast Asian Nations (ASEAN) and the three Northeast Asian states of China, Japan, and South Korea during the post-Cold War era. Special attention is placed on tracing the origins, discerning the features, and analyzing the prospects of the ongoing institutionalization processes as one of the key phenomena shaping regional order and prosperity in twenty-first-century Asia-Pacific.

Institutional activities have remarkably transformed East Asia, a region once known for the absence of regionalism and regime-building efforts. Of special note has been the leading role played by the Association of Southeast Asian Nations (ASEAN). ASEAN has, for example, been instrumental in the creation and development of the ASEAN Regional Forum (ARF), the Asia-Europe Meeting (ASEM), and the Forum for East Asia-Latin America Cooperation (FEALAC). It has also supported the Asia-Pacific Economic Cooperation (APEC) and the Council for Security Cooperation in the Asia-Pacific (CSCAP). Ever since the outbreak of the financial crisis in July 1997, there has been a particular explosion of region-building efforts among the 13 states of East Asia mentioned above (ADB 2010; Ba 2009; Emmers 2012; Dent 2010; Green and Gill 2009). Such efforts include the ASEAN Plus Three (APT) in December 1997, the respective ASEAN Plus One mechanisms, and the East Asia Summit (EAS) in 2005.

Yet, there also remain outstanding questions about this new regionalism in East Asia. Among the most prominent of these have been, for example, what constitutes "effective" institutions and what kinds of products should we expect to see from institutionalization processes. Such issues have raised further questions about ASEAN's influence and de facto role as the institutional hub of regional activity in East Asia. Meanwhile, the geographic scope of participation has also varied. "East Asian" cooperative activity has intensified, but the expansion of frameworks such as the East Asia Summit to include actors like the United States and Russia also speak to unresolved intra-East Asian geopolitical tensions that may also complicate institutionalization processes and region-building efforts in East Asia.

The book thus aims to address several interrelated questions: In what ways and to what extent has East Asian region-wide cooperation been institutionalized over the past two decades? Why has institutionalization of inter-state cooperation in some geographical areas and functional domains progressed in a faster and deeper manner than others? What drives and constrains the degrees and forms of institutionalization of East Asian cooperation? What are the effects and limits of institutionalized cooperation in East Asia? Has greater institutionalization led to greater and deeper cooperation among the 13 countries? How so, and why so? And in what areas?

The basic assumption and starting point of the book is that, while inter-state cooperation often involves some degree of institutionalization, the two are not necessarily linked. In other words, it is not inevitable that institutionalization will follow cooperation. Similarly, while there are factors at the bilateral, sub-regional, regional, as well as global levels that at times facilitate and expedite the seemingly natural progression from cooperation to institutionalization, those same factors may at other times also limit, fragment, delay, or even derail the process.

This introductory chapter performs three primary tasks. First, it elucidates the focus of inquiry and the scope of the book. Second, it offers a conceptualization of "institutionalization" that can be operationalized as a framework to guide the research and analysis of individual chapters of the volume. Third, it outlines the structure of the book and briefly discusses the central ideas of each chapter.

Mapping and re-configuring "East Asian" cooperation

In order to study the institutionalization of East Asia in a more systematic manner, this book focuses on two interrelated aspects of the phenomenon: the dynamics of "mapping" and "re-configuring" regional cooperation. By mapping, we refer to the process of locating, predicating, and settling on a particular (but evolving) geographical area (e.g. the maritime Southeast Asia, the entire Southeast Asia, particular segments of "East Asia" or "Asia-Pacific") within which a certain cluster of "regional" inter-state cooperation takes place. By re-configuring, we refer to the process by which substantive institutional arrangements of regional cooperation manifest in certain issue domains, policy levels, and institutional designs.

Both processes are dynamic. They are also contested and constantly subject to the interplays of various political, economic, strategic, and functional pressures at different levels. In brief, while mapping (and remapping) is about the evolving geographical area in which a given regional cooperation takes place, configuring (and re-configuring) is about the evolving substantive institutional arrangements (i.e. domains, levels, and institutional designs) of a given regional cooperation. Mapping and re-configuring, accordingly, are the two different sides of the institutionalization coin.

As noted, region-wide frameworks and cooperation have arrived relatively recently to East Asia. In general, they may be considered post-Cold War phenomena and even then, cooperation along distinctly "East Asian" lines – that is, as the 10 ASEAN states plus the three states of Northeast Asia – was slow to emerge. It was not until the 1997 Asian Financial Crisis (AFC) that region-wide cooperation among the 13 East Asian states really began to intensify and manifest in more regularized frameworks like the ASEAN Plus Three (APT). As regards East Asian cooperation and frameworks, the AFC had a number of effects. One was to call attention to East Asian states' interdependence and common vulnerability to global forces. For example, while the effects of, and reasons for, the economic turmoil varied from country to country, the crisis also called attention to shared challenges: (1) an over-reliance on short term foreign borrowing by private firms and banks; (2) over-investment in real estate; (3) inadequate supervision of financial institutions; and (4) over-dependence on the U.S. dollar. In August, Thailand entered into an agreement with the International Monetary Fund (IMF) for an emergency stand-by credit, in exchange for the adoption of stringent fiscal austerity and a range of structural reforms. Still, by the time of the APT's first informal summit meeting in Kuala Lumpur December 14, 1997, "many were helpless spectators to a mauling of their currencies, stock markets and economies in general by forces they barely comprehended" (Economist 1997).

The AFC also had implications for existing regional frameworks, especially APEC and ASEAN. APEC's response – despite being a body comprised of all the key regional and global actors – was practically non-existent. As for ASEAN, East Asia's most established institution, a confluence of challenges – political instability and regime collapse in Indonesia, a political coup in Cambodia, environmental haze – suggested an ASEAN in disarray and seemed to confirm the longstanding conclusions of ASEAN's naysayers about the weakness of the "ASEAN Way" of regional cooperation based on noninterference and aversion to "hard" enforcement mechanisms.

On the other hand, while the AFC clearly demonstrated the limitations of both APEC and ASEAN, it also generated new institutional activity. ASEAN states pursued new regional initiatives designed to deepen ASEAN regional integration that would culminate in a new ASEAN Charter. Most significantly, the same limitations that challenged ASEAN and APEC mobilized new interest and support for the nascent APT process and new East Asia-wide cooperation, which intensified especially during the first decade of the twenty-first century. Since then, regional cooperative activity has also continued under a new East Asia Summit (EAS) and ASEAN Defense Ministers' Meeting (ADMM) Plus frameworks, though the expansion of those frameworks to include states outside the 13 countries of East Asia also calls attention to unresolved geopolitical and historical tensions between East Asian states, as well as functional challenges associated with ASEAN and its approach to regional cooperation.

In short, East Asia has become the site of some very interesting institutional activity. Such activity also takes place at a time when contemporary regionalism has become more prominent in questions of global governance. Interest in region-wide cooperation has clearly grown in the years since the AFC, but where this cooperation is heading and the forms it will take remain evolving, contested, and contingent processes. To appreciate fully the institutional activity ongoing in East Asia and its challenges, it is first necessary give attention to what we mean by institutionalization.

Conceptualizing "institutionalization"

The International Relations (IR) literature on regional cooperation and institutions has been shaped very much by neoliberal definitions that see institutions as synonymous with the formalized rules and conventions of official standing bodies created for specific functional purposes. Yet extant conceptualizations of institutions are in fact diverse, and theorists of different stripes have cautioned against equating institutions with legal or physical structures.

Oran Young, for example, clearly distinguishes between "organizations," which are "material entities possessing physical allocation (or seats), offices, personnel, equipment, and budgets," and "institutions," which are "social practices consisting of easily recognized roles coupled with clusters of rules or conventions governing relations among the occupants of these rules" – that is, "rules of the game that define the character of social practices" (Young 1989: 32, 1994: 28). Douglass North similarly defines institutions to be inclusive of both "informal constraints and formal rules" that together "provide the rules of the game of human interaction" (North 1990: 384). Even Robert Keohane (1989), whose work has been so central to elevating more narrow, contractual definitions, has similarly defined institutions as sets of rules that are "formal and informal."

Thus, the literature has defined institutions to include activity that is less official and less formal. At the same time, as the above also underscores, institutions are not ad hoc. Informal or formal, institutionalized practices are those that happen with regularity and are reflective of dependable expectations and assumptions about how something like cooperation should be pursued. Put another way – and as suggested by Young and North's "rules of the game" characterization – institutions are most of all systems of regularized exchange and expressions of rules and constraint.

For the purpose of this volume, then, we choose to define institutions and institutionalization processes more broadly. We define *institutions* as durable rules that shape expectations, interests, and behavior. These range from formal obligations to informal norms and understandings of what constitutes acceptable behavior. Our definition thus aims to capture not only the kinds of formal cooperation and contractual institutional expressions emphasized by many; it also accounts for activity that may be less formal, but no less regularized (see also, ADB 2010).

Similarly, *institutionalization* is defined as a process of regularizing and harmonizing behavior among a group of sovereign actors, from which emerges agreed-upon rules, norms, and mechanisms from which it is difficult to deviate. Further, "institutionalization may occur and manifest through various processes – for example, formal coordination, legalization, and the creation of bureaucratic structures, but also education and training, modes of discourse, and socialization" (Ba 2012: 123).

In this volume, we also have a particular interest in regional cooperation. Thus, we are interested in processes of institutionalization as it pertains to regularized cooperation and cooperative institutions in East Asia. Further, the chapters in this volume begin with the premise that East Asian states have come together based on the assumption that regional cooperation is a worthwhile goal and in their common interest. In this sense, cooperative activity in East Asia is itself part of the process of institutionalization – that is, the regularization of cooperative behavior. This process takes place between a group of individual states but it has also in important ways defined more generally ASEAN's engagement of Northeast Asian states in regional institutions. Here, there are also similarities to Evelyn Goh's conceptualization of "enmeshment" and "omni-enmeshment," where enmeshment refers to a "process of engaging with a state so as to draw it into deep involvement into international or regional society, enveloping it in a web of sustained exchanges and relationships, with the long-term aim of integration" (Goh 2007/8: 120–121).

In short, institutions may be formal or informal. They can be expressed as material and legal structures, but they are first and foremost social structures. Institutionalization is the process of creating commonly understood rules of the game, expected paths of action and behavior, and also understood constraints.

Structure of the book

In line with our focus on the dynamics of *mapping and reconfiguring* as put forth at the outset, this book is structured into three main parts: "evolution," "domains," and "levels" of cooperation centered on East Asian states. The first part consists of two chapters. In Chapter One, Alice Ba focuses on the origin and institutionalization of Southeast Asian regionalism. It details the key events and factors leading to the creation of ASEAN in 1967, its developments in the subsequent decades during the Cold War, as well as its enlargement and deepening institutionalization throughout the post-Cold War era. The chapter evaluates the much talked about notion of "ASEAN centrality" from the perspective of the numerous institutional frameworks in which ASEAN is implicated. Chapter 2 by Md Nasrudin Bin Md Akhir and Sueo Sudo, then traces geographically-expanded institutionalization processes at the East Asian level, that is among the 10 member countries of ASEAN and the three Northeast Asian states. Specifically, the chapter analyzes the evolution, features, and driving factors of both APT cooperation since 1997 and EAS cooperation since 2005.

Part two of the volume focuses on domains of East Asian cooperation and consists of four chapters covering specific functional issue areas. In Chapter 3, Sueo Sudo and Tham Siew Yean trace East Asia's evolving efforts at institutionalized economic cooperation and consider their functional effectiveness and future prospects. Among the key economic institutions and arrangements covered by the chapter are: AFTA, APT, the ASEAN Economic Community (AEC) proposal, ASEAN Plus One, and various FTA networks in the region, as well as the Trans Pacific Partnership (TPP) and the Regional Comprehensive Economic Partnership (RCEP) negotiations. Complementing Sudo's and Tham's chapter on East Asian economic cooperation is Cheng-Chwee Kuik's chapter on security cooperation. In that chapter, he considers the evolution, features, and drivers of East Asian institutionalization in the security sector. Among the key security institutions covered are: ARF, APT, EAS, ADMM+8, as well as various Track 1.5 and Track 2 processes.

These two chapters are then followed by Tavida Kamolvej's chapter on disaster management, which highlights how institutionalized cooperation in this domain has tended to be a reactive, as opposed to proactive, process. In Chapter 6, Chanintira na Thalang and Pinn Siraprapasiri offer a contrasting discussion on ethnic conflict management in Southeast Asia. Specifically, the chapter investigates the limited success that ASEAN and APT frameworks have had in ethnic conflict management. The authors propose that ethnic conflict management can be understood as a case of non- or, at best, limited institutionalized cooperation.

The volume's third and last section considers different levels of cooperation. The two chapters comprising this section consider the ways that cooperation has been regularized (or not) at levels "below" and "above" conventional "Southeast Asian" and "East Asian" regional conceptualizations. In Chapter 7 Nguyen Quoc Viet considers cooperation at the sub-regional level. In his discussion, the Greater Mekong Sub-region Cooperation (GMS) provides a notable example of broader regional trends towards more rule-based and formally institutionalized cooperation by a sub-regional group of states. In contrast, the chapter that follows by Yulius Purwadi Hermawan considers the institutionalization of cooperation at the *interregional* level through the cases of the Asia-Europe Meeting (ASEM) and the Forum for East Asia-Latin America Cooperation (FEALAC). These two chapters highlight the important point that cooperation taking place at subregional and interregional levels is generative and can give rise to varied institutional expressions.

The volume then concludes with both a summary and a reflection upon the chapters' major themes. It also identifies some key sources for the different patterns of institutionalization exhibited across sectors and levels, before discussing the prospects of institutionalizing East Asian cooperation in the years to come.

References

Asian Development Bank (ADB). 2008. *Emerging Asian Regionalism: A Partnership for Shared Prosperity*. Manila: ADB.

Asian Development Bank (ADB). 2010. *Institutions for Regional Integration: Toward an Asian Economic Community*. Manila: ADB.

Ba, Alice D. 2009. *(Re)Negotiating East and Southeast Asia: Region, Regionalism, and the Association of Southeast Asian Nations*. Stanford, CA: Stanford University Press.

Ba, Alice D. 2012. ASEAN Centrality Imperiled? In Ralf Emmers, ed., *ASEAN and the Institutionalization of East Asia*. London: Routledge, pp. 114–129.

Calder, Kent E., and Francis Fukuyama, eds. 2008. *East Asian Multilateralism: Prospects for Regional Stability*. Baltimore, MD: The Johns Hopkins University Press.

Dent, Christopher M. 2008. *East Asian Regionalism*. London: Routledge.

Dent, Christopher M. 2010. *Organizing the Wider East Asia Region*. Asian Development Bank Series on Regional Economic Integration, No. 57. Manila: Asian Development Bank.

The Economist, December 20, 1997–January 2, 1998, pp. 48–49.

Emmers, Ralf, ed. 2012. *ASEAN and the Institutionalization of East Asia*. London: Routledge.

Goh, Evelyn. 2007/8. Greater Powers and Hierarchical Order in Southeast Asia. *International Security* 32(3): 113–157.

Goldstein, Avery, and Edward D. Mansfield, eds. 2012. *The Nexus of Economics, Security, and International Relations in East Asia*. Stanford, CA: Stanford University Press.

Green, Michael J., and Bates Gill, eds. 2009. *Asia's New Multilateralism: Cooperation, Competition, and the Search for Community*. New York: Columbia University Press.

Keohane, Robert. 1989. *International Institutions and State Power*. Boulder, CO: Westview Press.

Koremenos, Barbara, Charles Lipson, and Duncan Snidal. 2001. The Rational Design of International Institutions. *International Organization* 55(4): 761–779.

North, Douglass. 1990. Institutions and Their Consequences for Economic Performance. In Karen S. Cook and Margaret Levi, eds, *The Limits of Rationality*. Chicago, IL: University of Chicago Press: 383–401.

Young, Oran R. 1989. *International Cooperation: Building Regimes for Natural Resources and the Environment*. Ithaca, NY: Cornell University Press.

Young, Oran R. 1994. *International Governance: Protecting the Environment in a Stateless Society*. Ithaca, NY: Cornell University Press.

Part 1

Evolution of
inter-state cooperation

1 The institutionalization of Southeast Asia

ASEAN and ASEAN centrality

Alice D. Ba

Introduction

The Association of Southeast Asian Nations (ASEAN) has been a key driver and primary expression of regional cooperative activity in Southeast Asia. As such, it has come to be inextricably linked to the institutionalization of regional cooperation in Southeast Asia. Created in 1967, ASEAN began with five states (Indonesia, Malaysia, Philippines, Singapore, and Thailand) and has since expanded to include Brunei in 1984, Vietnam in 1995, Laos and Myanmar in 1997, and Cambodia in 1999. Known for its voluntarism, its consensus decision-making, and also its defense of noninterference norms, ASEAN has also been associated with the stabilization of relations and growing cooperation in Southeast Asia. Today, ASEAN institutionalism has been extended to East Asian and Asia Pacific frameworks, such that ASEAN provides an institutional hub for a network of cooperative frameworks in East Asia. At the same time, ASEAN's norms and practices have also long been criticized for hindering a more "effective," "action oriented" regionalism in pursuit of various functional and political objectives (Ravenhill 2008; Frost 2008). Explaining and understanding ASEAN institutionalism – what it does and how it does it, and just as important, what it does *not* do and what its limitations are – thus forms an important starting point for most discussions on the institutionalization of not just Southeast Asia but also East Asia more broadly. This is especially the case as regards institutionalized cooperation expressed as "regional organizations" and official (state-driven/"Track 1")[1] "regional frameworks."

As will be clear, the question of how best to conceptualize institutionalization is central to explanations and assessments of ASEAN as a regional organization and mechanism of regional cooperation. Towards illuminating the forms and drivers of institutionalized cooperation in Southeast Asia, this chapter proceeds as follows. First, it considers ASEAN's historical origins and how its founding premises bear on ASEAN as an institution. This first section also elaborates on the need for expanded definitions of cooperation and institutionalization if the variety of ASEAN's cooperative activity is to be fully accounted for. Second, this chapter considers how those premises have come to be institutionalized in ASEAN norms, practices, and decision-making – that is, what regional cooperation looks like – as well as ASEAN's economic and security cooperation agendas past and present.

Third and finally, the chapter elaborates on "ASEAN centrality," a term that refers to ASEAN's institutional prominence and influence in larger frameworks, inclusive of Northeast Asian and Asian Pacific powers. This section considers the ways in which the centrality of ASEAN is both regularized and challenged in East Asian and Asian Pacific institutional settings.

Institutionalizing ASEAN-Southeast Asia

Institutionalization can take many forms. To capture that variation, institutionalization is defined here as the process by which modes of behavior are made more dependable and durable. Importantly, such a definition expands beyond the legalistic, contractual forms of institutionalized cooperation ("formal cooperation") that is both typically emphasized by theoretical accounts, and long eschewed by East and Southeast Asian states. While many academic discussions may equate "institutionalization" with materially consequentialist rules (i.e., rules backed by clear threat of sanction) and "cooperation" with "centralized coordination," the reality and practice is more varied. Indeed, some of the most durable ("institutionalized") practices are not products of such legal or centrally enforced structures at all, but rather the disciplining norms and social conventions of a given community. In the case of Southeast Asia, cooperative activity is quite extensive and regularized, but the predominant form it takes has been more informal-personalistic than legal-contractual. An expansive, rather than overly restrictive, view of both institutionalization and cooperation is thus important if we are not to remove from view the different kinds of practices and the varied cooperative activities taking place in the region or how differences in development, position, or culture might affect what cooperation looks like.[2]

In addition to being more inclusive of different *forms* of cooperation, a more expansive definition, as that above, is also more open to differences in *purpose* and *function*. Questions of form and purpose – the *how* and the *why* of cooperation – are inextricably linked. They are also not value-free, even if often conceptualized as such. Political values strongly influence what states want and consequently the cooperative agendas that get pursued and institutionalized in Southeast Asia, yet discussions of cooperation often assume, rather than problematize the values and priorities driving regional cooperation. For example, underlying International Relations (IR)'s emphasis on formal, centralized institutionalization in international relations are unreflected normative assumptions about the state – its liberal rationalities, moral purpose, and functional capacities.[3] But while such assumptions may be true of more established states (i.e., in Europe and North America) they may be less true of post-colonial states, which are products of different historical, developmental, cultural, and geopolitical conditions. Such differences – both empirical and socially constructed – bear on conceptualizations of security that then affect a range of other considerations, activities, and policy preferences. For example, compared to more established states, Southeast Asian regional conceptions of security have historically been defined more comprehensively, with greater attention to internal, sub-state security concerns, and economic and political dimensions of security than the IR literature has typically highlighted. Similarly, just as liberal values and an individualist ethos tend to inform the emphasis placed on contractual obligations in Europe and North America, a normative, communitarian concern for the unity of the state and as a collective tends to inform state purposes and, in turn, how regional cooperation is expressed in East and Southeast Asia.

Such comprehensive and state-centric security conceptualizations have come to be especially institutionalized in ASEAN. Such conceptualizations also provide the basis for some of ASEAN's most defining cooperative practices, especially its norms of noninterference and consensus decision-making. The dominance of these practices in Southeast Asia, however, was not a foregone conclusion; rather, they *became* dominant because ASEAN's own development gave them a larger significance. Put another way, ASEAN *made* these practices what they are as much as these practices made ASEAN. As ASEAN's early history has been well-covered, the discussion below focuses on a few key points about ASEAN's early development as a way to provide insight into the conditions and processes that made some practices and not others so prominent.

The 1963 creation of Malaysia, inclusive of the British territories of North Borneo, Sarawak, and also Singapore, provided the immediate context for ASEAN's founding. The events surrounding it also proved for many, the interdependence of domestic, regional, and global insecurities in Southeast Asia. Most dramatically, Indonesia, seeing neo-colonialist plots at play, launched a low level war against Malaysia. Volatile domestic politics and economic crisis provided the domestic conditions for Indonesia's radicalized foreign policy; they also intensified the specter of great power mischief, especially from China, which was undergoing its own period of domestic instability and foreign policy revisionism. Joining Indonesia's campaign of *Konfrontasi* was the Philippines, which also severed relations with Malaysia over its inclusion of North Borneo. The fragility of both inter-state and intra-state relations was given additional illustration by race riots and communal violence that helped end Singapore's contentious and short-lived union with Malaysia. Meanwhile, interlinked foreign and civil wars also raged in Indochina, proving the relationship between internal division and external intervention.

The history above serves to underscore a few key points as regards this discussion on institutionalization in Southeast Asia. First, it serves to illustrate the contentiousness of not just states, but also Southeast Asia as a basis for organization and cooperation in the 1960s. In fact, were it not for a regime change in Indonesia and the commitment of specific regional elites, the possibilities of regional cooperation might have proven elusive. This includes the creation of ASEAN in 1967. Preceded by the failures of at least three attempts at regional organization,[4] the tenuousness of ASEAN's regional cooperative enterprise was additionally affirmed by the persistence of inter-state tensions in the years immediately following ASEAN's creation. These included the suspension of relations (once again) between Malaysia and the Philippines upon the former's discovery of the latter's plan to forcibly retake North Borneo/Sabah, as well as persistent political tensions between Malaysia and Singapore. In Indonesia, Singapore's executions of Indonesian marines captured during *Konfrontasi* provoked a nationalist backlash that was contained only because of the restraint exercised by President Suharto and leading Indonesian elites.[5]

By the same token, as a contrast to the Southeast Asia of today, this history also serves to underscore just how normalized and regularized – how *institutionalized* – Southeast Asia as a basis for regional cooperation has become, with ASEAN, again, the primary expression of such. Today, intra-Southeast Asian differences certainly remain and continue to govern how regionalism and regional cooperation is expressed in Southeast Asia; nevertheless, given the history above, it remains no less remarkable just how much "ASEAN" has become a shorthand for "Southeast Asia" across a spectrum of activity, from politics, to trade, to finance and banking, to investment portfolios, to civil society organizations, to global governance. This shorthand can be criticized for over-homogenizing important differences among those in Southeast Asia. However, the point here is that ASEAN-Southeast Asia has become an institutional and empirical fact in government agencies, business strategies, financial and trade portfolios, developmental programs, and so on, and as such, has helped to institutionalize Southeast Asia as a basis for organization and action.

Second, the historical challenges of intra-regional relations – both empirical and socially constructed – have provided referents for ASEAN elites that have invoked this history as a cautionary lesson for today's more stable and prosperous Southeast Asia. In particular, as elaborated elsewhere (Ba 2009), this history has provided ASEAN its legitimating arguments and discursive frames about the perils of domestic and regional division, their association with extra-regional intervention, and the importance of respecting one another's nation-building enterprises. These linkages would find particular expression in Indonesian ideas of national and regional *resilience*, a conceptualization broadly shared among ASEAN's founding states. Such political challenges serve to illustrate the normative drivers behind regional cooperation, regional integration, and regional organization in Southeast Asia. This contrasts with those who conceive the drivers of institutionalization and institutionalized cooperation as a response to pre-existing functional interests. For example, a common assumption is that states pursue regional cooperation because of a functional need to manage or pursue established sovereign interests. Similarly, it is assumed that a pre-existing interdependence drives the demand for cooperative mechanisms that can reduce transaction costs. Yet, in ASEAN, such conditions of economic interdependence and political affinity, especially in its earliest years, were weak at best. Rather, the historical drivers of ASEAN cooperation have been less the *management* of an *existing* regional interdependence or *defense* of *existing* state sovereignty, so much as it has been about *creating* and *substantiating* them.[6] As elaborated below, institutional purpose and form are often linked. The above political and historical dynamics are thus important because they bear on ASEAN's cooperative agenda and its defining institutional features – that is, what is institutionalized.

Institutionalizing norms and practices in ASEAN

The contestedness of states, especially as a source of national insecurity and intra-regional tension, contributes to a cooperation that values national autonomy as a principle of interstate relations and, in turn, noninterference as a practice. It bears emphasizing that the dominant pattern of inter-state relations in pre-ASEAN Southeast Asia was *interference*, not *noninterference*. Just as important and as noted above, these conditions and challenges are made politically significant by founding narratives that link inter-state interference to not just regional instability but also domestic/regime insecurity and heightened vulnerability to extra-regional interference.

Such challenges, as conceived and constructed, made noninterference, in particular, an important starting point for "good neighborliness" (ASEAN Declaration 1967) and the basis for a modus vivendi. As an expression of respect for another's national autonomy, noninterference, at a minimum, offered states and their national elites critical space to pursue their own national development priorities and establish regime legitimacy, which was considered a foundation of not just national stability but also regional stability. Of ASEAN norms and practices, non-interference has become the one especially associated with ASEAN (see, especially, Acharya 2001).

These concerns and priorities are reflected in ASEAN's early documents, as well as its early cooperative initiatives. ASEAN's 1967 founding declaration was notably short but in the span of two pages it nevertheless made clear the importance of national development and national independence, as well as security from external interference – be it from extra-regional states or neighboring states – as the basis for their common and regional security. The 1976 Declaration of ASEAN Concord made these connections between national development and regional stability, and between national and regional resilience, even more explicit. Noninterference was also given rare legal expression in ASEAN's first (and until 1995 only) treaty in 1976, namely, its Treaty of Amity and Cooperation (TAC). In short, ASEAN's first decade saw the gradual and incremental formalization and solidification of noninterference as a principle in ASEAN.

Noninterference, as an expression of respect for national autonomy, also affected the kind of cooperation ASEAN pursued. In particular, ASEAN's early documents and initiatives tended to emphasize individual national efforts in service of a larger regional cooperation agenda. This emphasis, however, has great significance for ASEAN as an institution. Specifically, while ASEAN's cooperative enterprises were clearly collaborative, the emphasis on national efforts also projected a cooperation that was far from being centrally coordinated or necessarily harmonized in the sense of standardization or homogenization.

The design of ASEAN's secretariat is illustrative. Typically, organizational secretariats provide a political and organizational expression of the collective; they also provide the bureaucratic support necessary to coordinate and implement collective decisions. ASEAN, however, in 1967 eschewed a central, "regional" secretariat in favor of five independent "national secretariats" "to carry out the work of the Association on behalf of that country" (ASEAN Declaration 1967); nor was there any body authorized to coordinate those different national units. It was not until 1976 that states, in fact, established an *ASEAN* secretariat, including a Secretary-General. Still, that secretariat remained a minimalist one, thus affirming the primacy of the national unit. The constraints faced by ASEAN's secretariat thus offer another illustration of how ASEAN norms affect how cooperation is expressed. Here, as above, the kind of cooperation institutionalized and regularized is a kind of decentralized collaboration as opposed to centralized coordination.

The understood interdependence of national and regional security and the tensions it produces manifest also in ASEAN's mode of decision-making. ASEAN makes decisions based on consensus. Consensus decision-making contrasts with majority-rules decision-making where minority states must subordinate their own concerns to that of the majority. Consensus is about respect for national self-determination and mutual accommodation towards an outcome that all can support. Indeed, of all ASEAN practices, consensus-making may best express states' dual and interdependent concerns for national and regional unity – in a word, *resilience*, which has provided ASEAN cooperation one of its most defining normative drivers (see also Eaton and Stubbs 2006). Consensus-seeking is, after all, the pursuit of a common position – regional unity – but it also maintains full respect for national autonomy. As should be clear, consensus in the ASEAN context is more than just a mode of decision-making; rather it is an institutional expression of core political values, especially resilience. At one and the same time, it institutionalizes the importance attached to expressing Southeast Asia as a collective, but also the primacy of national autonomy as the basis for Southeast Asia's modus vivendi.

Both noninterference and consensus – and more generally, the drive for resilience – also reflect a critical underlying premise, namely, the fragility of both states and intra-regional relations. To be sure, such concerns can be exaggerated, but the point here is that such challenges, as constructed, have meant that ASEAN states have generally avoided more ambitious and coercive agendas for fear that they will have disunifying effects – be they for the national or regional unit. The result is a more cautious kind of regionalism and a cooperation that is incrementalist, collaborative, and based on voluntarism, as opposed to extensive, centrally coordinated or based on legally compelled compliance.

Such cooperation has not been without its challenges. As elaborated below, an important critique of ASEAN institutionalism has been that its eschewal of more contractual, "binding" mechanisms has allowed states too much flexibility, especially as regards specific cooperative agreements – resulting in what some characterize as a culture or habit of noncompliance in ASEAN (see, for example, discussion in Sukma 2008). In making the national unit the normative centerpiece of regional security and stability, ASEAN institutionalism has denied ASEAN as an institution the normative and material capacity to compel compliance and to offer a more responsive and immediate response to challenges of common concern – for example, in cases involving transnational challenges, destabilizing challenges emanating from a particular member state, or Southeast Asia's global and regional economic challenges and competitiveness. Instead, ASEAN states have historically had to rely on mechanisms that are more informal-personalistic than legal-contractual. In particular, states exercise quiet, nonconfrontational diplomacy in an effort to persuade and at times, exert peer pressure on a recalcitrant state, but at the same time, practicing mutual respect and sovereign equality (Leifer 1999: 27–29; Haacke 2003; Katsumata 2003; Narine 2002: 31–33).

ASEAN's consensus decision-making can also be a very slow and belabored process. This has led to characterizations of ASEAN as "all talk; no action" and as an organization that is more "process driven" than "outcomes driven" (Jones and Smith 2007). As noted, ASEAN's consensus decision-making does indeed constrain the ambitiousness of proposals because the organization can only go as fast and as far as its most reluctant member is willing. Thus, it is often said that ASEAN initiatives are reduced to states' "lowest common denominator." At the same time, while the policy outcomes may be constrained, the process versus outcomes characterization is also in an important way a false dichotomy. As highlighted above, ASEAN processes are not just for process' sake; they are processes that serve ASEAN's prioritized outcomes and shared political values – namely, self-determination and national autonomy, regional resilience, regional consensus, and unity (see Ba 2011 and 2013: 142–146). One can debate the appropriateness of those outcomes, but the point is that ASEAN's processes are just as purposeful as more contractual expressions of cooperation. Another problem with the process versus outcomes dichotomy is that it ignores the indirect and cumulative effects of ASEAN cooperation. For example, ASEAN's consultative and negotiated processes may be slow, but they have also created cumulative points of agreement that make possible later cooperative norms and institutional practices.[7]

Still, these constraints have led many to characterize ASEAN as an instance of "weak institutionalism." However, it is "weak" only if institutionalization is defined narrowly – with legal and contractual forms of cooperation as the main measure. Again, institutionalization is the process by which practices are made more dependable. As many argue, arrangements that involve certain material sanctions *can* help make more dependable the practice of cooperation; however, such mechanisms can also provide deterrents to cooperation for those less certain about a particular enterprise. In such cases, consensus, because it is often more incrementalist, can also lower the threshold for cooperation just enough to make cooperation acceptable. Perhaps, even more important, contractual arrangements are not the only way to more durable practices; other kinds of mechanisms can be just as strong (and sometimes, stronger) in compelling certain kinds of action or activity. In the case of ASEAN, for example, its well-established normative commitments to respecting national autonomy may lack formal compliance mechanisms, but they nevertheless exert strong regulatory pressures on the kinds of cooperation states are able to pursue in East and Southeast Asia.[8] In fact, the strength of ASEAN's personalistic practices, conceptualizations of national and regional resilience, and sovereignty-affirming modes of cooperation – that is, their *strong institutionalization* in the culture and structure of ASEAN as an institution – has been an important reason for the difficulty encountered by those seeking to move ASEAN towards more contractual forms of cooperation (see discussion below).

In short, the above suggests a need to consider the critical question of *what kind of cooperation* has been institutionalized. In the ASEAN case, it is clear that more contractually constraining forms of cooperation as practice remain under-institutionalized. What have been institutionalized very well, however, are cooperative practices and modes of decision-making based on a mutual respect for national priorities as a basis for regional resilience and regional cooperation.

ASEAN's cooperative agendas

The norms and practices of self-determination, noninterference, consensus, and resilience also affect ASEAN's cooperative agendas. For example, the understood comprehensiveness and interdependence of states' security and developmental challenges mean that ASEAN is not a single-issue, functionally defined organization; it is also difficult to delineate between functional areas. Instead, it is a multi-issue organization with a broad interest in helping its member states build national capacities towards better responding to the complex mix of security challenges they face. Today, the ASEAN cooperative framework involves regular meetings of ministers and directors responsible for no less than 22 different functional ministries or units.[9]

Most of all, ASEAN cooperation, consistent with states' concern for resilience, has displayed a strong developmental focus. That focus is especially apparent in ASEAN's economic and trade agendas. For example, ASEAN's early economic agenda focused on cultivating national industries, capacities, and resources, as well as a more interconnected regional economy, in "the spirit of [regional] assistance" (ASEAN 1976). It is worth underscoring here that the conditions of ASEAN's economic cooperation agenda have been quite different, for example, from more developed regions like Europe, where national economies are more established, and where economic cooperation responds to an already high level of regional economic interdependence. Neither of these conditions existed in 1960s and 1970s Southeast Asia. Thus, in contrast to the market-driven trade liberalization that has driven regional economic schemes elsewhere, the emphasis in ASEAN has historically been placed on trade facilitation where the state maintains a role in identifying development priorities and defending prioritized domestic arrangements in service of both stronger national economies and expanded intra-regional economic ties/integration. In this vein, ASEAN's early economic agenda also saw cooperative schemes aimed at building greater economic/trade complementarity, as well as transportation and communications access and infrastructure.

Moreover, while founding states have experienced considerable economic development since those early days of ASEAN, both resilience and a developmental ethos continue to inform ASEAN's contemporary economic agendas. For example, they condition how ASEAN states approach not just their own economic agreements but also agreements with others (e.g., ASEAN's bilateral FTA agreements with China, Japan, South Korea, and others, as well as how states approach trade liberalization agendas in Asia Pacific Economic Cooperation (APEC), the Trans-Pacific Partnership (TPP), and also the Regional Comprehensive Economic Partnership (RCEP)). In these negotiations, the state-managed trade facilitation approach preferred by most ASEAN states can sit in tension with the market-led trade liberalization agendas preferred by more established economies. Similarly, concerns about national and regional resilience (and by extension, fears of regional division) are especially at play in ASEAN's contemporary emphasis on regional "connectivity." In particular, "connectivity" reflects an explicit concern about "development gaps" and the emergence of a two-tier ASEAN in which ASEAN's less developed, newer member states are left behind to be picked off by other (generally, larger) actors.

The above norms and concerns also shape ASEAN's security agenda and the forms that cooperation takes in ASEAN. Concerns about regional resilience and the fragility of relations, for example, have affected ASEAN's ability to mediate conflicts between its members. Specifically, ASEAN has been governed by an informal understanding that states should not bring bilateral territorial disputes to ASEAN. This was partly because such disputes often involved sensitive domestic concerns, which, as noted, have historically constrained how interventionist ASEAN as an institution is able to be. Initially, the practice also reflected a concern that the fragile ASEAN cooperative enterprise would not be able to withstand the pressures or politics of directly addressing such disputes (Leifer 1999: 29), and though a dispute resolution mechanism (the ASEAN High Council) was created in 1976, it has never been used.[10] Instead, those with territorial disputes with others in ASEAN were to pursue conflict mediation/resolution bilaterally or through other arrangements. Notably such practices were not contrary to "regional cooperation" as conceived. As Amitav Acharya has explained, the practice of keeping bilateral disputes out of ASEAN – in a sense, insulating the organization from potentially destabilizing disputes – reflected, in its own way, a regionalist kind of thinking, or as Acharya (1997) puts it, "thinking multilaterally but acting bilaterally." Similarly, while states' recent turn to non-ASEAN bodies like the International Court of Justice (e.g., in the case of Indonesia's and Malaysia's dispute over Ligitan/Sipadan) or the International Tribunal for the Law of the Sea (e.g., as when Manila turned to that body for arbitration over South China Sea claims, especially vis-à-vis China) is seen by some as an ASEAN failing, the practice is actually quite consistent with the norms and practices that have governed ASEAN.

In short, while some refer to ASEAN's "passivity" towards particular bilateral and territorial disputes (ICG 2011), it is also not quite right to say that ASEAN is without effect. For example, Ramses Amer characterizes ASEAN as playing more of a facilitating role than a mediating role – that is, ASEAN facilitates conflict moderation/mediation efforts, as opposed to playing the more direct role of third-party mediator (Amer 2001–2). Similarly, ASEAN is commonly characterized as playing a "conflict management" role in contrast to being a "conflict resolver"

(Caballero-Anthony 1998; Askander 1994).[11] Mostly, however, ASEAN's institutional role has been indirect (see also Narine 1998: 202). Specifically, ASEAN's institutional role is to preempt and neutralize drivers of conflict – for example, by generating norms and principles of mutually respectful inter-state conduct, by providing an institutional setting supportive of economic and national development, by facilitating dialogue, increased political exchange and economic integration between states – all of which are understood to serve security by encouraging self-restraint and more region-regarding policies. While the "ASEAN way" of conflict management may not guarantee self-restraint, it has, by and large, created a more stable and secure regional environment for its member-states. Its approach is also reflective of its political and institutional values. The challenge for ASEAN, however, is that ASEAN has fewer established, at-the-ready mechanisms available to it when crisis does break out or when states misbehave in ways that destabilize ASEAN as an institution or Southeast Asia as a whole.

In addition to the understood political sensitivity of intra-regional relations, fundamental differences about strategic priorities and responses have also historically complicated ASEAN security cooperation. So contentious was the prospect of "security cooperation" that the 1967 ASEAN Declaration made no mention of it. In fact, security was not made an official ASEAN area of cooperation until 1992 – though ASEAN was clearly a political-security organization from the start. These differences clearly complicate a regional response – it is partly why, for example, there has been no "ASEAN alliance" or ASEAN collective security mechanism – but those differences are also, then, what make the importance states attached to a collective response to regional challenges notable. States' negotiations between the understood need to respect national priorities and the normative interest in a regional response have produced a series of ad hoc, adaptive and incremental compromises that today lay the foundations for ASEAN's contemporary security cooperation.

The first instance may be found in the 1967 Bangkok Declaration itself. Negotiations were stymied by critical differences over questions of national and regional autonomy and the roles played extra-regional security guarantors. Specifically, the status of US foreign bases in the Philippines proved an especially thorny sticking point between the Philippines, a US treaty ally, and Indonesia, a state long-interested in projecting an independent ("free and active") foreign policy. Their compromise was finally captured in ASEAN's 1967 Declaration's reference to the "temporary" status of foreign bases and their existence "only with the expressed concurrence of the countries concerned," as well as the explicit directive that foreign bases would not be used "directly or indirectly to subvert the national development and freedom of States" in pursuit of "their national development" (ASEAN Declaration, 1967).

Similar debates also plagued ASEAN's 1971 Declaration on a [Southeast Asian] Zone of Peace, Freedom, and Neutrality (ZOPFAN). A declaration of normative purpose, not a legally binding treaty, the ZOPFAN Declaration affirmed the necessity of both the collective group and collective action, even at the same time that its brevity (barely a page) was a clear indication of outstanding disagreements – in particular, disagreements about how such a zone would be secured, especially as regards the relative responsibilities and contributions of extra-regional versus Southeast Asian powers.[12] Another example was ASEAN's response to Vietnam's 1978 intervention into, and subsequent occupation of, Cambodia (then Kampuchea) (1979–1989), which similarly put on display intra-ASEAN differences over the question of external security guarantors. Differences between Thailand (which felt most immediately threatened and sought strategic assistance from China) and Indonesia (which feared China more than Vietnam, and was most wary of extra-regional alignments) were especially sharp.[13] Thus, it was notable that states managed to fashion an "ASEAN response," even if the consensus produced was clearly limited. Moreover, the "ASEAN response" – even while affirming the importance of a collective ASEAN security response – did not really reconcile, so much as combine two distinct approaches involving a military prong led by Thailand with Chinese strategic assistance, and a more diplomatic prong – most notably, via the Jakarta Informal Meetings (JIMs) – led by Indonesia.

ASEAN's intra-mural negotiations over US bases in 1967, ZOPFAN in 1971, and Vietnam in 1978 are illustrative of the strategic differences that have challenged and in many ways, defined ASEAN security cooperation. At the same time, to the extent that the normative emphasis on collective action demands compromises, each of these cases also highlight important points of commonality – in particular, a shared concern about threats of extra-regional intervention, even if orientations might fundamentally diverge. In this sense, it may be said that ASEAN states have been united by a general and principled concern about the threat of extra-regional intervention, as opposed to agreement about a specific threat or the specific policy response. Thus, in each of these cases, states maintained their normative commitment to *regional* autonomy from extra-regional powers and at the same time, their *national* autonomy from each other as regards specific security policy choices.

Such compromises and negotiations clearly have affected the kinds of security initiatives produced – for example, security declarations on principle and general rules of conduct as opposed to specific operational plans of action. Or perhaps more accurately, regional initiatives establish cooperative purposes and parameters but leave the operational aspects of security commitments to each individual state. These compromises also lay the normative and practical groundwork for today's contemporary security matrix in which regional cooperative frameworks coexist with US bilateral arrangements and other sub-regional and bilateral security cooperation.

Adaptive compromises made in fashioning an ASEAN response to Vietnam's 1978 intervention have been especially cited for providing precedent for a number of practices being debated and developed in response to more recent challenges. For example, the Vietnam/Cambodia case is sometimes cited as establishing an informal ASEAN practice of deferring to the "frontline state" while also keeping diplomatic avenues open. Some have suggested that the Vietnam/Cambodia case has offered a kind of referent in ASEAN's efforts to respond to South China Sea tensions in the 2000s (see, for example, Amer 2014) – though the South China

Sea disputes have been additionally complicated by the number of claimants involved (i.e., technically, there is more than one "front line state").[14]

The Vietnam case may also have created the precedent for another ASEAN practice – namely, the practice of relying on individual states, less ASEAN itself, playing a mediating or facilitating role in conflict amelioration. Such instances include Indonesia's role in creating the Track II South China Sea Workshops that began in the 1990s (which has parallels with the JIMs Indonesia created during the Vietnam/Cambodia conflict); Malaysia's playing a mediator role in Manila's conflict and negotiations with the Moro Islamic Liberation Front (MILF) in Mindanao since 2001; and Indonesia's offer of good offices in the case of Cambodia's and Thailand's renewed border dispute and tensions over Preah Vihear temple in 2008–2013. Another example (elaborated below) was Indonesia's quick initiative in facilitating intra-ASEAN agreement over a set of common principles (the six basic principles on the South China Sea) following ASEAN's divisions at its 2012 AMM (Emmers 2014; Oegroseno 2013).

Finally, another example may be found in the ASEAN Troika mechanism which was first proposed as a way to facilitate the Paris Peace Accords ending the Vietnam/ Cambodia conflict. The ASEAN Troika was formally instituted as an ASEAN mechanism in 2000 and invoked as a possible policy option (not always success-fully) in subsequent crises – including the political crisis in Cambodia in 1997, East Timor in 1999, the political situation in Myanmar in 2000 and 2013, the challenges of terrorism in 2001, and even North Korea in 2013[15] – suggesting some normalization of the mechanism as a viable ASEAN policy response, even if not its regularization as practice.

As noted above, ASEAN states have tended to emphasize ASEAN's role in neutralizing the sources of conflict before conflict breaks out, rather than as a responder to conflict, after the fact. The ASEAN Troika mechanism suggests some effort to respond to that particular institutional limitation, though its operation remains considerably limited by the demands of consensus and thus far from institutionalized as standard practice (see Teh 2004). Together, these instances of ASEAN states playing conflict mediating or facilitative roles have contributed to their more formal institutionalization in the ASEAN's 2007 Charter which expli-citly cites as one option available to disputing states that the "Chairman of ASEAN or the Secretary-General of ASEAN" (as well as other ASEAN and non-ASEAN states) might, at the request of parties, act "in an ex officio capacity, to provide good offices, conciliation or mediation" (Article 23).

Institutionalizing (and defending) "ASEAN centrality"

Over the course of the 1990s and into the 2000s, ASEAN practices extended to the remaining mainland Southeast Asian states, and also to new frameworks inclusive of Northeast Asian and Asian Pacific states, setting the stage for what is now frequently referred to as "ASEAN centrality."[16] These two important devel-opments in the 1990s marked a new stage of cooperation and institutionalism for ASEAN. They also represented a consolidation and a validation of ASEAN norms and practices. Indeed, it was a remarkable achievement that formerly adversarial states, on two different sides of the Cold War, were now members of the same organization.

No less an achievement was the fact that ASEAN's organization of small to medium powers now found itself the institutional hub in a network of new, post-Cold War cooperative frameworks in East Asia. Such post-Cold War frameworks include the ASEAN Regional Forum (ARF) – a framework made notable for being the first regularized, official ("Track I") political-security framework in East Asia for the range of states it included (27 members) and for the fact that it was inclusive of both the United States, the status quo regional and global power, and China, East Asia's resident rising power. Also of note were the Asia-Europe Meetings (ASEM) created in 1995 to regularize formal, cooperative ties between East Asian states and European Union members (see Chapter 8 in this volume); the ASEAN Plus Three (APT) meetings which held its first informal summit in 1997 (see Chapter 2); the East Asia Summit (EAS), a larger grouping established in 2005 and comprised of APT states plus Australia, New Zealand, and India that, in 2010, expanded to include also the United States and Russia; and also the ASEAN Defense Ministers' Meetings Plus (ADMM+) created in 2010 and comprised of the same states as the expanded EAS (see Chapter 4). In each of these individual arrangements, ASEAN's grouping of small powers has enjoyed unexpected influence over questions of membership, agenda, and pace of cooperation. As noted below and in the chapters to follow, ASEAN centrality is not without its challenges; nevertheless, ASEAN has emerged as a kind of institutional hub or focal point for overlapping institutional arrangements.

Moreover, the principle of ASEAN centrality has also become increasingly formalized and regularized in both ASEAN and ASEAN plus arrangements over the last two decades. In ASEM, ASEAN determines the critical question of who constitutes "Asia."[17] In the ARF, APT, and ADMM+8, ASEAN's pride of place is affirmed by both the name and structure of frameworks that conceptualize other members as extensions and partners of collective ASEAN. The institutionalization of ASEAN centrality is evident in other ways as well. These include the provision that an ASEAN state always co-chair the ARF, that different frameworks (the ARF, APT, EAS, and ADMM+) adopt or affirm ASEAN's TAC as their code of conduct, and the practice of dovetailing larger ASEAN-plus meetings after ASEAN's. More recently, these regional frameworks affirm, as a matter of course, ASEAN's interest in making ASEAN-linked frameworks the region's primary cooperative frameworks. In 2007, the ASEAN Charter formally endorsed the position that ASEAN "maintain the centrality and proactive role of ASEAN as the primary driving force in its relations and cooperation with its external partners" as one of ASEAN's driving purposes. Especially since 2007, recognition of ASEAN centrality has become a standard part of the statement of purpose in the preambles of ASEAN and ASEAN Plus Statements and Declarations.

New economic arrangements similarly reinforce a picture of ASEAN centrality. This is evident in the matrix of free trade agreements that have emerged around ASEAN. Specifically, ASEAN, over the course of the 2000s, has negotiated FTAs and economic agreements with six of its dialogue partners – China, Japan, South Korea, India, and Australia/New Zealand. While the economic weight in East Asia is clearly Northeast Asian and there is stated interest in a more "regional" East Asian FTA, economic cooperation in East Asia nevertheless finds its primary expression in an ASEAN-centric hub and spokes pattern.

Thus, similar to the above political-security frameworks, ASEAN has emerged as a regional and institutional focal point for cooperative economic activity. In both security and economic arenas, this pattern of ASEAN institutional centrality reflects a combination of political and historical-institutional factors. Partly, ASEAN owes its centrality to the fact that relations between the non-ASEAN states (especially, Northeast Asian states) have been more politically fraught, making it difficult for others to assume a more central or leading role. But partly also, ASEAN centrality can be traced to the system and structure of ASEAN's dialogue partner arrangements begun in the late 1970s, and the role that system has played in generating ASEAN-centric frameworks. Indeed, ASEAN's dialogue partnerships themselves – there are now 10 such partnerships[18] – might be characterized as an early precursor of "ASEAN centrality."[19] From that system emerged the first institutionalized and practical expressions of ASEAN centrality – namely, regularized "ASEAN+1" Ministerial Meetings and then ASEAN's Post-Ministerial Conference (ASEAN PMC). Established well before "ASEAN centrality" entered into the ASEAN lexicon as a formal principle or objective, these arrangements have provided important foundations for contemporary cooperative frameworks.

In particular, the ASEAN PMC process, expanding beyond its original economic and developmental focuses to include political security concerns, provided the institutional foundations for the ASEAN Regional Forum.[20] Similarly, the structure of ASEAN+1 arrangements was instrumental to the above-noted series of FTA and economic partnerships that emerged in the 2000s. In addition, these ASEAN FTAs have since provided the starting points for the Regional Comprehensive Economic Partnership (RCEP). Currently comprised of ASEAN's 10 states and the six states with which it has negotiated economic partnerships, RCEP aims to harmonize East Asia's different FTA agreements even at the same time as it seeks to affirm "ASEAN centrality in the regional economic integration process."[21] RCEP, as elaborated below, contrasts with the Trans-Pacific Partnership (TPP) negotiations that are simultaneously taking place with fewer negotiating parties and that have become US-driven.[22] In that one does not ordinarily expect smaller powers to have such influence, ASEAN centrality has become a curious fact of the East Asian and Asian Pacific institutional landscape. Some characterize this as reflective of ASEAN's unique "convening power" (Abad 2007; Stubbs 2014).

Challenges and opportunities

With the extension and expansion of ASEAN frameworks, however, come also new and different challenges for ASEAN, ASEAN institutionalism, and ultimately,

ASEAN centrality. While ASEAN states have been instrumental in bringing a diverse set of states to the table, diversity has also heightened the challenges of achieving consensus, the result being heightened questions about ASEAN's institutional efficacy and, in turn, about the appropriateness of ASEAN's centrality. Within ASEAN itself, ASEAN expansion in the 1990s had nearly doubled its membership from six (inclusive of Brunei which joined in 1984) to 10. The APT has 13; the EAS and ADMM+ have 18. Both APEC and the ARF are especially challenged with over 20 members. Just as important, in both ASEAN and "ASEAN plus" arrangements, new participants of ASEAN processes came to the table often with very different developmental and political experiences than that of original members.

While the technical challenges of achieving consensus are similar in both ASEAN and ASEAN-plus settings, an important point of contrast regards the latter's inclusion of much more materially capable actors who are also critical strategic and economic partners to the ASEAN states. Thus, in ASEAN-plus arrangements, the difficulties of consensus lie not just in the greater number of states, but also in the fact that these larger actors may feel less inclined to work at consensus given other material options that might be available to them. Their political priorities as regards regional cooperation may also vary. Additionally challenging to the achievement of consensus are the relations *between* the larger powers which are complicated by a heightened sense of strategic competition and, in the case of intra-Northeast Asian relations, also the burdens of perceived historical wrongs done them.

Such diversity in both ASEAN and ASEAN-plus arrangements challenges ASEAN's interest in centrality in a few key respects. For one, ASEAN centrality increasingly hinges on ASEAN itself being able to present a united front and common position, which expanded membership, as noted, makes more difficult. Yet the fact that there are non-ASEAN states that disagree with ASEAN's institutional priorities makes the need for unity all the more imperative. A divided ASEAN weakens their individual and collective ability to shape the cooperative agenda; it also opens Southeast Asia to divide and rule tactics by outside powers. In this sense, ASEAN's expanded efforts at economic integration and push for ASEAN connectivity serve not just the contemporary purpose of centrality, but also ASEAN's historical one of resilience.

Within ASEAN, however, expansion has complicated a larger institutional trajectory of intra-Southeast Asian cooperation. For example, the 1990s saw ASEAN's founding states – now more comfortable with one another and more developed – pursue more ambitious trade integration schemes like the ASEAN Free Trade Area (AFTA) and now the ASEAN Economic Community (AEC). As most will attest, these new frameworks are considerable improvements over the Preferential Trade Agreements (PTAs) ASEAN pursued in the 1970s – though the strongly institutionalized national autonomy expectations noted above plus the structure of ASEAN trade (especially, their continued reliance on external markets) and their associated domestic interests also continue to constrain both the content and pace of economic liberalization in ASEAN. Expansion has introduced to ASEAN members that are less developed, newer to market-driven export-led growth strategies, and thus even more cautious about economic liberalization schemes. Similarly, as regards intra-ASEAN security cooperation, ASEAN expansion adds four continental, mainland states to an organization that had previously been dominated by maritime states (Thailand being, for a long time, the lonely continental state in ASEAN). With that addition also come different strategic orientations and dependencies, especially vis-à-vis China versus the United States, that can complicate ASEAN's ability to achieve consensus.[23] Different Cold War histories also accentuate that strategic diversity. These differences can also result in different appreciation for the need for a united ASEAN front, whatever their differences. Such differences were on dramatic display at ASEAN's 2012 AMM, when ASEAN ministers, for the first time since 1967, were unable to produce a joint communiqué. At that meeting, Cambodia – as chair of that year's meeting, the last member to join ASEAN, and a state with extensive relations with China – proved either unwilling or unable to facilitate an ASEAN consensus.

Such concerns combine with a series of crises since the late 1990s to compel new reflection and debate about the kinds of cooperation that should be institutionalized in ASEAN. Among the most defining of those crises was the 1997–8 Asian Financial Crisis (AFC), which destabilized economies and regimes and posed the most serious existential challenge faced by many states since independence. A lesson in interdependence, the AFC created pressure for new mechanisms that might allow states to better oversee the tremendous transnational flows taking place between them. Also of note were a number of political crises involving domestic politics. These included the crisis in East Timor following the collapse of the Suharto regime in Indonesia; destabilizing factional politics in Cambodia, including a 1997 coup that pushed that country's ASEAN membership back two years; and also political crackdowns in Myanmar that made human rights an annual source of tension between ASEAN and its most important partners. Also of note have been environmental and humanitarian crises affecting air quality, public health, transportation, tourism, and other commercial interests. Domestic political changes and liberalization pressures have also created new and different pressures on ASEAN's state-centric institution to change.

In each of these cases, the dilemma for ASEAN has resided in the fact that these challenges were technically domestic issues but affected the stability and material fortunes of not just one country, but the region as a whole. And by the norms of noninterference, such challenges were supposed to be off the ASEAN agenda or at least treated with particular caution. There were at least two issues. The first, as suggested, regarded what ASEAN could do in cases involving regionally destabilizing domestic practices and policies. The second issue was functional and practical. As highlighted above, ASEAN's nationalist institutionalism has meant a more decentralized kind of cooperation in Southeast Asia that has historically prioritized the political and the principled, not the functional and the operational. However, the transnational economic, security, and environmental challenges above called for, at minimum, expanded cooperative agendas and closer collaboration, if not coordination. As suggested above, the question of ASEAN's functional efficacy was made additionally salient by the politics of ASEAN expansion within Southeast Asia (e.g. to Cambodia, Laos, and Myanmar) and beyond Southeast Asia (e.g., ARF, APEC, APT) arrangements. In the latter case, tensions were especially sharp in the ARF which included such actors as the United States, Europe, Australia, Canada – whose economic and political development were differently conditioned, for whom internal fragmentation and autonomy were not particular preoccupations, who came from different political traditions, and who consequently had different ideas about what regional arrangements should do and how they should operate. Frustrations about the ARF's particular difficulties in moving beyond confidence building to a more active, preventive diplomacy generated growing questions about the appropriateness of both ASEAN institutionalism and ASEAN's institutional centrality in Asia-Pacific processes (Kuhonta 2006; Yuzawa 2005; Beeson 2009; Cossa 2009; Searight 2010; Aggarwal and Chow 2010). Adding to these questions has been the heightening of major power tensions between the United States and China and between China and Japan, especially after 2009.

In ASEAN-plus arrangements, these differences have meant heightened differences over both the purpose and form of regional cooperation – that is *what* the cooperative agenda ought to be and *how* best to pursue it. This has resulted in important dissatisfactions on the parts of key participants – the United States, Australia, Canada, and Japan – who downgraded their participation in the ARF and pursued non-ASEAN-centric possibilities, especially during the early 2000s. While US policies, including its "rebalance to Asia" under President Obama (2009–2016), have renewed US commitments to ASEAN and ASEAN-related arrangements, and in so doing, interest from other states and actors, the questions about ASEAN institutionalism and the challenges to ASEAN centrality remain.

In short, the above domestic, intra-regional, and extra-regional pressures presented ASEAN states and a historically state-centric organization with at least two related challenges as regards institutionalized cooperation: 1) how to expand the collective and *regional* authority of ASEAN as an institution vis-à-vis the national; and 2) how to strengthen ASEAN's institutional capacity in ways that will provide states "common agency" (Capannelli 2013) to implement decisions and coordinate action in ways that were both more timely and functionally impactful. Both challenges push ASEAN to move beyond its nationalist bounded institutionalism that had been so defining to the organization. As Joakim Öjendal (2004) put it, "The difficulties in dealing with these (and other) issues have opened up for critical questioning of ASEAN's role and effectiveness in practice, and the real significance of institutionalized regionalization in South-East Asia."

Among ASEAN's more significant efforts has been states' 2007 adoption of an ASEAN Charter, which was ratified in late 2008 by all 10 ASEAN members, and its subsequent "community blueprints" (Economic, Political-Security, and Socio-Cultural). Towards making ASEAN into a more "rules based" and "more integrated entity," the Charter has mandated single chairmanships for "key high level ASEAN bodies" and taken steps to strengthen the ASEAN Secretariat by enhancing its monitoring and review functions, as well as diplomatic role (ASEAN

Secretariat 2008; ASEAN 2007). In this vein, the ASEAN Community Blueprints and their "Community Councils," as well as the midterm reviews produced for each pillar,[24] also suggest a more "methodological" as opposed to "political" approach to cooperation (Tay 2008: 155, 160). Also officially approved was a moderated consensus ("ASEAN Minus X") principle for issues concerning economic integration – a principle that, in theory, allows individual states to opt out of an agreement, thus allowing the rest to move forward. Similarly, a qualified majority has been introduced to "day-to-day operational issues" involving "functional institutions such as the ASEAN Infrastructure Fund, the ASEAN+3 Chiang-Mai Initiative Multilateralization (CMIM) and the Credit Guarantee Investment Facility" (Capannelli 2013).

Such moves point to a growing interest in expanding beyond ASEAN's historic state-centrism to a more regional approach – in particular, a need to strengthen ASEAN's *institutional* capacities and not just the national capacities of individual states as they have historically done. In a similar vein, recent developments also suggest a more "functional" turn in ASEAN's institutional development – that is, there is a greater emphasis on functional efficacy and "practical" cooperation that will have more immediate effects on a situation. In particular, the ASEAN Defense Ministers' Meetings (ADMM) and ASEAN Defense Ministers' Meetings Plus (ADMM+), which involve the participation of defense ministers and senior defense officials (as opposed to foreign ministers), has been indicative of new cooperation – more "work shop" than "talk shop" (Tan 2011, 2013). Similarly, the ARF, which, as noted, has been especially criticized for its inability to move beyond confidence building, has seen some interesting developments that include, for example, greater (even if still "cautious") coordination and collaboration in areas of maritime security, piracy, and disaster relief (Haacke 2009; Tan 2013; see also Chapter 5 in this volume). At the same time, it is important not to lose sight of the indirect role that existing ASEAN mechanisms have played in generating the kind of "functional" cooperation that its critics would like to see. This is the point that See Seng Tan makes, for example, in highlighting how ADMM+8 frameworks can be traced to consultations begun in the ARF (Tan 2013). In a somewhat different vein, he and Emmers (Emmers and Tan 2011) also note significant technical, actionable, and progressive collaboration in the security realm (and specifically, "preventive diplomacy") associated with ASEAN itself and other ASEAN-related arrangements.

Nevertheless, ASEAN's institutional adaptations can still be criticized for their practical limitations. Efforts at both institutional change and new cooperation also remain considerably constrained, especially by ASEAN's intra-regional obligations to national autonomy. Consequently, each of the above measures have had a caveat: consensus requirements limit both the ASEAN Minus X principle and the ASEAN Troika mechanism in practice; the ASEAN secretariat remains grossly understaffed, underfunded, and undertrained;[25] the most destabilizing (and thus also most sensitive) security issues remain mostly off the table of ADMM and ADMM+ frameworks. Similarly, the creation of an ASEAN Committee of Permanent Representatives (CPR), originally introduced to strengthen and facilitate the coordinating functions of the ASEAN Secretariat (see Tay 2008: 160), has in fact proven to be more a mechanism of political micromanagement by states (Pitsuwan 2011; Chongkittavorn 2012).

In the final analysis, recent efforts to make ASEAN cooperation more functional and truly regional is best described as "partial" (Nesadurai 2009: 102). Nevertheless, they still represent a shift from "the traditional ASEAN way approach to inter-state relations and institutional development" and suggest an organization trying to adapt to new challenges (Evans 2004: 264; Ravenhill 2008; Katsumata 2004; Khong and Nesadurai 2007; Dosch 2008; Tay 2008). It also reflects some recognition that while the old norms have served Southeast Asia well, new transnational challenges in a range of policy realms (economic, societal, environmental, security, among others) demand institutional changes or ASEAN risks losing relevance vis-à-vis both its own members and others. Similarly, the ASEAN Charter, though falling well short of the ambitious plans laid out by the original working group, must be seen as a working, living document that also opens the door (normatively and practically) to new forms of cooperation (Caballero-Anthony 2008). In this vein, it is worth underscoring a point that is often underappreciated – namely, ASEAN's thus far remarkable ability to adapt and consequently survive tremendous changes that have taken place in Southeast Asia since the 1960s.

Conclusion

This chapter has highlighted ASEAN as a key example and generator of institutionalized Southeast Asian cooperation. The kind of cooperation most institutionalized in Southeast Asia has generally been personalistic, not legalistic; consensus-driven, not majority-rules; nationalist, not regionalist; more collaborative, less coordinated; differentiated, rather than homogenized. Reflective of the political, normative, and socially constructed imperatives of Southeast Asian states' most formative period of post-colonial, Cold War development – most notably, resilience concerns and values – those features have now been institutionalized in the structure and culture of ASEAN as an institution. In contrast to those who equate legalism with strong institutionalization, the ASEAN case illustrates that institutionalization can also involve more informal, less legalistic practices. In fact, it is precisely because those practices have been so strongly institutionalized in ASEAN that the move to more contractual forms of obligations has been so difficult.

This chapter has also highlighted new challenges confronting both ASEAN and ASEAN-style institutionalism, and critical steps taken that open the door to new kinds of cooperation in Southeast Asia. The tensions between old and new mean that what we see from ASEAN is institutional adaptation, as opposed to wholesale change. Partly, this is, as suggested, because the old norms and drivers of cooperation have been so strongly institutionalized in both the structure and culture of the organization. But this is also partly because the old norms and drivers have not completely lost their relevance or value within ASEAN. Indeed, ASEAN-style cooperation has paid states "high political dividends" – stabilizing intra-regional relations, providing the basis for new cooperation, justifying platforms on which to engage uncertain actors, and substantiating ASEAN centrality (see Petri and Plummer 2014: 10; Haacke 2003: 218–223). Thus, new challenges have not delegitimated ASEAN's cooperative norms and practices, so much as called for their adjustment. Still, while longstanding ASEAN norms and practices have served states well, ASEAN's recent institutional moves nevertheless reflect some recognition that today's transnational economic, political, societal, and security challenges also call for different cooperative practices that move from nationalist collaboration and more towards "regional governance" (Capannelli 2013). Adding to the functional arguments for change are also now heightened political and normative concerns and questions about "ASEAN centrality" from the very partners whose recognition ASEAN states seek.

Notes

1 See discussion in Chapter 4 of this volume.
2 For expanded, but different, discussions on the need for broader definitions of cooperation, see Introduction and Chapter 1 in Ba 2009, and also Ba 2014.
3 This contrast in state rationalities has been explored by different authors for different settings. See, for example, Hameiri 2012, and Beeson and Jayasuriya 1998.
4 Maphilindo (a failed effort by Malaysia, the Philippines, and Indonesia at regional cooperation based on Malay ethno-nationalist ties), the Association of Southeast Asia (ASA – a failed cooperative effort by Thailand, Malaysia, and the Philippines), and the Southeast Asia Treaty Organization (SEATO – a US-hegemonic led effort at security organization that convinced only two Southeast Asian states to join). For a detailed overview of ASA and Maphilindo, see, especially, Jorgensen-Dahl 1982.
5 See discussion in Chapter 2 in Ba 2009.
6 On this point regarding ASEAN economic cooperation, see Ba 2009: 93; and more generally, 32, 33.
7 See Ba 2009 which systematically traces the incremental changes that have produced new security and economic cooperation in ASEAN.
8 For a book-length treatment of the regulatory effects of ASEAN norms on ASEAN, see Acharya 2001.
9 See ASEAN website (www.asean.org/asean/asean-structure/asean-sectoral-ministerial-bodies).
10 It seems likely states' avoidance of the High Council also reflected outstanding questions states might have had about the neutrality of other members, who, given the contestedness of states, might also have outstanding disputes with the parties involved.
11 Though it should be noted that conflict resolution is technically a category of conflict management.
12 For an extended discussion on intra-ASEAN negotiations on ZOPFAN, see Hanggi 1991.
13 See Antolik 1990, which continues to provide the best book-length treatment of the intra-ASEAN negotiations and challenges faced by ASEAN in trying to respond to Vietnam's intervention and occupation.
14 There is an argument to be made that the Philippines, as well as Vietnam, might be considered the "frontline" states as they have been more affected than other claimants (namely, Malaysia and especially Brunei).
15 Hun Sen, as ASEAN chair, apparently offered to convene an ASEAN Troika to conduct shuttle diplomacy on the Korean Peninsula following North Korea's underground nuclear tests in 2013. See Dalpino 2013.

16 For discussions that trace some of the origins of the term and what it entails, see Caballero-Anthony 2014; Ho 2012; and also Petri and Plummer 2014: 10–27.
17 Yang Razali Kassim, "Asia-Europe summit to debut in March in Bangkok," *Business Times* (May 4, 1995).
18 They are China, Japan, South Korea, United States, Russia, Australia, New Zealand, India, Canada, and the EU.
19 My thanks to Sueo Sudo for this observation about ASEAN's dialogue partnerships as distinct, institutionalized expressions of ASEAN centrality.
20 ASEAN had also unsuccessfully pushed to make the ASEAN-PMC the basis for the Australia-initiated Asia Pacific Economic Cooperation forum (APEC).
21 See Joint Declaration on the Launch of the Negotiations for the RCEP, Phnom Penh, Cambodia, November 20, 2012.
22 For a discussion of ASEAN centrality in relation to RCEP, the TPP, and the US–ASEAN economic relationship, see Petri and Plummer 2014.
23 See, for example, Collins 2003, who contrasts Southeast Asia's mainland and maritime security complexes. See also Emmerson 1996.
24 A midterm report was produced for both the ASEAN Economic Community (2012) and the ASEAN Socio-Cultural Community (2014) pillars. A "status report" for the ASEAN Political Security Community pillar was produced in 2009.
25 According to Capannelli (2013), the ASEAN Secretariat in 2012 had a budget of US $16 million and a staff of 300, a far cry from the US$220 million and 1600 employees that the ADBI projects will need by 2030.

References

Abad, M.C., Jr. 2007. Constructing a Social ASEAN. ASEAN website (June 4). www.asean.org/resources/item/constructing-the-social-asean-m-c-abad-jr.
Acharya, Amitav. 1997. Ideas, Identity, and Institution-building: From the "ASEAN Way" to the "Asia-Pacific Way"? *Pacific Review* 10(1): 319–346.
Acharya, Amitav. 2001. *Constructing a Security Community in Southeast Asia*. London: Routledge.
Acharya, Amitav. 2004. How Ideas Spread: Whose Norms Matter? Norm Localization and Institutional Change in Asian Regionalism. *International Organization* 58(Spring): 239–275.
Aggarwal, Vinod and Jonathan Chow. 2010. The Perils of Consensus: How ASEAN's Meta-regime Undermines Economic and Environmental Cooperation. *Review of International Political Economy* 17(2): 262–290.
Amer, Ramses. 2001–2. The Association of Southeast Asian Nations and the Management of Territorial Disputes. *IBRU Boundary and Security Bulletin* (Winter): 81–96.
Amer, Ramses. 2014. The Dispute Management Approach of the Association of Southeast Asian Nations: What Relevance for the South China Sea Situation? In Shicun Wu, ed., *Non-Traditional Security Issues and the South China Sea*. Burlington, VT: Ashgate, pp. 47–72.
Antolik, Michael. 1990. *ASEAN and the Diplomacy of Accommodation*. Armonk, NY: M. E. Sharpe.
ASEAN. 1976. ASEAN Joint Press Statement of the 2nd ASEAN Economic Ministers Meeting, March 9.
ASEAN. 2007. ASEAN Leaders Sign ASEAN Charter (Press Release). November 20. www.asean.org/news/item/media-release-asean-leaders-sign-asean-charter-singapore-20-november-2007.

ASEAN Secretariat. 2008. ASEAN Embarks on New Era: ASEAN Charter Fully Ratified (Press Release). October 21. www.asean.org/news/asean-statement-communiques/item/press-release-asean-embarks-on-new-era-asean-charter-fully-ratified-asean-secretariat.

Askander, Kamarulzaman. 1994. ASEAN and Conflict Management: The Formative Years of 1967–1976. *Pacifica Review: Peace, Security & Global Change* 6(2): 57–69.

Askander, Kamarulzaman, Jacob Bercowtch, and Mikio Oishi. 2002. The ASEAN Way of Conflict Management: Old Patterns and New Trends. *Asian Journal of Political Science* 10(2): 21–42.

Ba, Alice D. 2009. *(Re)Negotiating East & Southeast Asia: Regions, Regionalisms, and ASEAN.* Stanford, CA: Stanford University Press.

Ba, Alice D. 2011. ASEAN Centrality Imperiled? ASEAN Institutionalism and the Challenges of Major Power Institutionalization. In Ralf Emmers, ed., *ASEAN and the Institutionalization of East Asia.* Abingdon and New York: Routledge, pp. 114–129.

Ba, Alice D. 2013. The Association of Southeast Asian Nations: Between Internal and External Legitimacy. In Dominik Zaum ed., *Legitimating International Organizations: Practice and Problems.* Oxford: Oxford University Press, pp. 131–162.

Ba, Alice D. 2014. Institutional Divergence and Convergence in the Asia Pacific? ASEAN in Practice and Theory. *Cambridge Review of International Affairs* 27(2): 295–318.

Beeson, Mark. 2009. ASEAN's Ways: Still Fit for Purpose? *Cambridge Review of International Affairs* 22(3): 333–343.

Beeson, Mark and Kanishka Jayasuriya. 1998. The Political Rationalities of Regionalism: APEC and the EU in Comparative Perspective. *Pacific Review* 11(3): 311–336.

Caballero-Anthony, Mely. 1998. Mechanisms of Dispute Settlement: The ASEAN Experience. *Contemporary Southeast Asia* 20(1): 38–66.

Caballero-Anthony, Mely. 2008. The ASEAN Charter: An Opportunity Missed or One that Cannot be Missed. *Southeast Asia Affairs 2008.* Singapore: ISEAS, pp. 71–85.

Caballero-Anthony, Mely. 2014. Understanding ASEAN's Centrality: Bases and Prospects in an Evolving Regional Architecture. *Pacific Review* 27(4): 563–584.

Capannelli, Giovanni. 2013. ASEAN Principles Need Efficiency Updates. *East Asia Forum* (November 5). www.eastasiaforum.org/2013/11/05/asean-principles-need-efficiency-updates/.

Chongkittavorn, Kavi. 2012. Asean Secretariat Must be Strengthened. *The Irawaddy* (May 21).

Ciociari, John D. 2010. *The Limits of Alignment: Southeast Asia and the Great Powers Since 1975.* Washington, DC: Georgetown University Press.

Collins, Alan. 2000. *The Security Dilemmas of Southeast Asia.* Singapore: ISEAS.

Collins, Alan. 2003. *Security and Southeast Asia: Domestic, Regional and Global Issues.* Singapore: Institute of Southeast Asian Studies.

Cossa, Ralph. 2009. Evolving US Views on Asia's Future Institutional Architecture. In Michael J. Green and Bates Gill, eds, *Asia's New Multilateralism: Cooperation, Competition, and the Search for Community.* New York: Columbia University Press, pp. 33–54.

Dalpino, Catherine. 2013. Multilateralism in the Asia Pacific. *Comparative Connections* (May). http://csis.org/files/publication/1301qasia_regionalism.pdf.

Dosch, Jörn. 2008. ASEAN's Reluctant Liberal Turn and the Thorny Road to Democracy Promotion. *Pacific Review* 21(4): 527–545.

Eaton, Sarah and Richard Stubbs. 2006. Is ASEAN Powerful? Neo-Realist Versus Constructivist Approaches to Power in Southeast Asia. *Pacific Review* 19(2): 135–155.

Emmers, Ralf. 2003. *Cooperative Security and the Balance of Power in ASEAN.* London: Routledge.

Emmers, Ralf. 2014. Indonesia's Role in ASEAN: A Case of Incomplete and Sectorial Leadership. *Pacific Review* 27(4): 543–562;

Emmers, Ralf and See Seng Tan. 2011. The ASEAN Regional Forum and Preventive Diplomacy: Built to Fail? *Asian Security* 7(1): 44–60.

Emmerson, Donald K. 1996. Indonesia, Malaysia, and Singapore: A Regional Security Core? In Richard Ellings and Sheldon Simon, eds, *Southeast Asia in the New Millennium*. Armonk, NY: M. E. Sharpe.

Evans, Paul. 2004. Human Security and East Asia: In the Beginning. *Journal of East Asian Studies* 4: 263–284.

Frost, Ellen. 2008. *Asia's New Regionalism*. Boulder, CO: Lynne Rienner Publishers.

Haacke, Jürgen. 2003. *ASEAN's Diplomatic and Security Culture*. London: Routledge.

Haacke, Jürgen. 2009. The ASEAN Regional Forum: From Dialogue to Practical Cooperation. *Cambridge Review of International Affairs* 22(3): 427–449.

Hameiri, Shahar. 2012. Theorising Regions through Changes in Statehood: Rethinking the Theory and Method of Comparative Regionalism. *Review of International Studies* (December): 1–23.

Hanggi, Heiner. 1991. *ASEAN and the ZOPFAN Concept*. Pacific strategic papers. Singapore: ISEAS.

Ho, Benjamin. 2012. *ASEAN's Centrality in A Rising Asia*. RSIS Working Paper, No. 249. Singapore: RSIS.

International Crisis Group (ICG). 2011. *Waging Peace: ASEAN and the Thai–Cambodian Border Conflict*. Asia Report No. 215. Brussels: ICG.

Jones, David Martin and Michael L. R. Smith. 2007. Making Process, Not Progress: ASEAN and the Evolving East Asian Regional Order. *International Security* 32(1): 148–184.

Jorgensen-Dahl, Arnfinn. 1982. *Regional Organization and Order in South-East Asia*. London: Macmillan.

Katsumata, Hiro. 2003. Reconstruction of Diplomatic Norms in Southeast Asia: The Case for Strict Adherence to the "ASEAN Way". *Contemporary Southeast Asia* 25(1): 104–121.

Katsumata, Hiro. 2004. Why Is ASEAN Changing? From "Non-Interference" to "Open and Frank Discussions". *Asian Survey* 44: 2.

Khong, Yuen Foong and Helen E. S. Nesadurai. 2007. Hanging Together, Institutional Design, and Cooperation in SEA: AFTA and the ARF. In Amitav Acharya and Alastair Iain Johnston, eds, *Crafting Cooperation*. Cambridge: Cambridge University Press, pp. 32–82.

Kuhonta, Erik Martinez. 2006. Walking a Tightrope: Democracy versus Sovereignty in ASEAN's Illiberal Peace. *Pacific Review* 19(3): 337–358.

Leifer, Michael. 1989. *ASEAN and the Security of South-East Asia*. London: Routledge.

Leifer, Michael. 1999. The ASEAN Peace Process: A Category Mistake. *The Pacific Review* 12(1): 25–38.

Leifer, Michael. 2000. Regional Solutions to Regional Problems? In Gerald Segal and David S. G. Goodman, eds, *Towards Recovery in Pacific Asia*. London: Routledge, pp. 108–118.

Narine, Shaun. 1998. ASEAN and the Management of Security. *Pacific Affairs* 71(2): 195–214.

Narine, Shaun. 2002. *Explaining ASEAN*. Boulder, CO: Lynne Reinner.

Nesadurai, H.E.S. 2009. ASEAN and Regional Governance after the Cold War: From Regional Order to Regional Community? *The Pacific Review* 22(1): 91–118.

Oegroseno, Arif Havas. 2013. ASEAN as the Most Feasible Forum to Address the South China Sea Challenges (Panel: The Challenges for ASEAN: The South China Sea,

Investment Protection and Myanmar). *Proceedings of American Society of International Law* (April): 282–283.

Öjendal, Joakim. 2004. Back to the Future? Regionalism in South-East Asia Under Unilateral Pressure. *International Affairs* 80(3): 519–533.

Petri, Peter and Michael Plummer. 2014. *ASEAN Centrality and the ASEAN-US Economic Relationship*. East West Center Policy Studies No. 69. Honolulu, HI: East West Center.

Pitsuwan, Surin. 2011. ASEAN's Challenge: Some Reflections and Recommendations on Strengthening the ASEAN Secretariat. Report submitted to H. E. Marty Natalegawa, Chair ASEAN Coordinating Council, December 12.

Ravenhill, John. 2001. *APEC and the Construction of Pacific Rim Regionalism*. Cambridge: Cambridge University Press.

Ravenhill, John. 2008. Fighting Irrelevance: An Economic Community "with ASEAN Characteristics". *Pacific Review* 21(4): 469–488.

Reus-Smit, Christian. 1997. The Constitutional Structures of International Society and the Nature of Fundamental Institutions. *International Organization* 51(4): 555–589.

Searight, Amy. 2010. New Challenges, New Vision, Pedestrian Progress. *Comparative Connections* (April): 125–140.

Stubbs, Richard. 2005. *Rethinking Asia's Economic Crisis*. New York: Palgrave.

Stubbs, Richard. 2014. ASEAN's Leadership in East Asian Region-Building: Strength in Weakness. *Pacific Review* 27(4): 523–541.

Tan, See Seng. 2011. From Talkshop to Workshop: ASEAN's Quest for Practical Security Cooperation through the ADMM and ADMM-Plus Processes. In Bhubhindar Singh and See Seng Tan, eds, *From "Boots" to "Brogues": The Rise of Defence Diplomacy in Southeast Asia*. Singapore: RSIS.

Sukma, Rizal. 2008. The ASEAN Charter: Neither Bold nor Visionary. In Pavin Chachavalpongpun, ed., *The Road to Ratification and Implementation of the ASEAN Charter*. Singapore: Institute of Southeast Asian Studies.

Tan, See Seng. 2013. Future of ADMM-Plus: Asia's Growing Defence Engagements. RSIS Commentaries No. 158.

Tay, Simon. 2008. The ASEAN Charter: Between National Sovereignty and the Region's Constitutional Moment. *Singapore Year Book of International Law*: 151–170.

Teh, Benny Cheng Guan. 2004. ASEAN's Regional Integration Challenge: The ASEAN Process. *Copenhagen Journal of Asian Studies* 20: 70–94.

Thambipillai, Pushpa. 1985. ASEAN Negotiating Styles: Asset or Hindrance? In Pushpa Thambipillai and Johan Sarvanamuttu, eds, *ASEAN Negotiations: Two Insights*. Singapore: ISEAS, pp. 3–28.

Yuzawa, Takeshi. 2005. Japan's Changing Conception of the ASEAN Regional Forum: From an Optimistic Liberal to a Pessimistic Realist Perspective. *Pacific Review* 18: 4.

2 The institutionalization of "East Asian" regionalism

The critical cases of ASEAN Plus Three and East Asia Summit

Md Nasrudin Md Akhir and Sueo Sudo

Introduction

This chapter analyzes the key features and sources of the institutionalization of "East Asian" regionalism since the 1990s. It does so by focusing on the cases of the ASEAN Plus Three (APT) and the East Asia Summit (EAS). As an ongoing phenomenon with long-term implications for the international order, East Asian regionalism has been characterized by three unique features. First, the evolution of East Asian regionalism is a process that has been initiated by and centered at the minor and emerging middle powers in Southeast Asia, rather than the much more powerful countries in Northeast Asia. Second, the organizational structure of East Asian regionalism has been characterized by diffuse, overlapping, and multi-layered inter-state cooperation, rather than being a highly institutionalized entity with a centralized structure of organizational authority. Third, in terms of its membership and the underlying power relations, East Asian regionalism has been driven not just by functional geographical and economic factors, but also by geo-political and geo-strategic calculations, as evidenced by the membership of the EAS that includes not one but several players that are geographically outside of the "East Asian" region.

Each of these three features is counter-intuitive on its own terms. Together, they form a puzzle that must be addressed by students and scholars of East Asian Studies, that is: why has East Asian regionalism remained an integration process that is ASEAN-led, loosely institutionalized, and inclusive of players outside of the geographical boundaries of East Asia? Addressing this issue is key to a better understanding of the past, present, and future of East Asian regionalism. This is especially so in light of the ongoing shift in global economic power from West to East, the intensification of the U.S.-led Trans-Pacific Partnership (TPP) negotiations, and the institutionalization of cooperation among the three Northeast Asian countries in the recent years. The character of East Asia's "institutionalized" structure partly reflects a conscious decision to set aside ideologies and show the international community that despite national differences, the member nations can still cooperate with one another. For example, the structure offers China, Japan, and the Republic of Korea (ROK) a neutral platform by which to pursue greater cohesion or harmony. Recent global and regional developments, including the challenges of intra-Northeast Asian relations, however, have raised many critical questions, not least about whether and how long the current ASEAN-centered East Asian regionalism will last, and how soon alternative forms of regionalism will emerge.

We argue that the institutional features of East Asian regionalism are a product of the interplays between functional imperatives and power dynamics. By functional imperatives, we mean the necessity for cooperation among a group of sovereign states in order to pursue certain common and mutually beneficial goals, including development, prosperity, security, and stability at both national and regional levels. By power dynamics, we refer to the self-interested calculations of individual key players (both major powers and regional states) that are aimed at maximizing their own relative position and interest *vis-à-vis* others in the system. While functional imperatives necessarily manifest in collaborative actions over issues ranging from trade, financial, transportation, and energy cooperation to transnational crime, contagious diseases, and natural disaster management, power dynamics often involve a more zero-sum and competitive action–reaction dynamic among the self-interested state actors. As shall be discussed below, it is the interactions and tensions between these two imperatives that have shaped the eventual forms and degrees of institutionalization of APT and EAS, which, by virtue of their memberships and impact, have emerged as the backbone of East Asian regionalism since the mid-2000s.

It is important to first define "institutions" and "institutionalization." As elaborated in the Introduction, the term "institutions" is defined as durable rules that shape expectations, interests, and behavior, whereas institutionalization is a process of regularizing and harmonizing behavior among sovereign actors, which involves the adoption of some agreed-upon rules, norms, and mechanisms among them. Institutionalization, in other words, is a process of creating commonly understood rules, expected paths of action and behavior, and mutually recognized constraints.

An overview of "East Asian" regionalism: from APT to EAS

When the Cambodian conflict ended in 1991, a common perception about and within ASEAN was that it had lost political direction (Sudo 2005). To counter such views, ASEAN leaders convened in January 1992 and adopted the Singapore Declaration which contained four concrete agreements, namely:

> (1) move to a higher plane of political and economic cooperation to secure regional peace and security; (2) seek to safeguard its collective interests in response to the formation of large and powerful economic groupings; (3) seek avenues to engage member states in new areas of cooperation in security matters; (4) forge closer relations based on friendship and cooperation with the Indochinese countries, following the settlement of the Cambodian conflict.
>
> (ASEAN 1992)

Since then security cooperation, extra-regional engagement, and economic integration have formed the three main thrusts of the ASEAN agenda in the interest of greater regional stability.

The initial post-Cold War frameworks were not initially East Asian. For example, a combination of post-Cold War security concerns and an assortment of proposals forwarded by Russia, Australia, and Canada, pushed ASEAN countries to form the ASEAN Regional Forum (ARF) in 1993. The forum for multilateral security cooperation held its first meeting in 1994. ASEAN's interests and concerns were why the ARF was named the *ASEAN*, not Asian, Regional Forum (Kimura 1995). The proposal by Japan and others to employ Post Ministerial Conference (PMC) as a security forum also offered a way forward, facilitating a new regionalism and forum for the discussion of security and political issues (Acharya 2009).

Efforts to promote regional integration and expand extra-regional links took various forms. One of them was Malaysia's proposal to create an East Asian Economic Group (EAEG), later renamed the East Asian Economic Caucus (EAEC) (Md Nasrudin 2009). Indeed, a perception existed that ASEAN may become marginalized in terms of economy and security in the wake of the creation of the Europe Union (EU) and the North American Free Trade Agreement (NAFTA). The fifth ASEAN summit in December 1995 discussed other proposals and regional cooperation, such as the Trans-Asia Railway and the Mekong Basin Development (Gilson 2002). Furthermore, the inaugural Asia-Europe Meeting (ASEM) involving ASEAN and other East Asian countries with Europe was held in Bangkok in 1996, which marked the formation of a multilateral, inter-regional dialogue. These efforts and developments laid important foundation for a deeper regional integration in East Asia and beyond.

The 1997 Asian financial crisis and the institutionalization of APT

The financial crisis that started in Thailand in 1997 soon spread its contours to other countries – notably Indonesia and the ROK. Some commonly known factors of the crisis are: "(1) an over-reliance on short term foreign borrowing by private firms and banks; (2) over-investment in real estate; (3) inadequate supervision of financial institutions; and (4) over-dependence on the U.S. dollar" (Sudo 2002: 27). The crisis and its consequences provided an important impetus for the finance ministers of East Asian states to meet more frequently. This was done under the framework of APT.

In November 1997, the representatives from Australia, Brunei, Canada, China, Hong Kong, Indonesia, Japan, the ROK, Malaysia, New Zealand, the Philippines, Singapore, Thailand, and the United States met to discuss possible International Monetary Fund (IMF) solutions (ASEAN 1997) – even though the solutions provided by the IMF were disappointing for many, especially the crisis-affected countries. As an alternative, the crisis-affected countries as well as the ASEAN members started looking towards the major East Asian economies to play a role (Narine 2001; Stubbs 2002). Japan responded positively and proposed the Asian Monetary Fund (AMF) which was subsequently rejected by the United States.

Japan then came out with another proposal called the "New Miyazawa Initiative" – under this proposal, a package worth US$30 billion was offered, which proved helpful to the countries influenced by the crisis like the ROK, Indonesia, Malaysia, Singapore, the Philippines, and Thailand.

Following the outbreak of the financial crisis, efforts have been made to enhance cooperation among the East Asian countries (Rüland 2000) and as a result, various institutions have emerged, notably the APT in 1997. Since then, ASEAN member states have established networks of bilateral currency arrangements with China, Japan, and the ROK. The agreements have occurred under the Chiang Mai Initiative (CMI) framework to prevent future financial crises (Ravenhill 2008). This was an initiative announced by the APT finance ministers with the overall aim to collaborate in four principal quarters, namely: monitoring capital flows, regional surveillance, swapping networks, and training personal. This initiative "involves an expanded ASEAN Swap Arrangement that would include all ASEAN countries, and a network of bilateral swap and repurchase agreement facilities among ASEAN countries, China, Japan and the ROK" (ASEAN 2000).

Moreover, within the framework of APT, the finance ministers worked to introduce the Asian Bond Market Initiative (ABMI) in 2003. Evidently, ABMI proved an appropriate scheme for various other financial institutions namely, Asia Cooperation Dialogue (ACD), the Executives' Meeting of East Asia Pacific Central Banks (EMEAP), and the Asian Development Bank (ADB). In addition to the ABMI, the APT meeting has eventually become a viable platform to discuss future plans and crisis prevention.

Through these processes, Japan became a major player and firmed its commitment to establish financial structures independent of the U.S.A. It is APT that provided Japan with the tool to create a financial system – one that would attract economies in the region. Since 2000, APT finance ministers have held regular meetings to discuss issues that are of common concern. The APT framework has provided the mechanism to advance financial cooperation. The main initiatives regarding financial cooperation have been the bilateral trade agreements between ASEAN Plus Three countries, the CMI, and the ABMI.

The financial crisis had several effects on ASEAN – notably, it endowed liberalization with added momentum and conveyed that regionalism is not all about politics but economy as well (Camilleri 2003). It also conveyed that if member countries in a region approve desirable structural reforms with regards to transparency and accountability, they can turn a crisis into an opportunity – the 1998 Hanoi Summit is an example. Not long after the 1997 Manila agreement, the financial ministers of the ASEAN member states reached a decision to establish a peer surveillance system to supervise macroeconomic policies, financial regulations, and transparency of member countries. Moreover, on the eve of the 6th ASEAN summit in Hanoi, the "Hanoi Action Plan" was adopted calling for several plans of action to facilitate the ASEAN Vision 2020 – it consisted of a five-year timeline 1999–2004. With the adoption of the Hanoi Declaration of 1998 and the Hanoi Plan of Action, ASEAN provided a way forward for future and sustainable integration.

Thus, APT cooperation quickly began to regularize. Formally started in 1997 at the periphery of the 2nd ASEAN Informal Summit in Malaysia, the APT's institutionalization was evidenced in 1999, by a Joint Statement at the 3rd APT Summit in Manila – where leaders from APT countries urged a move forward and escalation of East Asia cooperation in various areas at various levels. Significantly, financial cooperation among the APT countries has been implemented in tandem with other forms of regional integration, including free trade agreements, comprehensive economic partnerships, and functional cooperation in areas like transportation, health, food security, combating transnational crime, youth exchange, environment and disaster management. A horizontal and vertical integration among the APT countries over the past 15 years has substantially deepened regional interdependence, benefiting individual member countries in various ways. These achievements are remarkable, especially considering the vast differences among the regional states. The APT countries, for instance, not only differ in terms of their political systems, religions, cultures, values, and size of their land areas, they also vary in terms of the size and growth rate of their respective economies.

APT is a regional process driven by ASEAN that includes ASEAN countries, Japan, China, and the ROK. All 13 members of ASEAN+3 vary with unique differences in terms of their adopted political system, religion, culture, and land area, in addition to many other characteristics. However, these countries exhibit a particularly apparent difference in the size and growth rate of their respective economies. The trade structure in the East Asian region was once considered vertical as Japan was the only country which exported manufactured products whereas other East Asian countries were mainly suppliers of raw materials (Yoshimatsu 2003). The intra-regional trade within East Asia later became also horizontal, displaying interdependence among countries in Southeast Asia (for example), thus expanding upon the vertical-structured trade orientation that initially characterized regional economic integration. Still, as mentioned by Taggart Murphy, Japan, China, and the ROK remain very much East Asia's economic powerhouses, as they, together, own "much of the world's productive capacity" (Murphy 2009). In fact, East Asian economies' contribution to the world GDP is one of the biggest in the world (World Bank 2012).

Judging by the progress within APT, the main agendas have been mostly on transnational issues which were largely believed to be affecting the region as a whole. For instance, until May 2008, identified areas of APT cooperation involved 20 sectors covering the coordination of political and security policies, economy, trade and investment, macro economy, currency and finance, agriculture, fisheries and forestry, energy, the environment, tourism, transnational crime, health, labor, arts and culture, science and technology, ICT, information, social welfare, youth, women, rural development and eradication of poverty, natural disasters, and natural minerals. As similarly highlighted in the last chapter on ASEAN, APT's multi-functional agenda may reflect in part the comprehensiveness and interconnectedness of challenges. This approach is also believed to provide a wide basis where the establishment of a regional community can be realized and developed.

As a comparison, NAFTA concentrates more on commercial orientation where priority is only given to efforts that accommodate significantly large economic transactions between members. NAFTA primarily functions as an area for region-ally beneficial economic gain (Abbott 2000), whereas the local context of APT serves the greater roles of peace, stability, and economic prosperity.

Thus, APT has been developed to be a beneficial entity to help promote and nurture the partner nations in order to work toward a peacefully stable region. In the "Second Joint Statement on East Asian Cooperation" announced at the end of the APT Summit in November 2007 in Singapore, it was admittedly apparent that numerous vital accomplishments had been achieved in terms of regional coopera-tion in East Asia since the 1997 financial crisis of Asia. It is reasonable to say that intra-APT cooperation should be encouraged in the next 10 years and it can equally be agreed upon that cooperation within APT is the main vehicle of realizing the formation of the East Asian Community (EAC).

During the 14th APT Summit held on November 18, 2011 in Bali, the member states showed their satisfaction with the developments under APT coop-eration through the execution of the 2nd Joint Statement on the work plan (2007–2017) set under APT cooperation. Earlier, at the 13th APT Summit held in Hanoi (October 2010), the member states reaffirmed that under the umbrella of ASEAN as the driving force, the member countries would continue to work towards establishing an East Asian community in order to provide a mechanism for long-term developments in the region. Not only that, the Summit also approved the equally balancing and reinforcing positions of the APT process along with other bodies such as the EAS and the ARF with the overall aim to encourage East Asian community building. The 12th APT Foreign Ministers Meeting in Bali (July 21, 2010) approved the Terms of Reference (TOR) towards the establish-ment of the East Asia Vision Group (EAVG) II. Furthermore, the 5th APT Min-isterial Meeting on Transnational Crime (AMMTC+3) held in Bali (October 12, 2011) acknowledged the need to combat transnational crime by implementing tangible schemes.

In an effort to meet beyond the framework of the APT while simultaneously working alongside the APT, China, Japan, and the ROK have also begun their own trilateral summit, the first of which was hosted by Japan in December 2008. The trilateral meeting was aimed at advancing wider regional cooperation frame-works such as APT, EAS, ARF, and Asia-Pacific Economic Cooperation (APEC) as well as addressing the serious challenges in the global economy and the financial markets (MOFA 2008). In conjunction with the annual Trilateral Summit, the three countries had more than 50 trilateral consultative mechanisms including 18 Ministerial meetings and over 100 cooperative projects in 2011. What is clear is that the ASEAN-centered approach to region building in East Asia promoted an unbiased space for regional cooperation among the three nations. Since 1999 the purpose of the trilateral cooperation is to establish a future-oriented and compre-hensive partnership, and to facilitate regional peace, co-prosperity, and sustainable development. The Independent Trilateral Summit and the Trilateral Summit Meeting at the occasion of APT are held annually on a rotational basis. Taking a positive-sum view of trilateral relations, East Asian regionalism should simultaneously encourage and strengthen developments to the extent that such arrangements and institutional frameworks facilitate confidence, cooperation, and trust-building bilaterally as well as multilaterally, although some constraints may occur along the path due to historical contexts and other geopolitical tensions among Northeast Asian countries.

The early stages of the Trilateral Summit focused especially on economic development, particularly with China's entry into the World Trade Organization (WTO) around that time. The three nations were also focused on joint research to be carried out by government-funded institutes. The initially more laid-back style of the trilateral meeting took a step towards a formalized organization in 2008. That year, the trilateral meeting, which normally met in conjunction with APT, held its first meeting, independent of an ASEAN meeting. Then, in 2010, states moved to create a secretariat for trilateral cooperation. The secretariat was to provide administrative support and secretarial services for various trilateral consultative mechanisms as well as explore new agendas for cooperation and actively engage in public diplomacy. The new Trilateral Cooperation Secretariat (TCS) was opened in Seoul in September 2011 (Yeo 2012).

However, the trilateral meetings continue to run into obstacles, complicating their independence from ASEAN, which has remained the institutional core of East Asian regionalism. In the years since its formation, the summit has run into trouble several times with conflicts between the nations causing the summit to be postponed. For example, in 2005 due to the then Japanese Prime Minister, Junichiro Koizumi's visit to the Yasakuni Shrine, the trilateral meeting was canceled and the leaders of the three countries did not meet again until 2007. Similarly, the 2013 trilateral meeting once again ran into a roadblock with China requesting the summit that was initially scheduled in May to be postponed due to tensions caused by China's territorial dispute with Japan over a group of islands in the East China Sea (Nam 2013). Despite the fact that the trilateral meetings were definitely a right step in improving the relations between the three countries, the complications highlighted above challenge any expectations that China, Japan, and the ROK might have a successful institution without ASEAN playing an impartial mediator role. As is the ASEAN way, there is no real issue of who is the leader of the region; rather the APT platform focusing on cooperation and multilateral agreement is still at best, the most possible answer for an East Asian regional block.

Institutionalization of EAS

In November 2004, when the APT countries decided to hold the first meeting of the proposed EAS the following year, several concerns emerged among the members. First, it was not clear who would be leading the summit, given the Sino–Japanese antagonism – although ASEAN made it clear its own central role. Second, it was not clear what role the summit could play in East Asian regionalism and how it would relate to the APT. Third, who would participate in the summit was unclear (Kim 2010; Reddy 2010).

Concerning the EAS's membership, the APT members debated whether non-East Asian countries should be admitted. China and Malaysia wanted the membership confined to those of APT (Siazon 2005), while Japan, Indonesia, and Singapore advocated the inclusion of Australia, New Zealand, and India into EAS. Indonesia in particular, did not want the East Asian Community to happen too soon, as that might undermine the importance of ASEAN's community-building efforts, besides the duplication problem of the APT Summit and EAS (Hersutanto 2006). After a heated debate, a consensus was reached at the APT Foreign Ministers' Informal Meeting in April 2005 that EAS would accept the participation of countries other than APT. The decision was apparently influenced by the politics of "institutional balancing" (He 2008). Initiated by Malaysia, ASEAN set forth three criteria for the EAS membership as a quid pro quo for the expansion of the membership. The countries: (1) must be full dialogue partners of ASEAN; (2) must be signatories to the ASEAN Treaty of Amity and Cooperation (TAC); and (3) must have substantial cooperative relations with ASEAN (Interview with a Malaysian Foreign Ministry official, December 2012). Among the countries that fulfilled the criteria were New Zealand, Australia, and India, which joined the inaugural EAS as full participants.

The 16 participants in the first EAS duly met on December 14, 2005. The meeting was relatively short and few specific decisions were made; the emphasis was on developing communication among the members. It was reported that Malaysia and China opposed the inclusion of the phrase "the creation of an East Asian Community" in the declaration, asserting that the phrase should only be inserted into the APT declaration. Japan and India strongly objected to the exclusion of the phrase from the declaration, and eventually compromised with the phrase "community building in this region." The main issues discussed during the Summit included the need for denuclearization of the Korean Peninsula, terrorism, avian flu, sustainable development, the need for progress in the Doha round of World Trade Organization negotiations, and the role which EAS should play as a complement to APT in the process of community building in the region. At the end of the meeting, the Kuala Lumpur Declaration on East Asia Summit was issued, which indicated that EAS will be a forum for dialogue on broad strategic, political, and economic issues of common interest and concern, and with the aim of promoting peace, stability, and economic prosperity in East Asia (ASEAN 2005). ASEAN can be said to be a beneficial institution in the pursuit of East Asian community, which has benefited from the work done through the mutual passions of the involved nations and the regularization of efforts to help facilitate the region's peace, security, and economy.

The Kuala Lumpur Declaration recognizes the shared view, as a principle of the community, that EAS will play an important role in the formation of the community in the region, and that it is necessary to support efforts for the formation of the ASEAN Community. The objectives of the community are clearly stated as:

- establishing the East Asia Summit as a forum for conducting dialogue for the purpose of promoting peace, stability, and economic prosperity in East Asia;

- ensuring that the efforts of the East Asia Summit to promote formation of a community in the region, together with actualizing, coordinating, and strengthening the ASEAN Community, form an indispensable part of the evolving regional framework;
- making the East Asia Summit a forum that is open, comprehensive, transparent, and extroverted; and
- having ASEAN collaborate with other countries at the East Asia Summit and be the propellant of collaboration, together with endeavoring to strengthen the global standards and universally recognized values.

Concerning the modality of the EAS, states decided upon the following four points: (1) participation is to be based on the participative standards which ASEAN sets; (2) the summit is to be held regularly; (3) the summit is to be hosted and chaired by the ASEAN country, and the summit is to be held immediately following the annual ASEAN Summit; and (4) the form of the East Asia Summit is to be reviewed by ASEAN and other participating countries.

The 5th EAS was held on October 30, 2010 in Hanoi, Vietnam. Commemorating the fifth anniversary of EAS, all the members noted the significant achievements recorded so far and stressed the importance of further strengthening the EAS process through reviewing the progress over the past five years, re-emphasizing the importance of EAS in fostering dialogue and cooperation in the region, and reaffirming their commitments to further consolidating and strengthening EAS. In this connection, the adoption of the Hanoi Declaration on the Commemoration of the Fifth Anniversary of East Asia Summit is noteworthy. Finally, they welcomed the expressed interest of the Russia Federation and the United States in the EAS in closer engagement, which resulted in the formal decision to invite their leaders to participate in EAS starting from 2011 (ASEAN 2010). This new development in membership suggests that EAS is becoming a part of Asia-Pacific cooperation akin to APEC.

The 6th East Asia Summit, held in Bali in November 2011, concluded with the adoption of two key documents, namely the Declaration of the EAS on the Principles for Mutually Beneficial Relations and the Declaration of the 6th East Asia Summit on ASEAN Connectivity (ASEAN 2011b). Most noteworthy was the participation of the United States for the first time. The decision to join the EAS is part of a recalibration of United States foreign policy *vis-à-vis* ASEAN-led multilateral institutions. This shift in policy reflects a broader attempt by the United States to re-engage with Southeast Asia and is equally related to China's growing influence in the Asia Pacific region. By joining the EAS, Washington is seizing an opportunity to reverse the perceived US disengagement from the region, which has allowed China to play a larger role in East Asian regional platforms. As the main issue of EAS suggests, active US diplomacy is the key to the maintenance of regional stability ever since its participation in 2011.

In response to active US diplomacy, China increasingly regards the US rebalancing as an attempt to constrain its growing power in East Asia. For Beijing, Washington is merely seeking to isolate China by strengthening its bilateral alliances and utilizing regional institutions. In particular, Washington is enhancing its involvement in the South China Sea and thus interfering in bilateral issues between Beijing and the Southeast Asian claimant states. China also considers growing Philippine activities in the disputed waters over the Scarborough Shoal in early 2012 to be influenced by Washington. As a result, China and the United States seek to prevent the over-militarization of the disputes. Beijing and Washington view the South China Sea as an issue that requires a diplomatic rather than a military solution and they are content, for now at least, to let ASEAN lead the conflict management process.

Established barely eight years ago, EAS remains in its infancy. The process of community building lags behind with no clear blueprint as yet for the actions and steps needed in achieving an ultimate aim, which is equally ambiguous. Some critics quickly pose a question of redundancy in promoting East Asian regionalism based on ASEAN's centrality. During this continual process of community build-ing highlighted above, although significant progress is made, occasional static periods are invariably met; but what is generally illustrated is that these efforts eventually yield the achievement of many positive milestones.

The key institutional features of East Asian regionalism

As we have seen above, the rapid emergence of regional institutions has been a particularly salient dynamic in the international politics of East Asia, especially in the post-Cold War period. It can be explained that these institutions have emerged as a response to the necessity of coordinating an expanding network of boundary-spanning exchanges heightened in the context of globalization, and also as an effort to mitigate strategic geopolitical uncertainty by enhancing dialogue, transparency, and socialization among state actors.

However, the attempt to understand regional institutions using the EU model would run into trouble in accounting for some of the more intriguing empirical scenarios that describe the contemporary status and purpose of East Asian regionalism. In fact, unlike the EU precepts, East Asian regionalism is character-ized by both the endurance of extant institutions and instances of institutional creation in East Asia despite the empirically demonstrated inefficiency of regional institutions in reaching their stated goals. Moreover, the gap is so substantial that many observers raise questions about the nature of East Asian regionalism. For instance, some observers (Jones and Smith 2007; Ravenhill 2009) have serious reservations concerning Asian regional integration, suggesting that process over-whelms substance. It is also interesting to note that a plethora of adjectives have emerged to qualify Asian regionalism, starting with the term, "open regionalism" (Ravenhill 2001) and moving more recently to concepts of "monetary regional-ism" (Dieter and Higgott 2003), "regulatory regionalism" (Jayasuriya 2009), "networked regionalism" (Jetschke 2009; Yeo 2010), and "strategic regionalism" (Gilson 2007).

Despite rapidly growing economic interdependence in the post-Cold War era, the US-centered hub-and-spoke bilateral security system, or the so-called San

Francisco Peace Alliance, has still remained the driving force, thereby undermining the formal institutionalization of East Asian regionalism (Hemmer and Katzenstein 2002; Aggarwal and Koo 2007). Accordingly, the United States as an offshore player has shaped the contours of East Asian regionalism. It is due to this US factor that East Asian countries have organized a regional forum with a wide geographic scope and weak institutionalization (Calder and Ye 2004).

Informal functional networks

Noting the diversity in political and economic conditions and the lack of mutual trust in the region, East Asian countries have invariably opted for informal networking rather than transforming highly interdependent economic relations into a formalized regionalism (Doner 1997). The weak institutionalization of East Asian regionalism has to do with East Asia's unique legal culture, as well as the underdeveloped concept of issue areas. As a result, we observe the mushrooming of disjointed networks that may be regularized but often without systematic linkages with each other. Contrasting analytical explanations have emerged to capture this unforeseen nature of East Asian regional institutionalization. Some researchers point out that East Asian institutions have evolved in decentralized, contradictory, and ad hoc ways rather than deepening and solidifying regionalism. These observers highlight this feature of East Asian regionalism by dubbing it "thin gruel" (Friedberg 1993), "soft regionalism" (Zhao 1998), or "informal regionalism" (Katzenstein 1997).

However, functional cooperation has been advanced, as APT has amply demonstrated. In trade for instance, East Asian countries have actively undertaken negotiations for free trade agreements (FTAs) in the first decade of the new millennium. As of 2010, East Asian nations were involved in a total of 79 deals. Out of these 79, 33 FTAs are currently in effect and five FTAs have been signed. The five largest economies in East Asia have extensively engaged in multiple FTA deals over the last decade. Singapore, which is the most enthusiastic about FTAs in East Asia, has concluded 12 FTAs, of which 10 are in effect and two are signed. In addition, five more are under negotiation and two have been proposed.

In finance as well, in the aftermath of the Asian financial crisis, East Asian countries were successful in eliciting institutionalized cooperation for liquidity provision in the event of any future crisis by creating the CMI in May 2000, or networks of bilateral currency swap agreements (Grimes 2006; Amyx 2008; Henning 2009). Although the CMI initially started with limited amounts of money and lending provisions congruent with IMF regulations, East Asian countries steadily expanded the CMI's swap line to US$90 billion by 2009. Subsequently, in May 2009, East Asian countries, once again facing the global financial crisis, succeeded in further elevating the CMI to the Chiang Mai Initiative Multilateralization (CMIM).

Witnessing a steady progress in economic cooperation, many scholars provide a rosy picture of East Asian regionalism, anticipating that the evolutionary dynamics of institutionalizing East Asia will unfold in the coming decades. They argue that

East Asian countries' turn to bilateral FTAs testifies to their increased interests in state-to-state engagement (Bowles 2002). Christopher Dent argues that lattice regionalism in East Asia, formed by a number of bilateral FTAs, ultimately takes a "bilateral to plurilateral and regional" path to institutionalization. In his view, bilateral FTAs will ultimately turn into region-wide FTAs even without a regional "nerve center," because interlocking and overlapping FTAs will inevitably generate high transaction costs (Dent 2003). These views remain relevant only if we look at one dimension, that is, functional imperatives.

Interplays between functional imperatives and power dynamics

East Asian institutions have been driven by national bureaucracies and diplomatic and political elites who use regional institutions for two goals: (1) for gaining benefits via association with international normative structures and discourses; and (2) for pursuing a range of realpolitik practices that emerge from their socialization in realpolitik ideology: hedging and balancing against rising powers like China. This contrast has been seen in the latest summits in 2012.

Functional imperatives: the case for economic cooperation

The 15th APT Commemorative Summit was held on November 19, 2012 in Phnom Penh, Cambodia. Given the fact that the Asia Financial Crisis of 1997 gathered momentum for a stronger regional cooperation in East Asia, the region could develop the APT cooperation into a framework that promotes practical cooperation including finance and economy which contributes to regional stability and growth. Especially, the summit noted that institutional efforts were materialized in CMI and have produced tangible results such as the Chiang Mai Initiative Multilateralization Agreement (ASEAN 2012a). It also stressed the effort to double the total size (US$120 billion) of the CMI as a positive measure. Most important was the decision to upgrade the APT Finance Ministers' Meeting to the APT Finance Ministers' and Central Bank Governors' Meeting. In the past, officials responsible for monetary and exchange rate policies were left out. This major gap has now finally been filled. As a result, institutionalization of financial cooperation has been enormously advanced.

In the field of food security, the Summit acknowledged the coming into force of the ASEAN Plus Three Emergency Rice Reserve Agreement (APTERR) on July 12. They also noted Japan's role in proposing the rice reserve at the APT Agricultural Minister's Meeting in 2001 and research on it. Expressing his delight, the Japanese Prime Minister promised to actively contribute to this APTERR effort by sending experts and other assistance in order to ensure the smooth implementation of cooperation stipulated in the agreement.

Most notable developments can be seen in the field of economic cooperation. The summit welcomed the launch of the Regional Comprehensive Economic Partnership (RCEP) during the ASEAN-related Summit and hoped to continue contributing to the realization of a comprehensive and high-quality RCEP, together with the forging of an APT Connectivity Partnership, which includes the building of the ASEAN Community and the enhancement of "People-to-People Connectivity." The idea of the RCEP was first introduced in November 2011 at the ASEAN Summit in Bali, as officials attempted to reconcile two existing regional trade architectures. China supported the East Asia Free Trade Agreement, which restricted the grouping to ASEAN, China, Japan, and the ROK, whereas Japan favored the Comprehensive Economic Partnership in East Asia, which added three countries: India, Australia, and New Zealand. ASEAN leaders struck a balance with the RCEP, adopting an open accession scheme that would allow other members to join as long as they agree to comply with the grouping's rules and guidelines. As it currently stands, only ASEAN and its FTA partners will participate in the negotiations. However, contrary to reports that claim the United States is barred from joining, membership is open to other countries. During the August 30, 2012 ASEAN Economic Ministers' Meeting in Cambodia, officials endorsed the RCEP's guiding principles. The RCEP will cement ASEAN's central role in the emerging regional economic architecture. It also seeks to harmonize the "noodle bowl" of differences between the various ASEAN FTAs.

Power dynamics and institutional balancing: the case for security cooperation

The 7th EAS was held on November 20, 2012 in Cambodia's capital city of Phnom Penh. The forum highlighted six priority areas for cooperation, including energy and environment, education, finance, global health issues and communicable diseases, disaster management, and ASEAN connectivity. Regional leaders believe that the summit is beneficial to create stronger economic ties in the Asia-Pacific area, help promote development, enhance mutual trust, reach consensus, and diminish gaps within the region. The summit adopted the Phnom Penh Declaration, which pledges to help narrow development gaps among ASEAN member states so as to achieve the ASEAN Community by the end of 2015 (ASEAN 2012b). It is the second time the United States and Russia have joined the Summit after the two were admitted to the regional forum in 2011.

At the meetings, US President Barack Obama backed China's rivals Vietnam and the Philippines, and called for a new structure to prevent flare-ups over territorial disputes in the South China Sea. Chinese Premier Wen Jiabao, meanwhile, expressed strong opposition to US intervention in the region. While Obama demanded that free navigation of the sea be maintained under international law, Wen stated that China "opposes any internationalization of the South China Sea issue. All problems will be resolved among the countries directly involved." These points were repeated by both leaders throughout the summit, and both appeared unwilling to yield (*Mainichi Shimbun*, November 21, 2012; *Straits Times*, November 21, 2012).

Beijing's assertiveness to shape the resolution of the South China Sea disputes was another dimension of the power game. It led to a replay of the proxy tussle, leading to internal divisions within ASEAN caused by host Cambodia's poor handling of the increasingly divisive issue. For the first time in ASEAN history, the

Chairman's draft closing statement had to be openly contradicted and corrected by fellow ASEAN leaders for its "inaccuracies." Hun Sen had wrongly claimed, reflecting his eagerness to please Beijing, that the leaders had reached a consensus not to "internationalize the issue" (Kassim 2012).

In a similar vein, Prime Minister Noda welcomed the success of the Expanded ASEAN Maritime Forum (EAMF) held in October 2012, which was proposed by Japan during EAS 2011. He also welcomed the productive discussions at the Forum and commended the efforts by the Philippines as Chair. Noda emphasized that this framework is of significance as a confidence building measure, and called for this effort to be endorsed by the EAS leaders. He looked forward to the continuance of this effort and expressed the hope that discussions would further deepen.

However, due to the growing interdependent relations, the non-claimant countries such as Cambodia, Laos, and Myanmar were expected to appease China by minimizing the internationalization of the South China Sea issue. The ASEAN Ministerial Meeting (AMM) in July 2012 is a case in point. During the 45th AMM held in Phnom Penh, ASEAN leaders could not issue a Joint Communiqué following heated political wrangling between the incumbent Cambodian Chair and other ASEAN member states over their South China Sea disputes (*Bangkok Post*, July 16, 2012). The Philippines' Foreign Minister had discussed the situation in the Scarborough Shoal in several ASEAN Ministerial Meetings in Phnom Penh and he simply wanted a Joint Communiqué to reflect the fact that those discussions took place. To this, several ASEAN members and the ASEAN Secretariat expressed their support. However, Cambodia, as Chair, consistently opposed any mention of the Scarborough Shoal at all in the Joint Communiqué. The Philippines further maintains that since the competing claims involve four ASEAN members, this dispute is not a mere bilateral conflict with a northern neighbor but a multilateral one and should therefore be resolved in a multilateral manner.

On November 8, 2014 Chinese President Xi Jinping announced that China would set up a Silk Road fund worth US$40 billion to support infrastructure, resources, industrial, and financial cooperation, in addition to other projects related to connectivity for countries along the "Belt and Road" (*Xinhua*, February 5, 2015). The initiatives involve a land-based belt from China via Central Asia to Europe and a maritime Silk Road through the South China Sea to the Straits of Malacca, India, the Middle East, and Africa. It is clear that China intends to play a major role in maritime security and trade as trends show relationships with ASEAN are expected to compete for influence in the region. Maritime disputes in the East and South China Sea provide an illustration of how power dynamics have shaped East Asian regional cooperation and the new regional order that East Asian regionalism is promoting moves towards peace, prosperity, friendship, and sharing of mutual gains.

The case for ASEAN centrality

Thus the power dynamics between the nations in the region become a lot more complicated when APT relations are taken into consideration. The conflicts that are difficult to resolve in a multilateral setting also influence the relationship in Plus One dynamics. For ASEAN, the dichotomy of the organization with the bigger East Asian countries was not a situation where it would be easy to take sides, be it with China, Japan, or ROK. ASEAN's Plus One summit with these nations reflects the reality that ASEAN is very much aware of its own interest and continues to pursue separate relations with each nation despite the existing platform of APT and the EAS. To play each individual relation against one another, it seems likely that ASEAN hopes to balance the outcome in terms of the benefit it may reap from each individual relation.

During the 15th ASEAN–China summit held in Phnom Penh, Cambodia, Economic Ministers of ASEAN and China signed two Protocols to amend the Framework Agreement on Comprehensive Economic Cooperation between ASEAN and China as well as the Trade in Goods Agreement under the said Framework Agreement. For ASEAN and China, despite the ongoing territorial dispute and the continued concern towards China's actions within the region, the economic benefit of the combined market with China is undeniable considering that ASEAN and China have the largest consumer market size with 1.9 billion population. Even with the tension that ASEAN countries face with China, they have maintained China–ASEAN nontraditional security alignment and cooperation in a range of issues, including piracy, smuggling, human trafficking, the drug trade, transnational criminal organizations, illegal immigration, cyber-piracy and cyber attacks, terrorism, subversion, and ethnic/religious movements (Arase 2010). Such a security framework allows military cooperation without outright military agreements. This set-up benefits the need to see to the "shared vulnerability" and for ASEAN to continue developing its relations with China without compromising its own relations with other large powers, especially with the United States.

The relationship between ASEAN and Japan is far less contentious as compared to ASEAN and China, and the first ASEAN–Japan summit in 1977 was merely a continuation of relations which had taken off much earlier. Japan has played a relatively low-key role in the region mostly due to fear about Japan's military past, thus much of the focus of the relationship remains economic and cultural. It was not until much later that security figured as a more prominent part in ASEAN–Japan relations and the role grew in the 1990s (Sudo 2002: 83). Though Japan will not likely take unilateral action regarding China, it is through its relations with ASEAN that Japan began to play a bigger role in the South China Sea conflict, as in 1995 when the Philippines' vice minister requested that Tokyo try to persuade Beijing to resolve the conflict through deliberation. Another landmark development in Japan–ASEAN relations and involvement in regional security was when Japan suggested a new security approach within the framework of the ASEAN PMC despite the objections of the United States (Sudo 2002: 89). Japan continues to be a strong supporter in the efforts of building an ASEAN community. Thus, during a meeting with Le Luong Minh, Secretary-General of ASEAN, at the sidelines of the 46th ASEAN Foreign Ministers Meeting, the Foreign Minister of Japan, Fumio Kishida, said that Japan would also consider the needs of ASEAN beyond 2015 to support the continued integration of ASEAN to ensure the region remained competitive and promote equitable development.

The APT has also helped cultivate relations with the ROK, which also stands to play an important role for ASEAN. As with China and Japan, the ROK presents a great economic benefit for both partners within the relationship and the ASEAN–Korea FTA is a cornerstone to relations, which have expanded since 1989 with the ASEAN–ROK Sectoral Dialogue Partner (ASEAN–KOREA Centre). The first ASEAN–ROK summit was held in 1997 and in the 13th ASEAN–ROK Summit held in 2010 in Hanoi, Vietnam, ASEAN–ROK relations were expanded into a strategic partnership. The ROK also plays a hand in security dialogue through their participation in the PMC and ARF however; it is still a little left behind relative to ASEAN's relations with other neighbors. The focus of the relationship between ASEAN and ROK had always been more inclined to soft power, with the latter expounding on its cultural exports and *hallyu* phenomenon. There is also an increasing number of expatriates from the ROK residing in ASEAN countries, though understanding of Korea needs to be further enhanced (Cabalza 2011).

Overall, ASEAN is not likely to forgo its Plus One relation with China, Japan, and ROK individually over the growing institutional platform of APT and EAS. The growing complexity of relations between the ASEAN and its partners needs to be observed *vis-à-vis* the efforts put into the regional platform. China, Japan, and ROK all present a unique form of relation for ASEAN and despite the multi-lateral layer that the APT presents, the seemingly but not quite bilateral relations in the ASEAN Plus One creates a separate form of engagement between ASEAN and the larger, more developed East Asian nations.

Conclusion

This chapter argues that the institutional features of East Asian regionalism are a product of the interplays between functional imperatives and power dynamics. While functional imperatives necessarily manifest in collaborative actions over issues ranging from trade, financial, transportation, and energy cooperation to transnational crime, contagious diseases, and natural disaster management, power dynamics often involve a more zero-sum and competitive action–reaction among the self-interested state actors. East Asian regionalism is a regional integration that has been driven not just by plain geographical and economic factors, but also by geo-political and geo-strategic calculations, as evidenced by the membership of the EAS that includes not one but several players that are geographically outside of the "East Asian" region. Although the tensions stemming from power dynamics have prevented further institutionalization of regional cooperation and compli-cated the task of handling certain trans-boundary issues, the mounting functional imperatives have nonetheless served to bind the regional states together, thereby sustaining the momentum for greater regional cooperation and integration. Therefore, the structural development within the East Asian region that has become an institutionalized framework to approach matters and concerns of the region from a neutral position supports the effort of regional integration to gradually encourage interaction among members of the community as well as nurture existing partnerships. In order to promote continued integration within the greater East Asian community, existing relationships must be maintained and new bonds should be developed with partners to further regional peace, stability, and economic development.

References

Abbott, Frederick M. 2000. NAFTA and the Legalization of World Politics: A Case Study. *International Organization* 54(3): 519–547.

Acharya, Amitav. 2009. *Constructing a Security Community in Southeast Asia: ASEAN and the Problem of Regional Order.* London: Routledge.

ADB. 2010. *Institutions for Regional Integration: Toward an Asian Economic Community.* Metro Manila: Asian Development Bank.

Aggarwal, Vinod K., and Min Gyo Koo, eds. 2007. *Asia's New Institutional Architecture: Evolving Structures for Managing Trade, Financial, and Security Relations.* Berlin: Springer-Verlag.

Amyx, Jennifer. 2008. Stocktaking on Regional Financial Initiatives Among the ASEAN+3. In Andrew MacIntyre, T. J. Pempel, and John Ravenhill, eds, *Crisis as Catalyst: The Dynamics of the East Asian Political Economy.* Ithaca, NY: Cornell University Press, pp. 353–380.

Arase, David. 2010. Non-Traditional Security in China–ASEAN Cooperation: The Institutionalization of Regional Security Cooperation and the Evolution of East Asian Regionalism. *Asian Survey* 50(4): 808–833.

ASEAN Secretariat. 1992. Fourth ASEAN Summit. www.asean.org/asean/asean-summit/item/the-fourth-asean-summit.

ASEAN Secretariat. 1997. *Joint Press Statement of the ASEAN–Japan Finance Ministers Meeting.* Jakarta: ASEAN Secretariat.

ASEAN Secretariat. 2000. *Joint Press Statement of the Fifth ASEAN Economic Ministers and the Ministers of People's Republic of China, Japan and Republic of Korea Consultation (AEM+3). Bandar Seri Begawan, Brunei Darussalam. September 14.* Jakarta: ASEAN Secretariat.

ASEAN Secretariat. 2001. *Press Statement by the Chairman of the 7th ASEAN Summit and the Three ASEAN+1 Summits.* Jakarta: ASEAN Secretariat.

ASEAN Secretariat. 2002. *Framework Agreement on Comprehensive Economic Cooperation Between the Association of Southeast East Asian Nations and the People's Republic of China.* Jakarta: ASEAN Secretariat.

ASEAN Secretariat. 2003. *The Joint Ministerial Statement of the ASEAN+3 Finance Ministers' (AFMM+3) Meeting. Shanghai, People's Republic of China.* Jakarta: ASEAN Secretariat. May 10.

ASEAN Secretariat. 2005. *Kuala Lumpur Declaration on the East Asia Summit, Kuala Lumpur.* Jakarta: ASEAN Secretariat. December 14.

ASEAN Secretariat. 2006. *Chairman's Statement of the Second East Asia Summit, Cebu, Philippines.* Jakarta: ASEAN Secretariat. January 15.

ASEAN Secretariat. 2007. *Chairman's Statement of the 3rd East Asia Summit, Singapore.* Jakarta: ASEAN Secretariat. November 21.

ASEAN Secretariat. 2009. *Chairman's Statement of the 4th East Asia Summit, Cha-am Hua Hin, Thailand.* Jakarta: ASEAN Secretariat. October 25.

ASEAN Secretariat. 2010. *Chairman's Statement of the East Asia Summit (EAS), Hanoi, Vietnam.* Jakarta: ASEAN Secretariat. October 30.

ASEAN Secretariat. 2011a. *ASEAN Plus Three Cooperation.* Jakarta: ASEAN Secretariat.

ASEAN Secretariat. 2011b. *Chairman's Statement of the 6th East Asia Summit Bali, Indonesia.* Jakarta: ASEAN Secretariat. November 19.

ASEAN Secretariat. 2012a. *ASEAN Plus Three Leaders' Joint Statement on the Commemoration of the 15th Anniversary of the ASEAN Plus Three Cooperation 19 November 2012, Phnom Penh, Cambodia.* Jakarta: ASEAN Secretariat.

ASEAN Secretariat. 2012b. *Chairman's Statement of the 7th East Asia Summit (EAS), 20 November 2012, Phnom Penh, Cambodia.* Jakarta: ASEAN Secretariat.

ASEAN Secretariat News. 2012. World's Biggest Consumer Market Deepens Commitment with Latest Protocols between ASEAN and China. www.asean.org/news/asean-secreta riat-news/item/world-s-biggest-consumer-market-deepens-commitment-with-latest-proto cols-between-asean-and-china?category_id=27.

ASEAN Secretariat News. 2013. Japan Continues to Strongly Support ASEAN Community Building Efforts. www.asean.org/news/asean-secretariat-news/item/japan-con tinues-to-strongly-support-asean-community-building-efforts?category_id=27.

Aslam, Mohamed. 2009. Japan's Reluctance in East Asian Economic Integration. *Asia Europe Journal* 7(2): 281–294.

Ba, Alice. 2009. Regionalism's Multiple Negotiations: ASEAN in East Asia. *Cambridge Review of International Affairs* 22: 345–367.

Bowles, Paul. 2002. Asia's Post-Crisis Regionalism: Bringing the State Back In, Keeping the (United) States Out. *Review of International Political Economy* 9(2): 244–270.

Caballero-Anthony, Mely. 2009. Evolving Regional Governance in East Asia. In N. Thomas, ed., *Governance and Regionalism in East Asia.* New York: Routledge, pp. 32–65.

Cabalza, Chester B. 2011. Is South Korea Open for Soft Power Diplomacy? *Executive Policy Brief* 1(13): 1–4.

Calder, Kent and Min Ye. 2004. Regionalism and Critical Junctures: Explaining the "Organization Gap" in Northeast Asia. *Journal of East Asian Studies* 4(2): 191–226.

Camilleri, Joseph A. 2003. *Regionalism in the New Asia-Pacific Order.* Cheltenham: Edward Elgar.

Chia, Siow Y., ASEAN Economic Research Unit, and Institute of Southeast Asian Studies. 1994. *APEC: Challenges and Opportunities: ASEAN Economic Research Unit.* Singapore: Institute of Southeast Asian Studies.

Chin, Kin Wah. 2007. Introduction: ASEAN Facing the Fifth Decade. *Contemporary Southeast Asia* 29(3): 395–405.

Dent, Christopher. 2003. Networking the Region? The Emergence and Impact of Asia–Pacific Bilateral Free Trade Agreement Projects. *The Pacific Review* 16(1): 1–28.

Dent, Christopher M. 2008. *East Asian Regionalism.* London: Routledge.

Dent, Christopher M. 2010. Organizing the Wider East Asia Region. ADB Working Papers. November.

Dieter, Heribert and Richard Higgott. 2003. Exploring Alternative Theories of Economic Regionalism: From Trade to Finance in Asian Co-operation. *Review of International Political Economy* 10(3): 430–454.

Doner, Richard. 1997. Japan in East Asia: Institutions and Regional Leadership. In Peter Katzenstein and Takashi Shiraishi, eds, *Network Power: Japan and Asia.* Ithaca, NY: Cornell University Press, pp. 197–233.

Emmers, Ralf. 2012. *ASEAN and the Institutionalization of East Asia.* London: Routledge.

Emmers, Ralf, Joseph Chinyong Liow, and See Seng Tan. 2010. *The East Asia Summit and the Regional Security Architecture*. Baltimore, MD: University of Maryland School of Law.

Friedberg, Aaron. 1993. Ripe for Rivalry: Prospects for Peace in a Multipolar Asia. *International Security* 18(3): 5–33.

Giegerich, Bastian. 2008. Chapter Three: Domestic Determinants of National Profiles: Constraints or Enablers? *The Adelphi Papers* 48(397): 59–82.

Gilson, Julie. 1999. Japan's Role in the Asia–Europe Meeting: Establishing an Interregional or Intraregional Agenda? *Asian Survey* 39(5): 736–752.

Gilson, Julie. 2002. *Asia Meets Europe: Inter-Regionalism and the Asia–Europe Meeting*. Cheltenham: Edward Elgar.

Gilson, Julie. 2004. Complex Regional Multilateralism: "Strategising" Japan's Response to Southeast Asia. *The Pacific Review* 17(1): 71–94.

Gilson, Julie. 2007. Strategic Regionalism in East Asia. *Review of International Studies* 33: 145–163.

Goh, Chock-Tong. 2005. Speech by Mr Goh Chok Tong, Senior Minister, at the Asia Society Conference in Bangkok. Singapore: Ministry of Foreign Affairs. June 9.

Green, Michael J., and Bates Gill. 2009. *Asia's New Multilateralism*. New York: Columbia University Press.

Grimes, William W. 2006. East Asian Financial Regionalism in Support of the Global Financial Architecture? The Political Economy of Regional Nesting. *Journal of East Asian Studies* 6(3): 353–380.

He, Kai. 2008. Institutional Balancing and International Relations Theory: Economic Interdependence and Balance of Power Strategies in Southeast Asia. *European Journal of International Relations* 14: 489–518.

Hemmer, Christopher, and Peter J. Katzenstein. 2002. Why There is No NATO in Asia: Collective Identity, Regionalism, and the Origins of Multilateralism. *International Organization* 56(3): 575–607.

Henning, C. Randall. 2009. The Future of the Chiang Mai Initiative: An Asian Monetary Fund? Peterson Institute for International Economics. Policy Brief.

Hersutanto, B. 2006. Prospect for Building East Asia Community. *The Indonesian Quarterly* 34: 143–157.

Ho, Benjamin. 2012. ASEAN at 45: A Case for Principled Realism. RSIS Commentaries, No. 188, October 8.

Hook, Glenn D. 2001. Japan's Role in the East Asian Political Economy. In G. D. Hook and H. Hasegawa, eds, *The Political Economy of Japanese Globalization*. London: Routledge, pp. 40–55.

Hunter, William C., George G. Kaufman, and Thomas H. Krueger. 1999. *The Asian Financial Crisis: Origins, Implications and Solutions*. Berlin: Springer.

Jayasuriya, Kanishka. 2009. Regulatory Regionalism in Asia–Pacific: Drivers, Instruments and Actors. *Australian Journal of International Affairs* 63(3): 335–347.

Jetschke, Anja. 2009. Institutionalizing ASEAN: Celebrating Europe through Network Governance. *Cambridge Review of International Affairs* 22(3): 407–426.

Jones, David Martin and Michael L. R. Smith. 2007. Making Process, Not Progress: ASEAN and the Evolving East Asian Regional Order. *International Security* 32(1): 148–184.

Karunatilleka, Eshan. 1999. The Asian Economic Crisis. House of Commons Library Research Paper 99/14. www.parliament.uk/documents/commons/lib/research/rp99/rp99-014.pdf.

Kassim, Yang Razali. 2012. East Asia Summit 2012: Power Game in Asia Unfolds. RSIS Commentaries, No. 217, December 3.

Katzenstein, Peter J. 1997. Introduction: Asian Regionalism in Comparative Perspective. In Peter Katzenstein and Takashi Shiraishi, eds, *Network Power: Japan and Asia*. Ithaca, NY: Cornell University Press, pp. 1–46.

Kim, Jae Cheol. 2010. Politics of Regionalism in East Asia: The Case of the East Asia Summit. *Asian Perspectives* 34: 113–136.

Kim, Samuel S. 2004. Regionalization and Regionalism in East Asia. *Journal of East Asian Studies* 4(1): 39–67.

Kimura, Michio. 1995. Multi-layered Regional Cooperation in Southeast Asia after the Cold War: Papers and Proceedings of a Symposium Held at the Institute of Developing Economies on November 9–10, 1994 in Tokyo. Institute of Developing Economies.

Koga, Kei. 2010. Competing Institutions in East Asian Regionalism: ASEAN and the Regional Powers. *Issues and Insights* 10(23), October.

Koizumi, Junichiro. 2002. *Japan and ASEAN in East Asia: A Sincere and Open Partnership*. Speech by Prime Minister of Japan. Singapore. January 14. Tokyo: Ministry of Foreign Affairs.

Komori, Yasumasa. 2009. Asia's Institutional Creation and Evolution. *Asian Perspectives* 33: 151–182.

Lee, Poh-Ping. 1999. Why Japan Stepped in to Alleviate Asia's Economic Situation. *New Straits Times*, July 10.

Mahathir, Mohamad. 2006. Let Asians Build their Own Future Regionalism. *Global Asia* 1(1): 13–15.

Md Akhir, Md Nasrudin. 2009. Japan in ASEAN+3: Towards the Creation of an East Asian Community. In Md Nasrudin Md Akhir and Geetha Govindasamy, eds, *Japan and East Asia: Diplomacy and Strategic Partnerships*. Kuala Lumpur: University of Malaya Press, pp. 31–50.

METI. 2003. *White Paper on International Trade 2003*. Tokyo, Japan: Ministry of Economy, Trade and Industry (METI). www.meti.go.jp/english/report/data/gIT03maine.html.

MOFA. 2006. *Joint Statement on East Asian Cooperation*. Tokyo: Ministry of Foreign Affairs.

MOFA. 2008. Joint Statement for Tripartite Partnership. www.mofa.go.jp/region/asia-paci/jck/summit0812/partner.html.

Murphy, R. Taggart. 2009. Will East Asia Rule the World Economy? Economic and Financial Lessons from the 1970s. *The Asia–Pacific Journal* 26(2).

Nabers, Dirk. 2005. Neuer Regionalismus in Ostasien: Das Forum der ASEAN+3. In Dirk Nabers and Andreas Ufen, eds, *Regionale Integration: Neue Dynamiken in Afrika, Asien und Lateinamerika*. Hamburg: GIGA, pp. 53–70.

Nakasone, Yasuhiro. 2007. Aiming For Multi-layered System of an East Asian Community and an East Asian Economic Cooperation Organization. CEAC Commentary. December 4.

Nam, In-Soo. 2013. China Asks to Postpone Japan, Korea Summit. *The Wall Street Journal*, April 18.

Narine, Shaun. 2001. ASEAN and the Idea of an "Asian Monetary Fund": Institutional Uncertainty in the Asia–Pacific. In Andrew T. H. Tan and J. D. Kenneth Boutin, eds, *Non-Traditional Security Issues in Southeast Asia*. Singapore: Select Publishing – IDSS, pp. 227–256.

Park, Chang-Gun. 2006. Japan's Emerging Role in Promoting Regional Integration in East Asia: Towards an East Asian Integration Regime (EAIR). *Journal of International and Area Studies* 13(1): 147–177.

Pempel, T. John. 1999. *The Politics of the Asian Economic Crisis*. Ithaca, NY: Cornell University Press.

Ravenhill, John. 2001. *APEC and the Construction of Pacific Rim Regionalism*. Cambridge: Cambridge University Press.

Ravenhill, John. 2008. Asia's New Economic Institutions. In V. K. Aggarwal and M. G. Koo, eds., *Asia's New Institutional Architecture: Evolving Structures for Managing Trade, Financial, and Security Relations*. Berlin, Heidelberg: Springer, pp. 35–58.

Ravenhill, John. 2009. East Asian Regionalism: Much Ado about Nothing? *Review of International Studies* 35: 215–235.

Reddy, G. Jayachandra. 2010. East Asia Summit: Interests and Expectations. *International Journal of Peace and Development Studies* 1: 35–46. December.

Ries, Philippe. 2000. *The Asian Storm: Asia's Economic Crisis Examined*. North Clarendon, VT: Tuttle.

Rüland, Jürgen. 2000. ASEAN and the Asian Crisis: Theoretical Implications and Practical Consequences for Southeast Asian Regionalism. *The Pacific Review* 13(3): 421–451.

Severino, Rodolfo. 2007. ASEAN beyond Forty: Towards Political and Economic Integration. *Contemporary Southeast Asia: A Journal of International & Strategic Affairs* 29(3): 406–423.

Siazon, Domingo L. 2005. ASEAN and the Formation of an East Asian Community. Speech at Japan National Press Club. April 6.

Stubbs, Richard. 2002. ASEAN Plus Three: Emerging East Asian Regionalism? *Asian Survey* 42(1): 4–10.

Sudo, Sueo. 2002. *International Relations of Japan and South East Asia*. London: Routledge.

Sudo, Sueo. 2005. *ASEAN at the Third Transition: Groping for a New Regionalism in East Asia*. Nagoya: Economic Research Center, School of Economics, Nagoya University.

Sudo, Sueo. 2009. Japan's ASEAN Policy: Reactive Or Proactive in the Face of A Rising China in East Asia? *Asian Perspective* 33(9): 137–158.

Suzuki, Sanae. 2004. East Asian Cooperation through Conference Diplomacy, Institutional Aspects of the ASEAN Plus Three (APT) Framework. APEC Study Centre Working Paper Series 03/04 – No. 7.

Tanaka, Hitoshi. 2008. The Strategic Rationale for East Asian Community Building. In Jusuf Wanandi and Tadashi Yamamoto, eds, *East Asia at a Crossroads*. Tokyo: Japan Center for International Exchange, pp. 90–104.

Terada, Takeshi. 2003. Constructing an "East Asian" Concept and Growing Regional Identity: From EAEC to ASEAN+ 3. *The Pacific Review* 16(2): 251–277.

Trinidad, Dennis D. 2007. Japan's ODA at the Crossroads: Disbursement Patterns of Japan's Development Assistance to Southeast Asia. *Asian Perspectives* 31(2): 95–125.

United Nations Economic Social Commission for Asia & the Pacific. 2005. Implementing the Monterrey Consensus in the Asian and Pacific Region: Achieving Coherence and Consistency. United Nations ESCAP.

Vogel, Steven K. 1999. Can Japan Disengage? Winners and Losers in Japan's Political Economy, and the Ties that Bind Them. *Social Science Japan Journal* 2(1): 3–21.

World Bank. 2012. *World Development Indicators 2012*. Washington, DC: World Bank Publications.

Yamakage, Susumu. 2004. A Changing ASEAN and the Implications for Japan. *Gaiko Forum* 4(1): 35–44.

Yeo, Andrew. 2012. China, Japan, South Korea Trilateral Cooperation: Implications for Northeast Asian Politics and Order. EAI Issue Briefing, November 6.

Yeo, Lay Hwee. 2010. Institutional Regionalism versus Networked Regionalism: Europe and Asia Compared. *International Politics* 47(3/4): 324–337.

Yoshimatsu, Hidetaka. 2003. *Japan and East Asia in Transition: Trade Policy, Crisis and Evolution, and Regionalism.* London and New York: Macmillan Press.

Zhao, Suisheng. 1998. Soft versus Structured Regionalism: Organizational Forms of Co-operation in Asia-Pacific. *Journal of East Asian Affairs*, 12(1): 96–134.

Part 2

Domains of East Asian cooperation

3 Institutionalization of economic cooperation in East Asia

Sueo Sudo and Tham Siew Yean

Introduction

The publication of *East Asian Miracle* by the World Bank in 1993 signifies the fact that countries in East Asia have achieved sustained economic growth through market-driven integration with the global markets. In fact, greater economic openness and globalization in the region has created regional concentration of trade and investment activities. Reflecting on this, economic regionalism in East Asia has been regarded as a relatively recent phenomenon. The outbreak of the 1997 Asian currency crisis was, however, a turning point in the movement toward economic integration. Now, East Asian countries are rapidly catching up with the global trend of regionalization, intensifying the economic ties among themselves. As a result, economic interdependence has been deepening, making closer regional cooperation essential. If economic integration means just an absence of any barriers for the free flow of goods, capital, and people, East Asia may be said to have already attained quite a significant degree of market-driven integration. As regards institutional arrangements, however, the region, compared to the European Union and other regions, remains far behind.

Although numerous scholars have examined the emergence of East Asian regionalism since the outbreak of the financial crisis, less attention has been devoted to the development of its institutional architecture (Baldwin 2006; Soesastro 2006; Capannelli and Tan 2012). It should be stressed that the regional architecture is related to but distinct from regionalism. Whereas regionalism examines processes such as the growth of network ties among regional actors, increasing economic interaction, or the development of a shared regional identity, the regional architecture is the institutional frameworks which loosely govern, either formally or informally, economic and security relations between states.

At the outset, we need to define the terms institutions and institutionalization. Consistent with the conceptualization developed in the Introduction, we define "institutions" as durable rules that shape expectations, interests, and behavior. Accordingly, we define "institutionalization" as a process of regularizing and harmonizing behavior among a group of sovereign actors, from which emerges agreed-upon rules, norms, and mechanisms that are difficult to deviate from.

Based on this definition, this chapter analyzes the origins, development, and prospects of institutionalization of East Asian economic cooperation initiated by the Association of Southeast Asian Nations (ASEAN). It begins with a review of the evolution of the ASEAN Free Trade Agreement (AFTA), which captures the achievements of ASEAN's economic integration efforts, leading to a wider and deeper integration, which is exemplified by the realization of the ASEAN Economic Community (AEC) announced in 2003. Exploring the underlying factors driving the extension of ASEAN FTAs beyond the AEC, a widening integration process that includes ASEAN+1 FTAs, bilateral trading arrangements, and region-wide economic integration, we will argue that these parallel developments have been major challenges to ASEAN, particularly its interest in an AEC by 2015 and efforts to broaden FTAs in East Asia through institutionalization.

How can we understand the sudden emergence of regional economic institutions in East Asia since the late 1990s? This chapter argues that it is ASEAN's role and centrality that is the driving force for the increasing institutionalization of economic cooperation in East Asia. Indeed, starting from the challenges resulting from the Asian Financial Crisis, the visible rise of regional institutional building efforts has been attributed to ASEAN's response to the external environment via domino effects and the internal dynamics of ASEAN via the ASEAN Way. The domino effect is a mainstream explanation for the institutionalization of regional integration. According to this perspective, Asia can be considered variously as the object of a positive demonstration effect, the successful emulation of FTAs implemented in other regions (Ravenhill 2003), or the object of a defensive "domino effect" (Baldwin 1995). As Baldwin explains, the domino theory of preferential trade agreements occurs where industries of countries that are excluded from the FTA network will lobby hard to get their government to launch FTAs so as not to suffer from trade diversion. These efforts thus drive regional states toward competition in trade agreements. In a similar vein, Solís, Stallings, and Katada find that competitive pressure (both economic and political) triggered many East Asian governments to rush into FTAs, thus leading to FTA proliferation (Solís, Stallings and Katada 2009).

The second category of arguments focuses on the ASEAN Way of organizing regional affairs. This unique style stems from the Malay cultural practice of *musyawarah* and *mufakat*, which represents an approach to decision-making that emphasizes consensus and consultation. Starting with this cultural disposition, ASEAN has developed its diplomatic style, characterized as "a process of regional interactions and cooperation based on discreteness, informality, consensus building and non-confrontational bargaining styles" (Acharya 2001: 64). As a regional organization of developing countries initially, the exercise of the ASEAN Way tends to be defensive in nature in order to maintain its centrality in regional affairs.

Market-driven interdependence, crisis, and institutionalization

During the Cold War era, the rapid growth of economic interdependence in East Asia was determined by the logic of the market rather than government policies.

As exemplified by electronic and automobile industries, the emergence of East Asian production networks is largely determined by firms' relocation decisions, independent from intergovernmental plans for regional cooperation. In other words, East Asian countries had been able to produce a trade–investment nexus, which played an important role in fostering economic development and growth in the region (Capannelli 2011: 3).

The advent of the AFTA in 1992 was thus a natural response to safeguard the region. For some ASEAN members it appeared inevitable in light of the changing regional and global environment at that time. With the conclusion of the General Agreement on Tariffs and Trade (GATT) Uruguay Round at the beginning of the 1990s, global trade liberalization became serious, with implementation of several regional trade liberalization initiatives, in particular the European Single Market, the North American Free Trade Area (NAFTA), and the Asia-Pacific Economic Cooperation (APEC).

As with its predecessor the Pacific Economic Cooperation Conference (PECC), the launch of the intergovernmental APEC in November 1989 affected ASEAN the most organizationally. As one scholar put it:

> The climate of the 1980s changed and while ASEAN has considered strengthening itself for ten years, there has been no real pressure to do so, and an attitude of "let nature take its way" has prevented any substantial change. Now, real competition has emerged, and ASEAN seems more determined to preserve what it has built.
>
> (Crone 1992: 83)

Indeed, with the decline of US hegemonic power, the rise of multipolarity, and the increasing trend toward regional economic groupings, ASEAN has found it necessary to reappraise carefully the impact of these changes on the organization's cohesiveness, collective bargaining power, and leverage.

From the outset, therefore, ASEAN has had reason to regard APEC with caution. These concerns were explained by Indonesian Foreign Minister Ali Alatas in the following six point statement, which has become known as the "Kuching consensus": (1) APEC should not dilute the identity or limit the role of any existing regional groups; (2) APEC should be based on principles of equality, equity, and mutual benefit; (3) APEC should not be made into an inward-looking trading bloc; (4) APEC should essentially remain a forum for consultation and cooperation on economic issues; (5) APEC should strengthen the capacity of participants to promote their common interests; and (6) APEC should proceed gradually and pragmatically (*The Nation*, July 28, 1993). Joining APEC thus symbolizes ASEAN's expectations and fears. Hence, ASEAN faces a dilemma in that it cannot totally reject APEC, simply because ASEAN knows that APEC is the best means of engaging Washington in Asian affairs.

Thus, when US President Clinton called for an APEC summit for the purpose of institutionalizing the organization, ASEAN gave a rather mixed response. This was demonstrated by the fact that Malaysia, as the leading advocate for an East

Asian economic grouping, did not send its leader to the summit as a gesture of protest. Nevertheless, the most critical concern has had to do with the fear that ASEAN could be subsumed as part of the global production and sourcing network of the larger economies, such as Japan and the United States.

Reflecting the view that APEC is too large and ASEAN too small, the initiative in favor of East Asian regionalism began in 1990 with Malaysian Prime Minister Mahathir Mohammed's proposal of an East Asian Economic Group (EAEG, later renamed East Asian Economic Caucus). However, the proposal was blocked by the United States, which preferred to use APEC for its dialogue with all East Asian economies. Chiefly because of the US position, Japan was cool to the EAEG proposal. China was viewed as being too preoccupied with its own transition to a market economy to give serious thought to such an initiative. All of these factors gave rise to further thought by East Asian countries, including ASEAN.

However, the nature of APEC's role between 1997 and 1999 changed significantly due to the East Asian financial crisis. The 1998 APEC meeting in Kuala Lumpur, for instance, contested whether domestic problems of the member countries were the main cause for the financial crisis, whereas the 1999 meeting was largely concerned with resolving the East Timor issue. As a result, together with the failed negotiations of the Early Voluntary Sectoral Liberalization (EVSL) the voices for dissolving APEC summit meetings have gained strength in East Asia.

Thus, broader region building in East Asia, in which ASEAN plays an increasing role, started to take shape after the Asian financial crisis of 1997–1998. It started with regional monetary cooperation, known as the Chiang Mai Initiative (CMI), which gave birth to the process of ASEAN Plus Three (APT), comprising ASEAN plus China, Japan, and the Republic of Korea. At the initiative of Korea early in the new century, this process was expanded to cover other areas of economic cooperation, the most notable example being the East Asian Free Trade Area (EAFTA), of which China was an important supporter at a later stage. In the meantime, ASEAN took further steps to strengthen and broaden regional cooperation in 2005 when the first East Asia Summit (EAS) was convened. At this point Japan saw the opportunity to propose another comprehensive economic partnership in East Asia (CEPEA, also known as ASEAN+6). As a result, ASEAN has become host to both ASEAN+3 and ASEAN+6 as key initiatives aiming to broaden regional economic cooperation in East Asia.

Since then, the EAS has also developed its own platforms for leaders to discuss various regional and global issues related to development of the region. ASEAN holds EAS summits back to back with APT, with the only differences being the number of countries participating and the issues they select to discuss. Overall, the two processes (EAFTA and CEPEA) have created real questions in East Asia, if not great confusion, about the way people look at the region, and have complicated the regional institutional landscape.

Without any doubt, the financial crisis was a watershed: it was the most significant triggering factor for regional economic and financial cooperation among East Asian countries in the last few decades (ADB 2008). The crisis made clear the limits of an approach to regionalism primarily based on market forces and compelled a reconsideration of the macroeconomic management pattern practiced by East Asian countries, which the crisis proved to be ineffective, too risky, and complacent. East Asian policymakers realized there was a lack of regional mechanisms which could have helped avoid the crisis and been used to prevent future crises. They also understood the intrinsic weaknesses of East Asian financial systems and their poor state of development. And as a result of extensive dialogue among ASEAN countries and the three Northeast Asian economies, they were able to create several new initiatives for regional cooperation.

East Asia's initiatives in support of regional economic cooperation and integration can be classified into four pillars: (1) trade and investment; (2) money and finance; (3) infrastructure and connectivity; and (4) regional public goods (ADB 2006). In trade and investment, Asian economies have been experiencing a proliferation of free trade and investment agreements (FTAs) involving regional members. In money and finance, significant developments were recently achieved with the multilateralization of the Chiang Mai Initiative (CMI) and the establishment of the ASEAN+3 Macroeconomic Research Office (AMRO). In infrastructure and connectivity, a growing number of initiatives have been started under the Greater Mekong Sub-region (GMS) and the Central Asia Regional Economic Cooperation (CAREC) programs, in addition to the ASEAN Infrastructure Fund and region-wide projects such as the Asian Highway and the Trans-Asian Railway, under the United Nations' Economic and Social Commission for Asia and the Pacific (UNESCAP). Finally, in the regional public goods' pillar, East Asian countries have been strengthening dialogue in areas such as natural disasters management, environment and climate change, energy security, prevention and management of communicable diseases, and drugs and human trafficking (ADB 2010).

Through the cases of APEC and AFTA, the nature of ASEAN's central role in regional integration processes can be explained. First, despite increasing the amount of intra-regional trade in East Asia, it was only after the Asian financial crisis that East Asian governments began to actively seek preferential trade agreements. With the exception of ASEAN, which began its first steps towards a free trade area in 1992, the only other visible free trade negotiations that many East Asian governments engaged in was through APEC, a loosely organized forum that in the mid-1990s established its goals to facilitate and liberalize regional trade by 2010 for advanced countries and by 2020 for its developing members.

Second, ASEAN's role is also associated with regional challenges that were not directly linked to the Asian financial crisis. One challenge was APEC's trade liberalization through the EVSL, which ultimately fell apart in 1997 (Krauss 2004). Moreover, it did not help when APEC failed to effectively address the Asian financial crisis (Wesley 1999). In the late 1990s, the multilateral trade regime under the World Trade Organization (WTO) also began to face challenges from its own weight of success as its membership expanded rapidly to include many developing countries, and as states moved to more contentious and political issues like agricultural liberalization. As the Seattle incident ("the Battle for Seattle") amply suggests, the trade liberalization forces of the WTO were confronted directly and visibly with counterforces at its Ministerial meeting in 1999. Since then, despite the launching of the Doha Development Round and the admission of China into the WTO in 2001, trade liberalization negotiations at the WTO level have stagnated.

Third, under those global and regional circumstances, East Asian countries embarked on FTA negotiations in the early 2000s. Many of the first steps towards FTAs took the form of feasibility studies. One of the earliest cases for Japan was the proposal by Korean President Kim Dae Jung during his visit to Japan in October 1998 to conduct studies on the possibility of negotiating Japan–Korea bilateral FTAs. A proposal from Mexico towards a Japan–Mexico FTA emerged at around the same time. For Southeast Asia, Singapore spearheaded the region's FTA boom first by engaging in FTA negotiations with New Zealand in 1999, and then by exploring FTA possibilities with Mexico, Chile, and Korea. The FTA negotiations in East Asia gained momentum in the fall of 2000. Japan's FTA overture to Singapore, which had begun in late 1999 in the form of joint FTA studies between the two countries, upgraded itself to an official negotiation in October 2000. After one year of negotiations, the Japan–Singapore New Age Economic Partnership Agreement was signed in January 2002 and came into effect in November 2002, following ratification by the two countries. More importantly for the region, the then-Chinese Premier Zhu Rongji proposed in November 2000 that China and ASEAN start exploring the possibility of an FTA between them. The framework agreement on this Comprehensive Economic Cooperation between the two entities was signed in 2002, leading China to offer early harvest measures to individual ASEAN members as it opens its market up for certain products ahead of schedule. For Korea, Chile became its FTA partner, with the negotiations starting in September of 1999, and the agreement coming into effect in 2004.

Fourth, although the timing of the post-Asian financial crisis rise of trade regionalism has coincided with that from the financial/monetary side, regional trade cooperation exhibits strikingly different features from those of regional financial cooperation. One of these is the specificity of regional membership, which is very clear in the context of APT in finance, but is not so clear in the context of trade. The FTAs thus far have been dominated by bilateral agreements, and many of the early FTA partners for those East Asian governments are from beyond the immediate region (Solís and Katada 2007).

The clash over the appropriate membership of the region-wide FTA in East Asia is an intriguing feature of regional trade cooperation. Contrary to the conventional argument carried out by international relations scholars (Mansfield and Milner 1999), the collection of FTAs thus far has not translated into regionalism in East Asia. The "spaghetti bowl" of FTAs that crisscross within and outside East Asia has become a challenge to East Asian integration due to complex and conflicting rules of origin, cumbersome transactions throughout the region, and the lack of a top-level management function (Dent 2006). Despite calls from regional academics, think tanks, and some government officials to create a broad East Asian FTA, no convergence of vision and approach emerged.

From AFTA to the AEC as a basis for institutionalization of economic cooperation in East Asia

This section traces the background and rationales for establishing AFTA as a vehicle for ASEAN economic cooperation and the subsequent progressive institutionalization of economic cooperation in the form of an AEC, and the ASEAN Master Plan on Connectivity for accelerating economic cooperation in East Asia.

Pre-AFTA

Although the constitution of ASEAN in its very beginning in 1967 included economic rationales, economic cooperation was confined to a mixture of sectoral and commodity-based concerns under the Foreign Ministers' Meeting in the initial organizational structure of ASEAN after the Bangkok Declaration (ASEAN Secretariat 1997). It was almost a decade later that the first economic ministerial meeting took place at the 1976 Bali Summit, prompted in part by the 1973–1975 recession in the UK and the USA.

ASEAN's approach towards economic cooperation was both cautious and slow due to the ASEAN Way and initial attempts focused on selective economic integration in industry and trade with the signing of the ASEAN Industrial Projects (AIP) and the Preferential Trading Arrangement (PTA) in 1976 and 1977, respectively (Kosandi 2012). Several other attempts at industrial cooperation were launched subsequently, such as the ASEAN Industrial Complementation Scheme (AIC) in 1981 (subsequently modified as the ASEAN Brand-to-Brand Complementation (BBC) and the ASEAN Industrial Joint Ventures in 1983). When these schemes did not progress well due to both expectation and implementation gaps (Wong 2003), some turned to sub-regional initiatives in the form of growth triangles that were meant to be private investment-led so as to exploit sub-regional economic complementarities. The progress of these sub-regional initiatives was also, however, affected by political, economic, and social challenges similar to those experienced in the industrial and trade cooperation schemes. These include perceptions of unequal benefits, inadequate infrastructure, complex decision-making structure, and restrictions on labor mobility.

Nevertheless, the ASEAN-5 member states registered sterling economic growth from 1985 to 1992, leading to their labeling as the miracle economies in East Asia by the World Bank. This spectacular growth performance was by and large attributed to their respective economic links with the developed world through foreign direct investment and trade rather than to any of the economic cooperation schemes at that time. For example, the direction of ASEAN's trade in 1993 indicated that their exports and imports were linked more with the USA, Japan, and the European Economic Community (EEC) rather than with each other (Table 3.1). Excluding Singapore, intra-ASEAN trade was estimated to range between 3 and 5%. Not surprisingly, ASEAN was not viewed as an integrated economic entity then.

The 1990s, however, brought about a renewed effort to forge closer economic cooperation within ASEAN in its "search for a common prosperity" (Lee 2003:

Table 3.1 ASEAN direction of trade, 1993 (%)

Country	USA	Japan	EEC	ASEAN, 1970	ASEAN, 1993
Export					
Brunei	1.2	54.2	17.8	83.2	19.2
Indonesia	14.2	30.3	14.4	21.1	13.4
Malaysia	20.3	13.0	14.5	25.4	28.2
Philippines	38.3	16.3	16.8	1.2	7.1
Singapore	20.3	7.5	14.0	29.4	23.9
Thailand	21.6	17.0	17.0	14.9	16.3
Vietnam	n.a.	32.3	19.6	n.a.	17.6
ASEAN	19.9	15.7	15.0	21.4	20.2
Import					
Brunei	20.2	5.4	27.1	49.4	38.3
Indonesia	11.5	22.0	19.9	7.6	9.3
Malaysia	16.9	27.5	11.6	22.5	20.0
Philippines	19.8	22.8	10.3	5.2	10.9
Singapore	16.3	21.8	11.5	26.7	21.8
Thailand	11.7	30.3	14.9	3.2	12.1
Vietnam	0.1	13.1	11.1	n.a.	29.4
ASEAN	14.9	24.4	13.3	16.3	17.5

Source: ASEAN Secretariat 1997.

194). This was due to both internal and external factors. Domestically, the strong economic performance in the second half of the 1980s boosted the confidence of the ASEAN member states (AMS) in their ability to withstand the increased competitive challenges that inevitably accompanies increased liberalization. Moreover, the trade strategies of these countries have shifted from import substitution to export orientation and a greater inclination towards a foreign direct investment (FDI)-led growth strategy, due in part to changes in economic thinking as well as increasing influence of international financial institutions on the domestic policy formulation of the AMS at that time (Lee 2008).

Externally, the prolonged negotiations of the Uruguay Round under GATT and the formation of the Single European Market and NAFTA seemed to indicate an uncertain future for multilateral liberalization and a converse rise in regionalism. The changing global economic environment also pressed for the development of "economic alliances" to strengthen the economic position of countries, thereby lending greater credence to the use of regional trade agreements. In addition, the development of regional production networks and increasing trade in parts and components due to the inflows of FDI into the region with their greater openness towards these capital flows further strengthened the need for greater economic cooperation. ASEAN as a region and a group clearly offered more to foreign investors in terms of a bigger market as well as a combination of advantages that no member possessed individually (Lee 2008). Recent estimates by the WTO showed that share of parts and components trade in ASEAN-5's exports increased from a mere 1.7% in 1967 to 17.0% in 1992 (Table 3.2). Therefore, in addition to the fear of trade diversion, there was also a fear of investment diversion to other regional groupings, as well as to emerging competitors for scarce global capital such as China and the former Soviet bloc as they were being freed from communism then (Lee 2008).

Consequently, the leaders of ASEAN embarked on what was then seen to be a new, bold, and credible initiative (within the context and history of ASEAN's economic cooperation), to maintain its vitality and relevance, which is the AFTA in 1992. The institutionalization of economic cooperation in the form of a free trade agreement also signaled ASEAN's desire to maintain its position as an important regional organization in the midst of emerging new regional initiatives such as greater European economic integration and the NAFTA (Bowles 1997).

AFTA

The main objectives of AFTA are to create a single market and an international production base, attract foreign direct investments, and expand intra-ASEAN trade and investments. AFTA represents a significant shift in the institutionalization of economic cooperation as it is the first formal rules-based commitment to reduce tariffs in ASEAN (Leviter 2010). Its actual implementation reflects the ASEAN way through the provision of a two-track tariff reduction scheme in the Common Effective Preferential Tariff (CEPT) that was instituted for scheduled tariff reduction. Thus the deadlines for tariff reduction are different for the older ASEAN-6 member states and the CLMV countries, namely Cambodia, Laos, Myanmar, and Vietnam (see Appendix 1). Furthermore, the reduction timelines are lengthy and there are also provisions for states to temporarily suspend reductions for specific production lines. Members could also appeal for an extension of their deadlines, which Malaysia did in the case of its commitments to liberalize its automotive sector. Nevertheless, the acceleration of the deadline for realization of

Table 3.2 Share of parts and components trade in ASEAN-5 exports, 1967–92 (million USD)

Year	Parts and components exports	Total exports	Share (%)
1967	154.9	8,867.0	1.7
1970	235.1	12,213.7	1.9
1980	3,905.2	135,657.5	2.9
1990	38,562.2	276,095.8	14.0
1992	60,637.9	356,829.4	17.0

Source: WTO 2011.

AFTA from its initial target of 2008 to 2003 and subsequently to 2002 reflects the members' commitment to AFTA when the AFTA project was overtaken by the members' respective commitments in the Uruguay Round of the WTO when it was finally completed in 1994.

Tariffs did fall as scheduled indicating the successful institutionalization of economic cooperation with the AFTA project (ERIA 2012). In 2010, the CEPT rates for the ASEAN-6 were virtually zero and had an average of 2.6% for the newer CLMV countries. However, studies on the impact of AFTA indicate mixed results. Some early studies suggested small or insignificant effects on intra-ASEAN trade and investment (see for example, Tongzon 2005; Tham 2005). This can be attributed to the low utilization of CEPT concessions in the early years due to the relatively low margins of preference, bureaucratic practices and inefficiencies in the implementing agencies, lack of awareness on the part of the business community, and lack of clear and transparent procedures for obtaining the tariff concessions as well as some backtracking in the commitments of some countries. Econometric studies by Elliot and Ikemoto (2004), also found that trade flows were not significantly affected by AFTA for the period immediately following the signing of the AFTA, up to 1999. A positive AFTA effect was found for intra-ASEAN trade, which though limited, did increase over time. It is therefore possible that the impact of AFTA has increased over time with better dissemination of information and improvement in bureaucratic processes as other studies seem to indicate a positive impact. For example, using a sample period of 1980 to 2010, Okabe and Urata (2013) found positive and significant trade creation effects from the tariff elimination for a wide range of products, thereby leading them to conclude that AFTA has been successful in promoting intra-ASEAN trade.

Since trade and investment are tied together, especially in the case of regional production networks that have dominated the industrial development of the original ASEAN-5 member states, a Framework Agreement on the ASEAN Investment Area (AIA) was signed in October 1998. The AIA's objective is to make ASEAN a competitive, open and liberal investment area by binding member countries to progressively reduce or eliminate investment regulations and conditions that may impede investment flows and the operation of investment projects in ASEAN. To facilitate economic cooperation, there is also the AFTA-Plus or the expanded AFTA framework, covering trade facilitation measures such as technical barriers to trade, harmonization of standards and conformance measures, customs taxonomy, valuation and procedures; and the development of common product certification standards (Tham 2008). In addition, services liberalization has also been pursued under the ASEAN Framework Agreement on Services (AFAS) that was launched in 1995, as numerous services are also essential for facilitating the movement of goods from port to port. These framework agreements, however, continue to reflect the ASEAN Way as their implementation is left to the member states, unlike AFTA. For example, services liberalization is voluntary as countries nominate the sectors that they wish to liberalize, and there is also a lack of clear time frames. Thus although intra-ASEAN trade did increase from about 17% in 1992 to 21% in 2001, intra-ASEAN investment amounted only to 11% of total

FDI in ASEAN from 1995 to 2001, while the services liberalization remains limited (Tongzon 2005; Tham 2005; CARI 2013).

Post AFTA: AEC and beyond

Following AFTA, the proposal to establish an ASEAN Economic Community (AEC) in 2002 signified a shift towards deepening economic integration within ASEAN. As noted in the ISEAS Concept Paper on the AEC, ASEAN leaders have been concerned with the increasingly competitive global environment after the AFC in 1997/98 (Hew et al. 2005). In particular, the rise of China was perceived to be a potential threat to the attractiveness of ASEAN as host economies. Such perceptions were fueled, for example, by the fact that ASEAN's share of FDI inflows as a percentage of developing countries fell progressively from 1992 to 2000 while total inflows into China had outstripped inflows into ASEAN since 1993. Deepening integration in ASEAN was also recommended by the ASEAN-ISIS (Track Two) Report as well as the ASEAN Competitiveness Study by McKinsey and Company, which was commissioned by the ASEAN Economic Ministers. In all three reports, the call to deepen and accelerate regional economic integration in ASEAN is premised on the need to elevate ASEAN's attractiveness as a global production base, which in turn, will contribute towards sustaining economic growth in the region as well as in the respective members' economies.

This proposal was subsequently accepted at the Bali Summit in 2003 (Bali Concord II), with a target deadline of 2020, which was later brought forward to 2015. The AEC is one of the three pillars of the ASEAN Community with the two other being the ASEAN Security Community and the ASEAN Socio-cultural Community. It is envisaged that the AEC would be a single market and production base, with a free flow of goods, services, investments, capital and skilled labor by 2015. The AEC thus provides a comprehensive framework to build on the existing ASEAN integration programs, such as AFTA, AFAS, and AIA. The old agreements are therefore galvanized and housed under a new concept or the AEC as a new form of regional institutionalization. In line with the ASEAN way, this new form is not a drastic change from the old form in that there is no move toward a creation of an EU-like common market but instead it is more like an AFTA-Plus project (Goron 2011).

In 2007, the lofty goals of the AEC were translated into action when the ASEAN Leaders issued the Declaration on the AEC Blueprint. The Blueprint is essentially a master plan formulated for guiding the achievement of an AEC by 2015 by means of detailing economic integration measures, commitments, targets, and timelines for their implementation into four pillars, namely, a single market and production base, a competitive economic region, equitable economic development and full integration into the global economy (see Appendix 2). There are two objectives: liberalization and facilitation and protection of investment, harmonization of laws and regulations, capacity building, and the like (Pariwat et al., 2011). Notably, financial services and capital flows are treated differently in the Blueprint as these are the only two sectors that are allowed flexibility in the liberalization plan (Appendix 2). This is due to large differences in financial development and capital account policies of member countries as well as the sensitive nature of this sector in view of its implications on the monetary policy of each country and its influence on other sectors of the economy. Furthermore, the Blueprint only focuses on "skilled labor," leaving out the bulk of intra-ASEAN migrant workers, who belong mainly to the semi-skilled or unskilled categories. The ultimate form of integration, however, is ASEAN's version of a common market. This is definitely not, however, of the same stripe as the EU common market since it is an integration based on flows of goods, services, and to a limited extent, capital and labor while there is no policy integration, unlike the EU. The Blueprint is also accompanied by a strategic schedule that maps out the timelines for the implementation of the measures. It also serves as the main focus of ASEAN's economic agenda.

In 2011, in recognition of the need for a well-connected ASEAN in order to achieve the goals of deeper economic integration and to reinforce ASEAN's position as a hub for East Asian economic integration, ASEAN launched its Master Plan on Connectivity. This Plan brought with it new concepts such as "physical connectivity" (pertaining to infrastructure building), "institutional connectivity" (pertaining to trade liberalization and facilitation), and "people-to-people" connectivity (pertaining to shared education, culture, and tourism). While the idea of enhancing connectivity to reduce investment and trade costs and to harmonize processes and procedures as well as to promote togetherness represents a novel new concept for economic cooperation, its implementation as in the case of the AEC remains in the hands of national governments, reflecting the continued use of the ASEAN Way for enhancing connectivity.

As the deadline for the AEC draws to a close, an ASEAN scorecard as well as a mid-term review of the implementation of the AEC Blueprint was rolled out in 2012. According to the AEC Scorecard, ASEAN had achieved 67.5% of its targets for the 2008–2011 period. The first pillar, namely a single market and production base was the worst performer with a score of 65.9%, while the fourth pillar, namely integration into the global economy, was the best performer with a score of 85.7% (Sanchita 2012). Although the scorecard is not without deficiencies,[1] it represents a serious attempt towards monitoring compliance. Similarly, the Mid-term Review that highlighted the achievements and challenges in the implementation of the AEC (ERIA 2012) is another step in monitoring the Blueprint targets. By 2013, however, an implementation gap has emerged as the actual implementation lags significantly behind the timelines of stated objectives (CARI 2013), indicating that the ASEAN way of providing flexibility for member states to liberalize at their own respective pace, will impede the attainment of the goals of the Blueprint.

Nonetheless, there are already on-going efforts to consider further deepening ASEAN's integration beyond 2015. The Economic Research Institute for ASEAN and East Asia (ERIA) in conjunction with inputs from Harvard University have already come out with a *Jakarta Framework on moving the AEC forward into 2015 and Beyond* (ERIA 2011). Economic cooperation and its institutionalization in ASEAN are therefore expected to continue to evolve beyond 2015, regardless whether the AEC goals will be achieved by 2015.

ASEAN Plus One and expanding East Asian FTA networks

The economies of the AMS have always been outward-oriented due to their trade and investment links and engagement in the production networks with the multi-nationals from the developed world, including East Asia. This outward orientation has contributed to their stellar economic growth before the AFC. But the AFC changed the growth trajectory of the AMS as ASEAN's average growth rate has declined from 7–8% per annum to 5–6% per annum before and after the AFC. ASEAN's growth had been reaccelerating gradually before the onset of the global economic crisis in 2008. The growth performance demonstrated clearly that ASEAN's prosperity depends very much on its ability to manage changes in the external environment by devising appropriate strategies to overcome the challenges posed by these changes as well as to seize the opportunities that came with it.

In this regard, there were four changes in the external environment that neces-sitated ASEAN's integration to take into consideration its economic relations with the external world, namely: stiffening competition, rapidly changing markets, increased requirements for regional cooperation, and shifting policy priorities (Petri 2009). Increasing competition comes from outside ASEAN in the form of China and India as well as from within ASEAN itself, as the CLMV countries have also been gaining rapidly on ASEAN's established exporters. The destinations of ASEAN's export markets have also been progressively shifting from the world's developed economies to the region's emerging markets as the economic center of the world is shifting eastwards. Increasing importance of regional pro-duction networks has also given rise to the necessity to reduce transactions and trade costs through economic cooperation. However, this cooperation is best developed in the context of "open regionalism" in order to take advantage of the larger global market. Finally, as noted earlier the stagnation of multilateral liberal-ization has driven liberalization at the regional and bilateral level. The AMS are also engaged in multiple tracks of liberalization and ASEAN integration has to be cognizant of this in order to manage its own integration and that with the world.

ASEAN therefore explicitly takes into account its outward orientation and the changing external environment in the fourth core element of the AEC, which is integration into the global economy (Appendix 2). As stated in the AEC Blue-print, it is crucial for ASEAN to look beyond the borders of its own community in order for ASEAN to be more dynamic and to attain a stronger position in the global supply chain. More importantly, "ASEAN Centrality" needs to be main-tained in its external economic relations, including its existing and future FTAs with other countries.

To date, ASEAN has signed FTAs with the three North East Asian economies, namely China in 2002 and Korea and Japan in 2008. There are also FTAs with Australia and New Zealand as well as another with India, all of which were signed in 2009. As explained in the introduction, the proliferation of these FTAs can be attributed to the fear of trade and investment diversion from other FTAs that are being proposed or signed, leading to a domino effect. Despite this proliferation of FTAs, there is as yet no East Asian FTA even though the APT process was officially launched in 1999. Instead, economic cooperation at the East Asian level focuses only on functional cooperation as explained in the second section of this chapter. Indeed, at the APT meeting in Phnom Penh in September 2003, the economic ministers suggested taking an evolutionary approach for the development of an East Asian Free Trade Area, which is a long-term goal, as it needs to take into account the different stages of social, economic, and cultural development in East Asian countries (Soesastro 2003). Consequently, as noted by Terada (2012), ASEAN, by virtue of its relative success in implementing AFTA and its network of ASEAN+1 FTAs, lies at the hub of the institutionalization of economic cooperation in East Asia.

TPP versus RCEP: politics of regional economic cooperation

By the late 2000s, the institutionalization of economic cooperation in East Asia had become a complicated noodle bowl as ASEAN had inked FTAs with each Northeast Asian economy, as well as with Australia and New Zealand, and with India, as mentioned earlier. Economic simulations on the economic benefits of different economic groupings indicated that an ASEAN+6 (i.e. including Australia and New Zealand as well as India) would lead to the most economic benefits for the member countries of this regional grouping (Petri 2009; Urata 2008). It should be noted that one question as regards ASEAN's role as the driver of economic cooperation in East Asia remains: whether economic cooperation is a +3 or +6 grouping. Also, the future shape of the new economic architecture in East Asia is not resolved by prospective economic benefits as there were divergences in opinions among states, with China favoring a +3 grouping and Japan favoring a +6 grouping. This dilemma, at least where economic cooperation was concerned, was resolved at the East Asia Summit in 2012. At that meeting, the leaders formally agreed to launch negotiations on the Regional Comprehensive Economic Partnership (RCEP), comprising all the 10 ASEAN members and the six countries with which it has FTAs, namely China, India, Japan, South Korea, Australia, and New Zealand. This decision was guided by the proposals from different study groups for an ASEAN+3 and an ASEAN+6 FTA.

RCEP has a combined GDP of about USD17 trillion and accounts for 40% of world trade. Negotiations started in May 2013 and are expected to conclude by the end of 2015. It is also meant to be an open regional grouping as it does not exclude other countries from becoming members in the future as long as they comply with the grouping's rules and guidelines. Its guiding principles seek to preserve the centrality of ASEAN by harmonizing the various FTAs that ASEAN has with the +6 countries. Accordingly, RCEP will cover trade in goods, trade in services, investment, economic and technical cooperation, intellectual property, competition, dispute settlement, and other issues that will be identified during the course of negotiations.

It is possible that the potential grouping will lead to minimal trade liberalization as the guiding principle of RCEP is cognizant of the different stages of development of the prospective members by including flexibility for special and differential treatment. Thus sensitive sectors may be excluded and flexibility based on the ASEAN Way may be used as a crutch against liberalization and reforms needed (Hiebert and Hanlon 2012). It is also unclear how the negotiations can be concluded if the new grouping is indeed to harmonize the existing FTAs as these have achieved different degrees of liberalization and are far from uniform.

The Trans-Pacific Partnership (TPP) Agreement, on the other hand, evolved from the Trans-Pacific Strategic Economic Partnership Agreement (or the P4) formed in 2006 by four APEC economies (namely Singapore, Brunei, Chile, and New Zealand). Since these are small, open economies with modest interactions with each other, the P4 was not meant to be exclusive but rather as a pathfinder for an inclusive Trans-Pacific effort (Petri et al. 2011). Subsequently, the grouping has expanded to include the United States, Australia, Peru, Vietnam, Malaysia, Mexico, and Canada. In July 2013, Japan formally joined the eighteenth round of negotiations for the TPP, although it has been observing the talks from the sidelines before making the decision to participate in the TPP negotiations. The TPP goes beyond the traditional trade agreements as it will also deal with behind-the-border impediments to trade and investment or what is known as deep integration since it will address the governance gap between countries (WTO 2011). This is expected to lower trade costs and provide shared benefits that some of the markets or national governments may have failed to offer. Like the RCEP, it also allows for expanded membership based on willingness to abide by what has already been agreed by existing TPP partners.

Economic simulations have shown that the TPP or an Asian (e.g., the RCEP) track of integration can have a positive impact on world welfare gains (Petri et al. 2011). The TPP is estimated to generate an annual welfare gain of USD104 billion while the RCEP will generate annual welfare gains of USD215 billion by 2025. Integration on both tracks will generate an even larger welfare gain of USD303 billion while an eventual region-wide agreement such as a Free Trade Area of the Asia Pacific (FTAAP), would generate USD862 billion in benefits by 2025.

However, the crucial difference between the two potential groupings is the role of ASEAN (Table 3.3). Clearly, ASEAN can only be a driving force for East Asian economic cooperation in the RCEP and not in the US-led TPP. This may weaken incentives within ASEAN to further deepen economic integration in the AEC. Thus concluding a TPP without the RCEP can have serious implications on the future of economic cooperation in the APT.

Conclusion – major tasks ahead

In conclusion, let us recapitulate the key points that have emerged from this analysis and link them to issues of institutionalization in East Asia. As we have observed above, having traversed from AFTA to RCEP, it is remarkable that ASEAN has advanced the ASEAN-led institutionalization of economic cooperation in East Asia. In particular, there has been increasing recognition of ASEAN's role and centrality in driving Asian economic integration. As a result, economic cooperation in East Asia has been institution driven, as seen in the surge in bilateral

Table 3.3 TPP vs. RCEP

	TPP	RCEP
Members	USA, Singapore, Malaysia, Vietnam, Brunei, Japan, Australia, NZ, Canada, Mexico, Peru, Chile	ASEAN10, Japan, China, South Korea, Australia, NZ, India
Leadership	US-led	ASEAN-led
Characteristics	Born out of P4 agreement Covers 21 areas (deeper and comprehensive)	Born out of ASEAN+1 FTAs Covers 17 areas
Concerns	Does not include China and India May divide ASEAN	Tension between China and US; ASEAN+1 FTAs have different depths of commitments and deadlines
Schedule	Started in 2011 and to be concluded by 2014	Started in 2013 and to be concluded by 2015

Source: compiled by authors.

and multilateral free trade agreements, economic partnerships, and comprehensive economic cooperation agreements.

Given these historical developments, institutionalization of economic cooperation in East Asia has been driven by two factors. The first factor is the domino effect, which drives member governments to generate a chain reaction of subsequent preferential trade agreements. From APEC to RCEP, the domino effect considerations have affected the level and pace of institutionalization of economic cooperation. The second is the ASEAN Way and centrality, which suggests its leading role in regional architecture by which the region's relations with great powers are conducted and simultaneously the interest of ASEAN community is promoted. From APEC to RCEP, ASEAN remains to be a driver in charting the evolving regional architecture. As a result, institutionalization in East Asia tends to progress slowly and defensively without heeding too much of its consequences.

The challenge for ASEAN is thus to work out a region-wide framework like RCEP in order to maintain momentum by extending regional economic integration to a group of partners with an appropriate measure of the gains associated with the AEC. In overcoming the challenge, ASEAN needs to address the followings: first, the array of Asia's institutions for regionalism has emerged as a result of ad hoc decisions undertaken by policymakers in response to perceived, narrow functional expectations, be they economic or security in orientation. The shaping of these institutions did not follow a regional grand design like in the case of the European Union. While the existing regional architecture has served the region well so far, the pressing challenges wrought by globalization and transnationalism have made clear that its current structure is insufficient to guarantee the continued success of the regions' economies in a way that is sustainable, equitable, and compatible with global structures (Capannelli and Tan 2012).

Second, the ASEAN Way has helped ASEAN to survive as a regional grouping thus far and the defensive actions are the progressive institutionalization of economic cooperation so that it can maintain its centrality. Nevertheless, the ASEAN Way has raised challenges in terms of the implementation and achievements of these economic cooperation efforts. It is unclear whether further institutionalization without any changes in the ASEAN Way can foster a more economically integrated ASEAN and East Asia.

Third, with the advent of the RCEP, the broadening process is also becoming more crucial to ensure ASEAN centrality. Certainly the RCEP must implement trade liberalization consistent with what will be done under the scope of the AEC and consolidation of the rules of origin resulting from overlapping FTAs. Trade in services, however, is still a difficult area for participating countries with different levels of development, so it needs to find its own path for development in the short run, with a clear strategy for its trade liberalization to be found in the long run. Investment issues could be developed in parallel with the ASEAN+1 process in the short run, but will become more important in the longer run as development into a comprehensive investment area should involve greater efforts and commitments from participating countries. Finally, ASEAN should not let the RCEP be undermined by development of the TPP, which seems to be a parallel development, at least in the short run, and despite the participation of several ASEAN members in such an agreement (Chirathivat and Srisangnam 2013).

Box 3.1 Salient features of CEPT

1   Based on reciprocity, that is, all countries must give the preferential tariff, once a good is accepted under the CEPT.
2   It is sectoral as members nominate the sectors for liberalization.
3   Fast track and normal track, with 15 products originally earmarked for fast track reductions.
4   CEPT product list is divided into inclusion list, temporary exclusion list, general exclusion list, and a sensitive list.
5   Longer timeline for the CLMV countries.

Compiled by authors.

Note

1   The scorecard only indicates whether a country has initiated policies to implement the Blueprint measures. Hence, while an absence of policies initiated can be taken to imply little progress, the converse may not hold as the scorecard does not examine the actual status of implementation of each measure. It also does not explain why policies are not initiated due to its mechanical nature.

Table 3.4 Key characteristics and core elements of the AEC blueprint

	Core Elements	Liberalization	Facilitation/Protection/Harmonization
A.	**Single Market and Production Base**		
A.1	Free Flow of goods (nine strategic approaches)	Eliminate tariffs: 2010 for ASEAN-6 and 2015 for CLMV; Eliminate non-tariff barriers: 2010 for ASEAN-5, 2012 for the Philippines and 2015 for CLMV	Simplify rules of origin, customs integration ASEAN Single Window; trade facilitation, standards of commerce
A.2	Free flow of services (three strategic approaches)	Allow 70% foreign equity in priority sectors (health, tourism, IT, transport by 2012), logistics by 2013 and all other services by 2015. Financial services: Liberalization according to readiness	
A.3	Free flow of investment (five strategic approaches)	Liberalization according to the ASEAN Comprehensive Investment Agreement	Investment protection and promotion
A.4	Free flow of capital (seven strategic approaches)	Progressive liberalization depending on members' readiness	Harmonize regulations
A.5	Free flow of skilled labor		Facilitate movements of professional labor through Mutual Recognition Agreements
A.6	Priority of integration sectors		Projects in 12 Priority sectors
A.7	Food, agriculture, and forestry		Harmonize best practices, such as safety and quality standards
B.	**Competitive Economic Region**		Introduce competition policies and develop regional networks and guidelines
B.1	Consumer protection		Develop regional networks and guidelines

Core Elements	Liberalization	Facilitation/Protection/Harmonization
B.2 Intellectual property rights		Implement IPT action plan, promote regional cooperation
B.3 Infrastructure development (10 strategic thrusts)		Facilitate multimodal transport and implement key infrastructure projects
B.4 Taxation		Complete bilateral agreements
B.5 E-commerce		Harmonize legal infrastructure
C. Equitable Economic Development		
C.1 SME development		ASEAN Blueprint of best practices
C.2 Initiative for ASEAN Integration		Capacity building for CLMV countries
D. Full Integration into the Global Economy		
D.1 Coherent approach		Enhance coordination and common approaches for trade agreements with dialogue partners
D.2 Supply networks		Adopt international best practices and standards, technical assistance

Source: Prakash and Isono, 2012; and Pariwat et al., 2011.

References

Acharya, Amitav. 2001. *Constructing a Security Community in Southeast Asia.* London: Routledge.

ASEAN Secretariat. 1997. *ASEAN Economic Cooperation: Transition and Transformation.* Singapore: ISEAS.

Asian Development Bank (ADB). 2006. *Regional Cooperation and Integration Strategy.* Manila: ADB.

Asian Development Bank (ADB). 2008. *Emerging Asian Regionalism: A Partnership for Shared Prosperity.* Manila: ADB.

Asian Development Bank (ADB). 2010. *Institutions for Regional Integration: Toward an Asian Economic Community.* Manila: ADB.

Baldwin, Richard. 1995. The Domino Theory of Regionalism. In R. Baldwin, P. Haaparanta, and J. Kiander, eds, *Expanding Membership of the European Union.* Cambridge: Cambridge University Press.

Baldwin, Richard. 2006. Managing the Noodle Bowl: The Fragility of East Asian Regionalism. CEPR Discussion Paper, No. 5561.

Bowles, P. 1997. ASEAN, AFTA and "the New Regionalism". *Pacific Affairs* 70(2): 219–234.

Capannelli, Giovanni. 2011. Institutions for Economic and Financial Integration in Asia: Trends and Prospects. ADBI Working Paper, No. 308.

Capannelli, Giovanni and See Seng Tan. 2012. Institutions for Asian Integration: Innovation and Reform. ADBI Working Paper, No. 375.

Chirathivat, Suthiphand and Piti Srisangnam. 2013. The 2030 Architecture of Association of Southeast Asian Nations Free Trade Agreements. ADBI Working Paper Series, No. 419.

CIMB ASEAN Research Institute (CARI) 2013. *The ASEAN Economic Community: The Status of Implementation, Challenges, and Bottlenecks.* Jakarta: CARI.

Crone, Donald. 1992. The Politics of Emerging Pacific Cooperation. *Pacific Affairs* 65: 68–83.

Dent, Christopher. 2006. *New Free Trade Agreements in the Asia Pacific.* Basingstoke: Palgrave Macmillan.

Economic Research Institute for ASEAN and East Asia (ERIA). 2011. Jakarta Framework on Moving the ASEAN Community Forward into 2015 and Beyond. www.eria.org/Ja karta%20Framework%20on%20Moving%20ASEAN%20Community%20Forward%20into %202015%20and%20Beyond%20Presented%20to%20the%20President%20of%20Republi c%20of%20Indonesia.pdf (accessed August 10, 2013).

Economic Research Institute for ASEAN and East Asia (ERIA). 2012. *Mid-Term Review of the Implementation of the AEC Blueprint: Executive Summary.* Jakarta: ERIA. www.eria. org/publications/key_reports/mid-term-review-of-the-implementation-of-aec-blueprint -executive-summary.html (accessed August 8, 2013).

Elliot, Robert J. R. and K. Ikemoto. 2004. AFTA and the Asian Crisis: Help or Hindrance to ASEAN Intra-Regional Trade? *Asian Economic Journal* 18: 1–23.

Goron, C. 2011. *Building an ASEAN Community by 2015. New Concepts for a Revival of the "ASEAN Way" towards Regional Integration.* European Institute for Asian Studies (EIAS) Briefing Paper. Brussels: EAIS.

Hew, Denis, et al. 2005. ISEAS Concept Paper on the ASEAN Community. In Denis Hew, ed., *Roadmap to an ASEAN Economic Community.* Singapore: ISEAS.

Hiebert, Murray and Liam Hanlon. 2012. ASEAN and Partners Launch Regional Comprehensive Economic Partnership. December 7. Centre for Strategic and International

Studies (CSIS). http://csis.org/publication/asean-and-partners-launch-regional-comp rehensive-economic-partnership (accessed August 10, 2013).

Kawai, Masahiro 2007. *Evolving Economic Architecture in East Asia.* ADB Institute Discussion Paper No. 84. Tokyo: ADBI.

Kosandi, Meidi 2012. Parallel Evolution of Practice and Research on ASEAN Economic Integration: From Paradigm Contestation to Eclectic Theorization. *Ritsumeikan Annual Review of International Studies* 11: 101–133.

Krauss, E. S. 2004. The US and Japan in APEC's EVSL negotiations. In E. S. Krauss and T. J. Pempel, eds, *Beyond Bilateralism.* Stanford, CA: Stanford University Press.

Lee, Poh Ping. 2008. AFTA, the New Regionalism, Globalization and the ASEAN Community. In S. Y. Tham, P. P. Lee, and O. Norani, eds, *Community in ASEAN: Ideas and Practices.* Bangi: UKM Press.

Lee, Tsao Yuan. 2003. The ASEAN Free Trade Area: The Search for a Common Prosperity. In S. Siddique and Sree Kumar (compiled), *The 2nd ASEAN Reader.* Singapore: ISEAS.

Leviter, L. 2010. The ASEAN Charter: ASEAN Failure or Member Failure? *International Law and Politics* 43: 159–210.

Lincoln, Edward. 2004. *East Asian Economic Regionalism.* Washington, DC: Brookings Institution Press.

Mansfield, E., and H. Milner. 1999. The New Wave of Regionalism. *International Organization* 53(3): 589–627.

Okabe, Misa and Shujiro Urata. 2013. *The Impact of AFTA on Intra-AFTA Trade.* ERIA Discussion Paper Series. ERIA-DP-2013–2005. Jakarta: ERIA.

Pariwat, Kanithasen, Jivakanont Vacharakoon, and Charnon Boonnuch. 2011. AEC 2015: Ambitions, Expectations and Challenges. Bank of Thailand Discussion Paper, DP/03/2011.

Petri, Peter A. 2009. Competitiveness and Leverage. In M. G. Plummer and S. Y. Chia, eds, *Realizing the ASEAN Economic Community: A Comprehensive Assessment.* Singapore: ISEAS.

Petri, Peter A., Michael G. Plummer, and Fan Zhai 2011. *The Trans-Pacific Partnership and Asia-Pacific Integration: A Quantitative Assessment.* East-West Center Working Paper Series, Economic Series, No. 119. October 23, 2011. Honolulu, HI: East-West Center.

Prakash, Anita and Ikumo Isono. 2012. ASEAN in the Global Economy – An Enhanced Economic and Political Role. Economic Research Institute for ASEAN and East Asia (ERIA) Policy Brief, No. 2012–2001, January.

Ravenhill, John. 2003. The New Bilateralism in the Asia Pacific. *Third World Quarterly* 24(2): 299–317.

Sanchita, Basu. 2012. A Critical Look at the ASEAN Economic Community Scorecard. East Asia Forum. June 1. www.eastasiaforum.org/2012/06/01/a-critical-look-at-the-a sean-economic-community-scorecard/ (accessed August 8, 2013).

Soesastro, Hadi. 2003. *An ASEAN Economic Community and ASEAN+3: How Do They Fit Together?* ANU Pacific Economic Papers No. 338. Canberra: Australia-Japan Research Centre, Asia-Pacific School of Economics and Government.

Soesastro, H. 2006. Regional Integration in East Asia: Achievements and Future Prospects. *Asian Economic Policy Review* 1(2): 215–235.

Solís, M., and S. N. Katada. 2007. The Japan–Mexico FTA: A Cross-Regional Step in Japan's New Trade Regionalism. *Pacific Affairs* 80(2): 279–300.

Solís, M., B. Stallings and S. N. Katada, eds. 2009. *Competitive Regionalism: FTA Diffusion in the Pacific Rim.* London: Palgrave.

Terada, T. 2012. Entanglement of Regional Economic Integration and ASEAN. Chapter 3 in *Japan Center for Economic Research (JCER) "Asia Report"*. Tokyo: JCER. www.jcer. or.jp/eng/pdf/2012asia_chapter3.pdf (accessed June 5, 2015).

Tham Siew Yean. 2005. FDI and the Free Movement of Investments in ASEAN. In Denis Hew, ed., *Roadmap to an ASEAN Economic Community*. Singapore: ISEAS.

Tham Siew Yean. 2008. ASEAN Economic Cooperation: Moving towards an ASEAN Economic Community. In S. Y. Tham, P. P. Lee, and O. Norani, eds, *Community in ASEAN: Ideas and Practices*. Bangi: UKM Press.

Tongzon, Jose, L. 2005. Role of AFTA in an ASEAN Economic Community. In Denis Hew, ed., *Roadmap to an ASEAN Economic Community*. Singapore: ISEAS.

Urata, Shujiro 2008. An ASEAN+6 Economic Partnership: Significance and Tasks. Asia Research Report 2007. Japan Center for Economic Research.

Wesley, M. 1999. The Asian Crisis and the Adequacy of Regional Institutions. *Contemporary Southeast Asia* 21(1): 54–73.

Wong, John. 2003. The ASEAN Model of Regional Cooperation. In S. Siddique and Sree Kumar (compiled), *The 2nd ASEAN Reader*. Singapore: ISEAS.

World Bank. 1993. *The East Asian Miracle*. Washington DC: World Bank.

World Trade Organization (WTO). 2011. *World Trade Report 2011*. Geneva: WTO.

4 Institutionalization of security cooperation in East Asia

Cheng-Chwee Kuik

Introduction

This chapter examines the institutionalization of region-wide security cooperation in East Asia, with particular focus on its evolutions, features, and factors.[1] By "East Asia," I refer to the region encompassing Southeast and Northeast Asia. By "institutionalization," I refer to a process in which a group of sovereign states seek to *regularize* and *harmonize* their cooperation in their pursuit of shared goals, through the adoption of certain formal mechanisms or informal practices, which, once in place, shape the states' expectations and actions.[2] To regularize means to fix or increase the frequency of the cooperative endeavors among the states, whereas to harmonize means to improve the qualitative aspects of the cooperative endeavors. Harmonizing cooperation is an effort where egoistic sovereign states with divergent interests come into agreement about what constitutes their shared goals and how best to pursue them collectively. The wider the scope of the shared goals and the stronger the collective action among the member states, the higher the degree of harmonization; the higher the degree of harmonization, the higher the degree of institutionalization. Different institutional arrangements – across sectors and across time – often exhibit different degrees of harmonization (and by extension, different degrees of institutionalization), for factors at various levels.

Based on these conceptions, the chapter seeks to address the following questions: In what ways and to what extent has regional security cooperation among the East Asian countries been institutionalized over the past few decades? What are the key factors that have shaped the forms, degrees, and pace of institutionalization of East Asian security cooperation?

As a *region-wide* inter-state cooperation that centers primarily – and not necessarily exclusively – on the 10 member states of the Association of Southeast Asian Nations (ASEAN) *and* the three Northeast Asian states of China, Japan, and South Korea, the East Asian security cooperation is a relatively recent phenomenon that has emerged only in the post-Cold War era.[3] The creation of the ASEAN Regional Forum (ARF) in 1994 marked the emergence of the first region-wide security cooperation that is initiated by and focused mainly on East Asian states, albeit with membership that involves non-East Asian actors. Security cooperation that is forged *exclusively* among the East Asian states, however, did not come into being until the late 1990s, when the 13 countries (i.e. the ASEAN-10 and the Northeast Asia-3) began to cooperate on security matters under the ASEAN Plus Three (APT) framework. This took place only after the countries had embarked on the East Asian-wide cooperation on economic issues in the wake of the 1997–98 Asian financial crisis (see Chapter 3 of this book).

As shall be elaborated, the institutionalization of security cooperation in East Asia has been marked by three characteristics. First, in terms of its organizing mode, East Asian-wide security cooperation has evolved primarily on the basis of "cooperative security," as opposed to "collective defense" (i.e. military cooperation that involves mutual defense commitment among the member states). These cooperative security arrangements have existed side-by-side with various US-led *bilateral* military alliances and partnerships that were mostly established during the Cold War. Second, in terms of scope, the East Asian-wide security cooperation has focused more on non-traditional security issues than on traditional security activities. Prior to and even after the creation of the APT, individual East Asian countries have chosen to forge military security cooperation with extra-regional powers, mainly the United States, rather than exclusively among themselves. When they do engage in military cooperation at the regional level, the platforms have always involved actors outside of the East Asian region. Examples are the ARF since 1994 and the ASEAN Defense Ministers' Meeting Plus (ADMM+8) since 2010. Third, in terms of structure, the East Asian security cooperation is a fragmented and weakly institutionalized collaborative process that consists of multiple multilayered and overlapped formal and informal forums. Most of these institutions – like the foreign ministerial-level ARF, the leader-level East Asia Summit (EAS), and the defense ministerial-level ADMM+8 – are initiated and led by the ASEAN states, whereas others – like the semi-official Shangri-La Dialogue (SLD) – are more oriented on extraregional players. These Track 1 and Track 1.5 forums are complemented by the Track 2 processes like the Council for Security Cooperation in the Asia-Pacific (CSCAP) and the Network of East Asian Think-tanks (NEAT).

What explains these institutional characteristics of the East Asian-wide security cooperation? I argue that the forms and extent of the institutionalization of East Asian security cooperation are, essentially, a function of several interrelated factors, ranging from the persistence of historical legacies and political problems, to the convergence and divergence in security perceptions across the regional states, and to the imperative of functional cooperation. It is the interplays of these push and pull factors that have shaped the way and the degree to which the East Asian security cooperation has been institutionalized since the 1990s.

This chapter proceeds in three parts. The first part analyzes the origin and evolution of various institutions that have constituted and supported security cooperation among the East Asian states. The second part illustrates the institutional features of East Asian security cooperation. The third and concluding part sums up the discussion.

Evolution

Before tracing the origins and developments of the region-wide security institutions in East Asia, it is useful to typologize these institutions. Based on the formality of their memberships, the institutions can be grouped into three categories (Capie and Evans 2002): (a) "Track 1" institutions, that is, formal meetings attended by government officials representing their respective countries, including the ARF (created in 1994), the APT (1997), the EAS (2005), and the ADMM+8 (2010); (b) "Track 1.5" institutions, that is, meetings attended by officials acting in their private capacities, security analysts, and academics, including the SLD (2002); and (c) "Track 2" institutions, that is, non-governmental and informal meetings attended by think-tank researchers and non-governmental security specialists, including the CSCAP (1993) and the NEAT (2003).

In order to better illustrate how the establishments of the above institutions have had important bearing on the evolving patterns of East Asian security cooperation at different junctures, I shall structure the discussion into three phases. They are: (a) Phase One (1990–1996): the initiation stage, which witnessed the creation and institutionalization of the ARF and CSCAP as the embryonic Track 1 and 2 platforms that allowed region-wide security cooperation to take place in the immediate post-Cold War era; (b) Phase Two (1997–2005): the accretion stage, which saw the establishment and gradual development of various regional institutions that augmented the earlier security regionalism platforms; and (c) Phase Three (2006–present): the parallel progression stage, which witnessed the creations of the ADMM and ADMM+8 mechanisms as "the defense track" that complements the other parallel pillars of Asia-Pacific security regionalism. These developments have in effect expanded the scope and extent of East Asian security cooperation, albeit with memberships that go beyond the 13 East Asian countries.

It is necessary to briefly discuss the situation during the Cold War before detailing each of these phases. As mentioned at the outset, the East Asian region-wide security cooperation is a relatively recent phenomenon that has taken place only in the post-Cold War era. During the Cold War, inter-state security cooperation in the East Asian region existed mainly in two forms. The first was the bilateral alliances and military partnerships between an individual East Asian state and an extra-regional power, for example the 1951 US–Philippine Mutual Defense Treaty, the 1960 US–Japan Treaty of Mutual Cooperation and Security, and the 1978 Soviet Union–Vietnam Treaty of Friendship and Cooperation (Leifer 1989; Yahuda 1996). The only military arrangements that were not bilateral but multilateral in their membership were the Southeast Asia Treaty Organization (SEATO) formed in 1954 (dissolved in 1977) and the consultative Five-Power Defense Arrangements (FPDA) that replaced the 1957 Anglo-Malayan Defense Agreement (AMDA) in November 1971 (Chin 1983; Storey et al. 2011).[4] Both were driven by extra-regional powers, that is, the USA in the case of SEATO and the UK in the case of FPDA. The second form of security cooperation during the Cold War was the *bilateral* border security agreements and defense links (including bilateral military exercises and intelligence-sharing) between ASEAN states, for example,

Malaysia–Thailand, Malaysia–Indonesia, Indonesia–Philippines, Singapore–Brunei, Thailand–Indonesia security cooperation (Acharya 1990; Antolik 1990).

These two forms of security cooperation were the dominant patterns of security cooperation in East Asia throughout the Cold War decades. There was no region-wide security cooperation exclusively among the East Asian states. It is true that the establishment of ASEAN in 1967 – after the demise of its two short-lived predecessors, the 1961 Association of Southeast Asia (ASA) and the 1963 Malaysia-Philippines-Indonesia (MAPHILINDO) – had provided a nascent framework for regional multilateralism. However, ASEAN was limited to the non-communist Southeast Asian nations in its membership, and confined to diplomatic, rather than military, endeavors (Leifer 1989; Acharya 2001; Haacke 2003; Ba 2009).

The absence of a region-wide framework for East Asian security cooperation throughout the Cold War period had to do with a variety of factors. Chief among them were: the ideological problems that divided the region into the communist and non-communist camps, the deep-seated historical animosities and political distrust among individual East Asian states, as well as the divergent threat perceptions and security outlooks among the regional actors (Buzan and Segal 1994; Hemmer and Katzenstein 2002). It was not until the end of the Cold War that some of these barriers gradually subsided, thereby presenting new opportunities for security regionalism.

Phase one (1990–1996): initiation

How did the ARF and CSCAP come about? What were the prime factors leading to the inceptions of these embryonic regional security institutions in the early 1990s? While the establishment of these institutions can be attributed to various factors, the principal driving force was the shared concern among the regional countries about the need to cope with the *strategic uncertainty* resulting from the dramatic systemic change following the end of the Cold War (Khong 2004; Goh and Acharya 2007: 6; Severino 2009: 3–6).

The unanticipated end of the Cold War produced mixed consequences for East Asian security. On the one hand, the collapse of communism in Eastern Europe and the dissolution of the Soviet Union between 1989 and 1991 had effectively terminated the four-decade-long East–West standoff. On the other hand, however, the demise of bipolarity and confrontation along ideological lines had also induced a high degree of unpredictability about the nature, sources, and forms of future conflicts and threats in the East Asian region. This sense of unpredictability was further deepened by a host of territorial disputes, historical controversies, and political problems among the East Asian countries that were submerged during the Cold War but re-surfaced in the 1990s (Acharya 1993; Friedberg 1993/94; Ganesan 1999). Adding to these sources of uncertainty was the perceived "power vacuum" problem. After America's withdrawal from the Philippine's Subic naval and Clark air bases by 1992, there was a widespread apprehension about the lone superpower's future strategic commitment in the post-Cold War Asia-Pacific (Roy 1995).

These developments, along with China's continuing rise as an economic and military power as well as Japan's growing aspirations, had all aroused concerns about the possible adverse effects of the uncertain distribution of power on regional stability and prosperity in the new era (Jeshurun 1993; Morada 2010). The concerns had at times developed into varying degrees of anxiety in the face of China's moves after 1992 to assert its sovereignty over the Spratly Islands in the South China Sea, which are also being claimed in whole or in part by Vietnam, the Philippines, Malaysia, Brunei, and Taiwan (Simon and Emmerson 1993; Valencia 1995). The ASEAN states' options were limited in meeting the perceived challenges. To begin with, the weaker states lacked the aggregate military means to balance against the giant neighbor. Besides, confrontational policies would only undermine their efforts to develop closer economic ties with China (Leifer 1996: 18). A multilateral framework that operates on the mode of cooperative security, by comparison, was seen as a more desirable approach.

Other regional developments further added pressure for ASEAN states to initiate a new framework to cope with emerging challenges and ensure its relevance in the post-Cold War era. These included the inception of the Australia-initiated Asia Pacific Economic Cooperation (APEC) in 1989, as well as the proposals promoted by Australia and Canada to establish a new platform for regional dialogue that was modeled on the Conference for Security and Cooperation in Europe (CSCE). According to Alice Ba, these developments were perceived as a challenge to ASEAN not only because the proposals "came from outside the region" but also because their push for Asia-Pacific arrangements "potentially could subsume ASEAN" (2009: 172). Ralf Emmers similarly observes that the changes in the immediate post-Cold War regional strategic environment had forced the Southeast Asian states to rethink their sub-regional approach to security. They realized that "the external origins of post-Cold War security challenges and the strategic and economic interdependence" have inextricably linked their sub-region to the rest of the Asia-Pacific (Emmers 2003: 31).

These shared concerns thus led to a consensus among the leaders of the six ASEAN states (Brunei, Indonesia, Malaysia, the Philippines, Singapore, and Thailand) about the need to go beyond the Southeast Asian ambit and establish *an Asia-Pacific-wide multilateral forum – one that is centered on ASEAN – as a platform for dialogues on regional security issues*. For the small- and medium-sized ASEAN states, such a consultative platform, with the involvement of major powers and regional players, would be a more viable modality than alternative arrangements such as a collective defense entity, or the CSCE-like mechanisms proposed by Australia and Canada, to reduce uncertainty by cultivating a stable power relationship in the post-Cold War Asia (Leifer 1996).

The reason for ASEAN's central role in driving regional multilateralism in the post-Cold War Asia-Pacific was in part "historical" (Khong and Nesadurai 2007), because it was, up until the early 1990s, the only institution that had demonstrated a noted security role in the region, chiefly by its concerted diplomatic efforts at the international level in attempting to reverse Vietnam's intervention and occupation of Cambodia in the 1980s (Morada 2010). ASEAN's role was also in part a result of "strategic convenience" (Sukma 2010: 113), because the Association, being a group of lesser powers, was seen as "an acceptable interlocutor to all the major powers" (Leifer 1996: 26).

In July 1991, at the ASEAN Ministerial Meeting (AMM) in Kuala Lumpur, the ASEAN leaders first raised the idea of using the ASEAN-Post-Ministerial Conferences (PMC) – a platform that has been used by ASEAN to discuss economic and development issues with their dialogue partners after the annual AMM since the 1970s – as a forum for regional security dialogue. On January 28, 1992, at a summit in Singapore, ASEAN leaders expressed their collective desire to intensify the group's external dialogues in political and security matters by using the existing ASEAN-PMC structure. By May 1993, however, a prevailing view among ASEAN states and their dialogue partners was that "it was not possible [for them] to hold high-level discussions on regional security without the participation of China, Russia and Vietnam" (Severino 2009: 11), the former foes of ASEAN states during the Cold War. This set the *inclusive, conciliatory, and non-confrontational tone* of the new forum. The three countries – along with Laos and Papua New Guinea as well as ASEAN's then seven dialogue partners (Australia, Canada, the European Union, Japan, New Zealand, South Korea, and the United States) – were all invited to a special session in Singapore in July 1993, which became the founding dinner of the ARF. On July 25, 1994, the first ARF meeting was convened after the AMM, but before the PMC.

The name "ASEAN Regional Forum" highlighted its status as an *ASEAN*-centered arrangement, its focus on *regional* issues, and its then intended aim of being a loosely institutionalized *forum*, that is, a platform with a minimal degree of institutionalization.

At the time of its founding, the ARF was an 18-member forum comprised of the six ASEAN countries, ASEAN's seven dialogue partners, ASEAN's two consultative partners (China and Russia), and three observers (Vietnam, Laos, and Papua New Guinea).[5] The forum was later joined by Cambodia in 1995, Myanmar and India in 1996, Mongolia in 1999, North Korea in 2000, Pakistan in 2004, Timor-Leste in 2005, Bangladesh in 2006, and Sri Lanka in 2007. The joinings of these new participants make the ARF a 27-member regional security forum as of 2013. Notwithstanding its enlarged membership that covers a wider geographical area beyond Southeast and Northeast Asia (the forum presently includes four participants from South Asia), the ARF has remained largely "East Asia" in its focus. This is most evidenced from the sorts of security issues raised at the forum, which have centered mainly on the South China Sea, the Korean peninsula, the Taiwan Straits, and various trans-boundary security problems in the East Asian region.

The 1994 meeting marked the birth of a multilateral forum that serves the functions of the balance of power at the regional level (Emmers 2003; Leifer 1996; Haacke and Morada 2009). As observed by Michael Leifer (1996: 19), the underlying goal of the ASEAN-centered forum was "to create the conditions for a stable balance or distribution of power among the three major Asia-Pacific states – China, Japan, and the United States – that would benefit regional order." Khong

Yuen Foong (1997: 290) put it succinctly: the raison d'etre of the ARF is to keep "(a) the United States in, (b) China and Japan down, and (c) ASEAN relevant and safe." That is, as a way of "keeping the United States engaged in the region, rising powers such as China and Japan restrained, and as a means to reassure the smaller ASEAN states" (Khong 1995: 52). The Chairman's Statement of the first ARF Meeting stated that the forum was aimed at cultivating "a more predictable constructive pattern of relationships for the Asia-Pacific." Alastair Iain Johnston (1999: 292) highlights the China factor, adding that ASEAN's ARF approach is one of "institutional engagement" so as to "acquire more information about Chinese intentions; link China's security interests to economic interactions with ASEAN making it more costly to 'defect' against ASEAN interests in security affairs; and change Chinese definitions of their own interests."

These raisons d'etre – specifically, ASEAN states' shared goals of ensuring their regional relevance and cultivating a more predictable pattern of power relations for the post-Cold War Asia-Pacific – dictate the overall *direction* and *degree* of institutionalization of the new forum. This is well illustrated by three institutional features of ARF: (a) led by smaller states; (b) low level of institutionalization; and (c) cooperative security as its organizing mode. We shall discuss the first two features here and leave the third to a later section (as cooperative security is a key feature common to all region-wide security institutions in East Asia).

The most striking feature of the ARF is that it is led by smaller and weaker states, rather than by major powers, as is often the case with regional institutions. Since its inception, the institutional development of the ARF has been driven by and centered on ASEAN states, a group of small- and medium-sized actors. ASEAN's centrality in the forum is formalized, among others, in the following aspects: (a) organizing, hosting, and chairing the annual ministerial ARF meetings (on a rotational basis among ASEAN states in alphabetical order); (b) co-chairing the inter-sessional support group (ISG) meetings with one non-ASEAN state; (c) setting the direction and future activities of the forum through the 1995 ARF Concept Paper; (d) determining the criteria for future ARF membership; and (e) extending ASEAN's norms – as enshrined in the 1976 Treaty of Amity and Cooperation (TAC), which emphasizes sovereign equality, non-use of force, nonintervention, and mutual respect – as the principles of conduct among the ARF participants (Leifer 1996; Johnston 1999; Haacke 2003; Sukma 2010). These institutional arrangements put ASEAN in the "driver's seat" of the ARF, making the forum an ASEAN-centric institution. The Chairman Statement issued after the second ARF meeting in 1995 stated that "ASEAN undertook to be the driving force." Such a position has afforded the ASEAN states a disproportionate leverage to influence the development of regional affairs and engage the stronger powers in an equal footing, thereby ensuring their regional relevance in the post-Cold War Asia-Pacific.

Another important and related feature is the low level of institutionalization of the forum. This is largely due to the prevalence of the ASEAN norms in the forum. The ASEAN norms – popularly known as the "ASEAN Way" – are a collective of practices that include the habits of dialogue, consultation, non-interference, quiet diplomacy, informality, and consensus-seeking in the conduct of international affairs. The pervasiveness of such practices as the prevailing normative structure makes the ARF – like ASEAN – a weakly institutionalized platform that is marked by flexible (vs. binding), incremental (vs. speedy), accommodative (vs. intrusive), and consensual (vs. majority voting) decision-making mechanisms (Khong and Nesadurai 2007; Ba 2009). The low level of institutionalization is indicated by various organizational aspects of the ARF: (a) the adoption of the term "partici- pation" rather than "membership" (countries taking part in the ARF are called "participants" rather than "members"); (b) the use of the terms "inter-sessional support groups" (ISG) and "inter-sessional meetings" (ISM), rather than the more commonly used term "working group," to label the groups tasked to undertake activities between the ARF ministerial meeting sessions (Johnston 1999: 287) – the ISGs and ISMs were considered necessary, because the ARF ministerial meetings typically only last for a few hours (Morada 2010); (c) the absence of a permanent secretariat – instead, the planning and coordination works of ARF activities are handled by the "ARF Chair" (the chair of ASEAN at a given year), which is assisted by an "ARF Unit" (established only in 2004, that is, 10 years after the creation of the forum) in the ASEAN Secretariat; and (d) the per- sistent avoidance of the forum to implement rules and mechanisms that are more intrusive in nature, for example to move from "Confidence-Building Measures" (CBMs) – the first stage of the ARF as outlined by its 1995 Concept Paper – to development of "Preventive Diplomacy" (PD) mechanisms, the second stage of the forum (Emmers and Tan 2012; Severino 2009: 112–125).

All in all, these signify *an increased frequency and regularity* of security coop- eration among regional countries, but one that was still marked by a *low level of policy harmonization.* That is, while the countries share the common goal of pre- serving peace and stability in post-Cold War Asia, they do not agree with each other as to how best to pursue them collectively, through what mechanisms, and at what pace.

Indeed, some observers have criticized that the ARF's reluctance to move beyond CBMs and implement PD is indicative of its institutional limitations as a "talk shop," unable or unprepared to deal with pressing regional security issues (Henderson 1999; Glosserman 2010). For other analysts, however, the ASEAN states' insistence on keeping the ARF less intrusive and under-institutionalized may not necessarily be a weakness. They contend that, at the initial stage of the forum at least, weak institutionalization has provided multiple benefits. Specifi- cally, the under-institutionalized features have enabled the ARF participants – a group of diverse states with very different interests and sensitivities, some of them being former foes – to develop habits of dialogue, build confidence, and forge cooperation among themselves, at a pace that is comfortable to all. The 1995 Concept Paper envisaged "a gradual evolutionary approach to security coopera- tion," which will take place in three stages, that is, promotion of CBMs, devel- opment of PD mechanisms, and development of "Conflict Resolution" mechanisms. The third stage was later modified as "elaboration of approaches to conflict" due to China's objections (Foot 1998; Johnston 1999). This served to ensure the continuing involvement of all key players, while allowing ASEAN states to learn their intentions and allowing the powers to constrain one another, thereby cultivating a predictable and productive pattern of power relations (Johnston 1999; Khong and Nesadurai 2007).

In retrospect, these two institutional features – smaller-states-led and low level of institutionalization – have had path-dependence effects on the institutional design of many of the subsequent regional institutions, particularly the APT, the EAS, and the ADMM Plus. These features make them the ASEAN-led institutions, which exist side-by-side with other non-ASEAN-based institutions such as the SLD, CSCAP, and NEAT. Together they have provided platforms for East Asian security cooperation.

The function of the ARF has been supported by its non-official counterpart, that is, CSCAP, which was formed in June 1993, about a month prior to the founding dinner of ARF (Ball 2010: 10). According to Sheldon Simon (2002), the establishment of CSCAP can be traced to the activities of the ASEAN Institutes of Security and International Studies (ASEAN-ISIS), themselves founded in the 1980s. The institutes organized regular meetings and collaborative efforts aimed at promoting "an alternative conception of security in the Asia-Pacific based on cooperation rather than military balances" (Simon 2002: 173; Wanandi 2006: 31–41). These efforts include supporting the annual Asia Pacific Roundtable (APR) in Kuala Lumpur, which has evolved into the forum for all CSCAP member institutes to meet and discuss their activities (Capie and Evans 2002: 214). Since 1993, CSCAP has functioned as the principal Track 2 mechanism to support the inter-governmental ARF activities and promote security cooperation through non-governmental efforts (Emmers 2003: 31).

ASEAN-ISIS, CSCAP, and other Track 2 processes have been an integral part of the institutionalization of region-wide security cooperation in East Asia, especially during the early stage. By 1995, there were 83 known Track 2 multilateral dialogues, as compared with 17 official Track 1 meetings (Singh 2003: 287). Despite and precisely because of their non-official status, Track 2 organizations have been able to play an instrumental role in initiating dialogues, proposing ideas, sponsoring activities, and facilitating mediations, thereby contributing to confidence-building and cooperation among regional countries (Acharya 1998; Simon 2010). As observed by Desmond Ball, the second-track organizations and dialogues possess full advantage of the "extraordinary vitality and fecundity of non-governmental organizations" that allow relatively "free discussion of diplomatically sensitive issues that could not be brought up in official fora," and at the same time secure the necessary official involvement to attract government resources and appreciation (Ball 2010: 10).

Phase two (1997–2005): accretion

Whereas the earlier phase was marked by the inceptions of ARF and CSCAP as the embryonic platforms that allowed region-wide security cooperation to take off in Asia Pacific, the period from 1997 to 2005 was highlighted by the creation of additional layers of institutions that have over time *augmented* the functions of the earlier platforms, in various domains and at various levels. These institutions are: the ASEAN Plus Three (APT) since 1997, the Shangri-La Dialogue (SLD) since 2002, and the East Asia Summit (EAS) since 2005. In effect, they have slowly contributed to increased frequency and *regularization* of security coopera- tion – and to some extent, some elemental level of *policy harmonization* – among the East Asian countries.

As discussed below, the APT, while started as a regional economic institution, has in due course played a regional security role as well. Specifically, it has served to complement the functions of the existing institutions in two ways, that is, pro- viding the first and only official avenue for security cooperation *exclusively* among the 13 East Asian countries, and offering an additional channel for inter-state cooperation on non-traditional security issues. The SLD, on the other hand, has supplemented other institutions by allowing *defense establishment personnel* from various countries to be involved directly in regional security cooperation, albeit in a semi-official setting. Finally, the EAS has offered *a platform at the summit level* that allows leaders from the wider "East Asia" region to forge a strategic dialogue on regional issues.

This is *not* to say that there was a deliberate, systematic effort on the part of the East Asian countries to promote and institutionalize regional security cooperation in a mutually complementary manner. The institutional developments in Asia during this phase – as that of the preceding and succeeding periods – emerged more by default than by design. That is, they were the outcomes that unfolded as regional states responded to the changing geoeconomic and geopolitical conditions at different critical junctures.

As highlighted in Chapter 2, 1997 was an important year in the development of *East Asian* regionalism. As a response to the Asian financial crisis that severely hit several East Asian economies that year, which highlighted regional contagion and growing interdependence among the Southeast and Northeast Asian countries, the leaders of ASEAN and their three Northeast Asian counterparts met in Kuala Lumpur in December for an informal summit. The summit initiated the APT cooperation. The *prevailing shared goal* then was to collaborate more closely on a wider regional basis (i.e. Southeast *and* Northeast Asia) in order to better respond to the common economic challenges of currency turmoil and financial instability, in the face of a perceived lack of assistance from key external actors, that is, the United States and the International Monetary Fund (Stubbs 2002; Cohen 2012: 41).

At the beginning, the APT process had focused primarily on economic and financial matters, as evidenced most notably by the adoption of the Chiang Mai Initiative (a bilateral currency swap arrangement) among the 13 countries in 2000. Over time, however, the APT cooperation has expanded and "spilled over" to other sectors, including political-security and transnational issues (Wu 2012: 96–119; Chalermpalanupap 2005). According to Gaye Christoffersen, Japan and China have been edging towards promoting APT as a security institution. At the third APT summit in 1999, Chinese premier Zhu Rongji remarked that China was ready for security to be placed on the agenda. In a joint statement at the end of the summit, the leaders pledged to accelerate economic cooperation, continue dialogue in the political-security arena, and strengthen collaboration in addressing common transnational concerns. In 2000, Japanese prime minister Yoshiro Mori suggested that APT activities should be expanded to include political and security cooperation, such as cooperation on combating maritime piracy. In 2001, in the wake of the September 11 terrorist attacks, China's Zhu put forward a five-point proposal to further institutionalize APT in areas including non-traditional security and terrorism (Christoffersen 2007: 130–131). In 2002, the sixth APT summit approved a final report submitted by the East Asia Study Group (EASG), which recommended the APT countries to, among other goals, strengthen mechanisms for cooperation on non-traditional security issues. In 2003, the first annual APT Senior Officials Consultation on Transnational Crime (SOMTC+3 Consultations) was held in Hanoi. In 2004, the first biennial APT Ministerial Meeting on Transnational Crime (AMMTC+3) was held in Bangkok.

Similar institutionalized efforts have also been taken in other domains, as more and more trans-boundary problems emerged and made the management of the non-traditional security challenges an urgent – and continuously mounting – *shared goal* among the APT countries by the mid-2000s, which required some *harmonized policy coordination* among the affected countries. For instance, during the 2003 SARS outbreak, health ministers from APT countries held meetings to fight the epidemic and prevent other infectious diseases. The meetings led to the inceptions of two regularized mechanisms: the APT Senior Officials Meeting on Health Development (SOMHD+3) and the APT Health Ministers Meeting. The 2004 tsunami in the Indian Ocean similarly led to the adoption of regional cooperative mechanisms in natural disaster relief among the APT countries (Wu 2012: 99–102).

The APT has been supported by its Track 2 vehicles, in the forms of the Network of East Asian Think-tanks (NEAT) and the East Asia Forum (EAF). Both were launched in 2003, in part as a response to the recommendations made by the East Asian Vision Group (EAVG) and EASG. The NEAT seeks to facilitate networking and research collaboration among think-tanks, whereas the EAF (in which the South Korean government played an instrumental role) brings together government officials, business persons, and academics at the semi-governmental level. Both vehicles serve to provide intellectual support and policy recommendation to the APT process (Komori 2009: 332–334).

The evolving security role of APT has been complemented by other subsequent regional institutions, including the SLD. First held in 2002 at Singapore's Shangri-La Hotel, the SLD – also known as the Asia Security Summit – is an annual forum organized by the London-based International Institute for Strategic Studies (IISS), but hosted by Singapore and backed by the United States. The SLD's role is complementary to that of the other regional security institutions in at least four aspects: (a) it involves more countries (unlike the APT, whose membership is confined to geographical East Asia); (b) it encompasses both traditional and non-traditional security cooperation (unlike the APT, whose activities fall outside the realm of traditional security), albeit in the form of discourse and not policy action; (c) it is designed to be a semi-official or Track 1.5 forum, with participation of both government and "non-official" delegates (unlike other more formal inter-governmental institutions like the APT and ARF, and unlike the Track 2 processes like CSCAP and NEAT); and (d) more importantly, the SLD is aimed at providing a platform that allows defense ministers and military professionals (although it is also attended by academics, think-tank analysts, journalists, and NGO representatives) to engage directly in regional security cooperation, alongside the ARF and APT, which involve primarily representatives from foreign ministry and other civilian establishments (Capie and Taylor 2010: 359–376; Singh and Tan 2011). Brendan Taylor observes that there are a number of reasons contributed to the apparent success of the SLD – to develop from a small conference to a key platform of defense diplomacy in Asia – within a relatively short period of time. Chief among them is the strong backing from Washington, in which the high-profile presence of a US delegation has added its credibility and status. Besides that, the SLD also received significant funding from both private and governmental players, including Australia and Japan (Taylor 2011: 54–56).

The creation of the East Asia Summit (EAS) in December 2005 added another layer of platform for regional security cooperation. How did EAS come about? The idea of establishing EAS was first stated in the EAVG report in 2001, which described the evolution of APT into an East Asia Summit as "a long-term objective." However, the objective was brought forward in 2004, when Malaysian premier Abdullah Badawi put forward a proposal at the APT Summit in Vientiane that year to hold the inaugural EAS in 2005 in Kuala Lumpur. Abdullah's proposal was supported by Premier Wen, and accepted by the Summit. During the run-up to the summit, while some regional countries advocated that the EAS be limited to the APT countries (i.e. ASEAN plus China, Japan, and South Korea), others insisted that the new forum should also include India, Australia, and New Zealand. In the end, it was the latter view that prevailed, when the 16 countries attended the inaugural EAS summit. The Chairman's Statement of the summit described the APT as the "main vehicle" for East Asia community building, and the EAS a "forum for dialogue" on broad strategic, political and economic issues of common interest and concern. The USA and Russia joined the EAS in 2010, making it an 18-member forum.

The EAS complements and augments the existing security institutions in two ways. First, its designated role as a forum for strategic dialogue (as spelt out in various chairman's statements of the EAS) as well as its membership – which includes all the big powers in the Indo-Pacific region – have allowed it to evolve into one of the key platforms for the management of major power relations in the twenty-first century. The size of its membership – larger than APT but smaller than ARF – helps the function of such a role. Second, the status of EAS as a summit-level institution – unlike the ARF that has remained a ministerial-level arrangement – has made it a high-profile platform for regional security cooperation, especially after Obama's attendance in 2011 (the first by a US president).

Phase three (2006–present): parallel progression

Up until 2005, the institutionalization of region-wide security cooperation in East Asia had been predominantly led by the region's *foreign policy* establishments (with Track 2 organizations playing the supportive role in the background). While the national *defense* establishments began to get involved in regional defense diplomacy activities in the mid-1990s, their involvement was under the ARF framework (a platform centered on foreign ministers), specifically through the ARF Defense Officials' Dialogue (ARF-DOD) and the ARF Security Policy Conferences (ASPC) processes (Tan 2011). The inception of the SLD since 2002 has brought a change to this by allowing defense ministerial personnel to directly engage in regional defense diplomacy on their own platform, but the forum has remained more a semi-official gathering than a formal institution. It was not until the 2006–2010 period – with the advents of the ASEAN Defense Ministers' Meeting (ADMM) and the ADMM-Plus – that the defense-ministerial-driven mechanisms have emerged as a parallel pillar, alongside the foreign-ministerial-driven forums, in promoting the institutionalization of security cooperation in the wider East Asian region. As more security cooperation activities are being conducted more regularly on the two tracks side-by-side, there has been some effort among the regional countries to harmonize their policy goals and outlooks (if not actions).

This development has been described by an analyst as "the late rise of Asia's defense diplomacy" (Capie 2013: 1–26). Another scholar views it as a case of "better late than never," interpreting the evolution as "an incomplete jigsaw puzzle that has just benefited from the addition of a key piece" (Tan 2013).

ASEAN countries were a prime mover of this key piece, even though their move may have been a long time coming to many. Until 2006, there was no regular meeting among the defense ministers from ASEAN member countries. Multilateral defense diplomacy among them was facilitated through mechanisms like the ASEAN Chief of Army Multilateral Meeting (since 2000), the ASEAN Chiefs of Defense Forces Informal Meeting (since 2001), the ASEAN Navy Interaction (since 2001), the ASEAN Air Force Chiefs Conference (since 2004), the ASEAN Military Intelligence Meeting, and the ASEAN Armies Rifles Meeting (Singh and Tan 2011: 8–9). After the Declaration of ASEAN Concord II (the Bali Concord II) in 2003 that called for the establishment of the ASEAN Security Community (ASC) by 2020, the institutionalization of ASEAN defense cooperation gained further momentum. The 2004 ASEAN Summit in Vientiane adopted the ASEAN Security Community Plan of Action, which provided for the convening of the annual ADMM.

On May 9, 2006, the inaugural ADMM was launched in Kuala Lumpur. It represented the first step in the realization of the ASC. In January 2007, the ASEAN leaders decided to bring forward the formation of the ASC to 2015. In November the same year, the leaders revised the ASC to the ASEAN Political-Security Community (APSC). The same month, the second ADMM in Singapore approved a concept paper on the "ADMM-Plus," which provided for the

ADMM's engagement with ASEAN's dialogue partners. Subsequently, the third ADMM in Pattaya in February 2009 approved another document, the "Concept Paper on ASEAN Defense Ministers' Meeting-Plus (ADMM-Plus): Principles for Membership," which reiterated the need for ADMM to engage its dialogue partners in order to draw on "the varied perspectives and resources of a wide range of non-ASEAN countries" in addressing the security challenges facing Southeast Asia (Tan 2011: 36–37; ASEAN Secretariat n.d.). The same meeting set three criteria for qualifying as a "Plus" country: (a) being a Dialogue Partner of ASEAN; (b) having "significant interactions and relations with ASEAN defense establishments"; and (c) capable of working with the ADMM "to build capacity so as to enhance regional security in a substantive manner" (Chalermpalanupap 2011: 21). In May 2010, the fourth ADMM in Hanoi adopted two more concept papers on ADMM-Plus, on "configuration and composition" and "modalities and procedures," respectively. The meeting made the decision to invite the eight dialogue partners of ASEAN, that is, Australia, China, Japan, India, New Zealand, Russia, South Korea, and the United States, to the inaugural ADMM+8 held in Hanoi on October 12, 2010. With the inclusions of the USA and Russia into the EAS in the same year, the membership of ADMM+8 coincided with that of the EAS.

The establishment of the ADMM+8 was an important milestone in the institutionalization of defense and security cooperation in East Asia, in that it created a common platform for the defense ministers from the ASEAN member countries to engage their counterparts from the world's major powers and the region's key players in a mutually productive manner (Desker 2010; Kassim 2010; Tan 2011). In the eyes of some analysts, the inaugural ADMM+8 gathering was "a historical meeting that will establish the basic modalities for a new regional security architecture designed to build confidence, practical cooperation among defense leaders and militaries, and promote peace and prosperity in the dynamic Asia Pacific region" (Bower 2010: 1–4).

Among the most promising roles of ADMM+8 is its potential for building regional capacity and re-enforcing the ASEAN centrality in East Asian institutional building. As observed by scholar See Seng Tan (2011), by engaging with the defense establishments of the world's major and middle powers under the ASEAN-led cooperative framework, the ADMM+8 provides a practical platform "for institutionalizing and possibly enhancing the existing forms of assistance from dialogue partner countries to the ASEAN members." This enables ASEAN states to benefit from the powers' technical know-how and resources, thereby enhancing their capacity to deal with various transnational security problems, especially in areas such as humanitarian assistance and disaster relief (2011: 30–31).

Features

The evolution of region-wide security cooperation in East Asia, as described above, highlights three institutional features: (a) an organizing mode of cooperative security; (b) a focus on non-traditional security issues; and (c) a multilayered, fragmented structure of multiple parallel platforms and overlapped mechanisms.

Cooperative security as the organizing mode

Organizing mode is a key aspect of institutionalization. It shapes the manner and degree to which the member states of an institution regularize and harmonize their cooperation in their pursuit of shared concerns, interests, and goals at a given time.

The organizing mode of all extant platforms of region-wide security cooperation in East Asia, thus far, has remained one of *cooperative security*. This is a contrast to the organizing mode of the US-led *bilateral* alliances in the region, which is one of collective defense. To a large extent, this has to do with ASEAN's central role in the formation and development of most of the institutions, as discussed. Jorg Friedrichs (2012: 756) observes that over the past two decades, ASEAN has been "the main crystallization point of security regionalism not only in Southeast Asia but also in East Asia more widely," and that "the most elaborate institutional fabric to meet East Asian security challenges is the cluster of regional institutions around ASEAN." Because those institutions are the extension of ASEAN and because cooperative security is the core of ASEAN's diplomatic norm (Leifer 1989, 1996; Haacke 2003; Jones and Smith 2007), it is perhaps only logical for those institutions to evolve and operate on the basis of cooperative security. The absence of a clear and immediate source of threat in post-Cold War Asia at large is another reason underpinning the salience of cooperative security – as opposed to NATO-style collective defense – as the prime organizing mode of East Asian security cooperation (including the SLD, a non-ASEAN-based forum). Crucially, such institutions have coexisted with various *bilateral* alliances and partnerships involving external powers (mainly the USA) that were mostly created during the Cold War.

Cooperative security refers to a security arrangement that entails the attributes of inclusivity (inclusion of both like-minded and non-like-minded actors), comprehensive (both military and non-military security issues), habits of dialogue, and reassurance (rather than deterrence) (Dewitt 1994; Capie and Evans 2007: 106–107). Such an approach is qualitatively different from "collective defense," which refers to a security arrangement among a group of states that is aimed at deterring and defending against a commonly perceived threat (Acharya 2007: 20). It is also different from "collective security," which refers to a security arrangement among a group of sovereign actors aimed at collectively deterring, confronting, and punishing aggression by any member of the group against another member (Capie and Evans 2007).

These three approaches involve different operating mechanisms. Collective defense necessarily counts on mutual defense commitment, collective security on mechanism for punishment, whereas cooperative security on mechanism for reassurance. The main distinction between cooperative security and the other two approaches is that, cooperative security does not entail any formal commitment to defend the security of the group members, or to punish aggression from within the group (Mearsheimer 1994/5; Acharya 2007).

Take the ARF as an example. The cooperative security approach has been formalized and implemented through the scope of its membership and activities (which are inclusive and comprehensive), as well as the underlying goals of its three-stage process (which are, fundamentally, geared towards fostering dialogue and promoting mutual reassurance among the forum participants).

As mentioned, the ARF has been inclusive from the very beginning. It has included not only countries of different ideologies and government systems, but also countries which are former foes and present rivals. In terms of activities, the ARF process has included both traditional security and non-traditional security cooperation. This can be observed from the scope of its inter-sessional activities (through ISGs, ISMs, and seminars), which range from defense policy positions, conventional arms register, and nuclear non-proliferation, to search and rescue, counter-terrorism, environmental security, and to infectious diseases, energy security, and maritime cooperation. All of these activities are considered as part and parcel of the confidence-building measures (CBMs) that are stage 1 of the three-stage process of the ARF.

The inclusive membership and the comprehensiveness of its activities are necessary for the ARF to perform its cooperative security functions of encouraging dialogue and promoting mutual reassurance, which, in turn, are central to the forum's goal of cultivating a predictable and productive pattern of power relations in the uncertain post-Cold War Asia-Pacific. Including all the key players into the new forum is deemed necessary in part because a wider dialogue promises a better dialogue, and in part because the alternative arrangement of excluding certain countries would only create unnecessary suspicion and distrust, hence running the risk of increasing uncertainty and destabilizing the region. Moreover, some of the emerging security issues after the Cold War are trans-boundary in nature, and cannot be handled effectively without the collaboration of other countries and other sub-regions. The growing salience of such transnational and non-traditional security issues in Asia has, naturally, necessitated the post-Cold War regional security cooperation to be more comprehensive in scope. In this respect, forging cooperation over the various traditional and non-traditional security issues in a *regularized* and somewhat *harmonized* manner – through the numerous ISG and ISM activities – has over time helped to cultivate a sense of partnership and a habit of cooperation, thereby building confidence and promoting reassurance among the forum participants. Khong and Nesadurai (2007: 37) observe: "Because the ARF included participants who distrusted one another for historical, ideological, and power political reasons, confidence building was viewed as necessary in its infancy." The CBM activities serve to reduce mistrust through regular consultations and cooperation at various levels, as well as the efforts to increase transparency, enhance exchanges, and achieve intra-group understanding. The 1995 ARF Concept Paper stresses that "the region is remarkably diverse" and that "the ARF should recognize and accept the different approaches to peace and security and try to forge a consensual approach to security issues." Alice Ba notes that the ASEAN-led cooperative process "is designed to preserve relations and keep everyone engaged, even if it is at the expense of collective and functional coordination" (2012: 124).

The nature of ASEAN-led forums as cooperative security institutions means that there is no provision that addresses the use of force in conflict and conflict resolution. Because of these institutional attributes, Leifer has described the ARF as "an extension of ASEAN's model of regional security." In his words:

> ASEAN's model has promoted an exclusively political approach to problems of regional security through multilateral dialogue. ASEAN's practice is based on diplomacy alone, and makes no provision for the institutional enforcement characteristics of models of collective security. Nor does it include formal mechanisms for settling disputes for fear of impairing political relationships.
>
> (Leifer 1996: 3–4)

There are other reasons why cooperative security has prevailed over other arrangements (e.g. collective defense) as the preferred mode of *regional* security cooperation in the post-Cold War Asia-Pacific. Chief among them is the changing nature of threats and differing threat perceptions among regional countries in the new era. Post-Cold War threats, especially the various non-traditional security problems, are more diffuse and indirect. Some of the military security threats, like territorial and maritime disputes, are perceived with different degrees of concern. Much of the security problems are sovereignty related and legacies of the past, and hence are unlikely to be resolved soon. These call for reassurance, rather than deterrence, as the dominant mechanisms for regional security. After all, given the deep-seated distrust among some of the regional countries, there is much need to reassure; and given the absence of a commonly perceived threat, there is no specific target to defend against on a regional basis. Cooperative security – precisely because of (not in spite of) its relatively low level of institutionalization – is hence the prevailing mode of regional security cooperation in Asia. It allows regional countries with divergent perceptions to forge and increasingly regularize their cooperation, with the hope of attaining – however gradual and problematic – some level of interest harmonization among them. This has been so not only for the ARF, but also other regional institutions that have been created after both the ASEAN-led and non-ASEAN-led forums.

This is not to say that cooperative security is the only organizing mode of institutionalizing security cooperation in East Asia. As noted, the US-led alliances in the region – US–Japan, US–Korea, US–Thailand, and US–Philippines – are all organized and function on the mode of collective defense. These alliances are all bilateral in their memberships; they are not region-wide security cooperation. Unlike in Europe, there is no NATO-like multilateral alliance in East Asia (Hemmer and Katzenstein 2002).

A focus on non-traditional security cooperation

In terms of scope, the East Asia-based security institutions have, by and large, placed relatively more emphasis on non-traditional security cooperation than conventional, military security matters. The reasons are multiple: (a) non-traditional security issues are far less contentious than military security problems; (b) many of the transnational security problems (e.g. SARS, the 2004 tsunami) are more pressing; (c) collectively addressing the cross-border security challenges is becoming a key shared goal among the regional countries (as no single country could cope with the problems alone); (d) the absence of a common military threat; (e) the divergent perceptions across the countries, and so on. Together, they necessitate more regularized inter-state cooperation and more harmonized policy coordination. Arguably, East Asian countries do not see cooperation on non-traditional security and cooperation on traditional security realms as mutually exclusive, but complementary. That is, strengthening non-traditional security cooperation may help to mitigate some of the conventional security problems, by virtue of enhancing confidence-building and capacity-building among them.

All of the regional security institutions discussed above have placed varying degrees of emphasis on non-traditional security cooperation. The ARF, while focusing largely on military CBMs in the 1990s, has gradually increased activities on trans-boundary security cooperation, especially after the September 11 terrorist attacks in 2001. The ARF has formed several ISMs on various NTS issues: counter terrorism and transnational crime, maritime security, and disaster relief (alongside non-proliferation and disarmament). Rodolfo Severino, the former Secretary-General of ASEAN, observes that although there were concerns that turning attention to non-traditional security issues might distract the ARF from its basic objective of dealing with inter-state conflicts, the discussions on non-traditional security issues at various levels "foster the acceptance of 'human security' as a fit subject of the ARF's attention and regional cooperation," which, in turn, helps to promote mutual confidence, transparency, a sense of common purpose, and net-working, thereby conceivably helping "to reduce the likelihood of conflict, a function that could contribute indirectly to conflict prevention" (Severino 2009: 63–64).

Within the APT, security cooperation among the 13 members has pre-dominantly been focused on non-traditional security issues, as noted. According to an analyst, the APT cooperation on non-traditional security exhibits the features of "soft regionalism": "It is not centrally orchestrated, lacks strong institutional sup-port, and involves few substantive arrangements, yet it has achieved the widest possible participation from APT countries and allows for flexible reactions to common challenges" (Wu 2012: 102).

Cooperation on non-traditional security often begins with an idea first pre-sented at a regional security institution, in response to a certain emerging transnational problem. For instance, at the SLD, the then Malaysian Defense Minister Najib Razak proposed in 2005 the initiative of the "Eyes in the Sky" (EiS), which called for joint maritime air and sea patrols by the littoral states of Malaysia, Indonesia, and Singapore, for tackling piracy and armed robbery in the Strait of Malacca. At the 2008 SLD that was held not long after the Cyclone Nargis in Myanmar and Sichuan earthquake in China, the participants agreed to three principles to guide humanitarian disaster relief in the region (Taylor 2011).

The EAS has similarly covered the non-traditional security issues, along with functional areas. The EAS Chairman's Statement in October 2010 outlined five priority areas: finance, education, energy, disaster relief management and mitigation, and avian influenza prevention.

A similar focus of activity can also be observed in ADMM. Since its inception in 2006, it has promoted cooperation on NTS, particularly on humanitarian assistance and disaster relief. The ASEAN Defense Ministers have adopted two concept papers to advance cooperation in this area: the "Concept Paper on the Use of ASEAN Military Assets and Capacities in Humanitarian Assistance and Disaster Relief (HADR)" and the "Concept Paper on Defense Establishments and Civil Society Organizations (CSOs) Cooperation on Non-Traditional Security." In 2011, the ADMM conducted a Table-Top Exercise in HADR under the Third Workshop of the ASEAN Defense Establishments and CSOs Cooperation in Non-Traditional Security (ASEAN Secretariat n.d.).

Its extension, the ADMM+8, has focused on five core transnational issues: disaster relief, peacekeeping, military medicine, maritime security, and counter-terrorism. According to Tow and Taylor (2010: 109), the reasons for such a focus include: the relative easiness of these non-sensitive issues to attain consensus and agreement; the need for immediate cooperation in these issues, as the security challenges are "beyond the scope of any country to handle alone"; and more importantly, addressing these non-traditional issues could nurture trusts and promote confidence building in East Asia. Another analyst adds that the ADMM and ADMM+8 processes:

> are better understood as narrow functional enterprises aimed primarily at developing the abilities of ASEAN militaries to respond comprehensively and systematically to complex challenges posed by transnational threats of a non-military nature, not least disaster management, maritime concerns, pandemics and the like.
>
> (Tan 2011: 30–31)

A multilayered, fragmented structure

In terms of structure, the East Asian security cooperation is a multilayered, fragmented, and weakly institutionalized collaborative process that consists of multiple overlapped platforms. As noted, most of these platforms – like ARF, EAS, ADMM, and ADMM+8 – are initiated and led by the ASEAN states, whereas others – like the SLD – are driven and backed by the United States and other players. Besides these Track 1 and Track 1.5 institutions, the structure of the region-wide security cooperation is also supported by Track 2 organizations and processes.

Such a structure has both advantages and weaknesses.

The main strength of the multilayered structure is that it allows for institutional division of labor across mechanisms and platforms, even though this role is more by default than by design. Because of their different scope of memberships and activities, the different regional institutions have over the years operated in a way that is mutually complementary, and perhaps even mutually reinforcing. This is so not only between the Track 1 and 2 mechanisms, but also among the ASEAN-led institutions, as well as between the ASEAN institutions and the non-ASEAN driven forums.

Track 2 organizations like ASEAN-ISIS and CSCAP complement the Track 1 institutions in various ways. Because of their unofficial status and membership compositions, Track 2 processes are able to provide expertise on issues of a long-term nature, engage in frank debate, discuss subjects that are deemed to be too sensitive or controversial for Track 1 meetings, offer a conduit between state and non-state actors, as well as provide a platform for socialization functions (Kerr and Taylor 2013: 236; Capie and Evans 2002: 213).

The multilayered structure also allows complementarities among the ASEAN-led institutions. An example to illustrate this would be the role of ADMM+8, EAS, and APT in the management of major power relationships in East Asia. As observed by Barry Desker (2010), the establishment of the ADMM+8 provides an opportunity "for the engagement of the U.S. and China, the two states at greatest risk of being engaged in a competitive relationship in East Asia, as well as major regional powers such as Japan, India, and Russia." He adds that by having the same dialogue partners as those of the EAS, the ADMM+8 have been viewed "as an overlapping institution designed to assuage the concern of the emergence of the APT as the basis of a Chinese-dominated security framework in East Asia that excludes the U.S." Although the creation of ADMM+8 has raised questions about the future viability of the SLD because the former replicates some of the key features of the SLD, the latter as a flexible Track 1.5 forum has continued to serve as a potential alternative to the ASEAN-centered institutions in shaping the direction of East Asian security cooperation (Taylor 2011: 58–59).

Overall, these multiple and mutually complementary mechanisms have combined to increase the frequency and regularization – and to some extent, policy harmonization – of security cooperation among the East Asian countries. Specifically, they have served, to varying degrees, the following functions: enhancing confidence-building and improving interstate trust (Tan 2011, 2013; Chalermpalanupap 2011), inducing meaningful cooperation (Khong and Nesadurai 2007), managing peaceful change (Friedrichs 2012), tackling trans-border security problems (Beeson 2009), creating the norm-based platforms to manage intra-regional security concerns and develop a regional identity (Acharya 2001; Ba 2009), as well as cultivating a stable balance of power and providing a common buffer mechanism to cope with the political and security challenges from the extra-regional powers at a time of strategic uncertainty (Leifer 1996; Khong 2004; Emmers et al. 2010; Ba 2012). These, in turn, allow the regional countries to concentrate on their domestic development and sociopolitical tasks, while preserving a degree of autonomy and national cohesion.

Notwithstanding these functions, the current arrangements for East Asian security institutions nonetheless suffer a number of weaknesses because a multilayered structure is also a fragmented structure. The existence of the ASEAN-led institutions and the non-ASEAN-centered forums, for instance, could create competition and friction. William Tow and Brendon Taylor have warned that "institutional duplication is potentially dangerous" because "what appears to be growing cooperation can actually be a reflection of increased competition – particularly between the great powers" (2010: 115–116). In other words, higher regularization of activities does not necessarily lead to higher harmonization of interests and actions. Taylor adds that a bifurcation could occur "wherein some countries (namely the United States and Australia) increasingly back the SLD whereas others (namely China and some ASEAN members) give stronger support to the ADMM+," and that such an outcome "would be potentially problematic in that it would likely render the prospects for region-wide cooperation in any genuine sense much more difficult in the defense sector" (2011: 61). Because of the weakly organized nature of the ASEAN-led institutions, which are marked by their lack of means for compellence, these institutions have been criticized as "talk shops without any teeth" (Garofano 2002: 502), leaning more toward "conflict avoidance" than conflict resolution (Jones and Smith 2007: 149). Ba (2012: 135) observes that some countries, like the United States, Australia, and Japan, have begun to view existing arrangements as "not inclusive enough of their concerns and priorities," while others have questioned "the ability of ASEAN processes to achieve specific functional ends."

Conclusion

This chapter reveals that the pace and patterns of institutionalization of East Asian security cooperation have been driven and limited by the interplay of multiple factors: enduring historical legacies, converging security interests, diverging geostrategic perceptions, and a growing functional need to cooperate on a wide range of transboundary challenges. It also reveals that regularization and harmonization – two micro-processes of institutionalization – do not necessarily progress in tandem. As discussed, while good progress has been made in terms of the frequency and regularity of cooperative activities thanks in large part to the creation of multiple institutions since the 1990s, the *substantive aspects* of regional security cooperation (i.e. the degree of policy harmonization) have been mixed. On the one hand, most regional states have come to agree more about their shared goals in forging regional cooperation, that is, to better respond to their common challenges of the post-Cold War strategic uncertainty, the contagion of regional financial instability, and the danger of transnational problems. These shared goals have led them to step up their collective actions in enhancing confidence building and in strengthening practical collaboration in non-traditional security issues. On the other hand, however, the regional states have not always seen eye-to-eye on *how best to pursue their shared goals collectively.* Disagreements have revolved around: in what way, to what extent, and at what pace they should and could institutionalize their collective effort to pursue their common goals. Examples include the efficacy of ASEAN Way in managing regional security issues, the complementarities among the various ASEAN-led institutions and other non-ASEAN forums, as well as the speed and scope of implementing preventive diplomacy, as noted. Divisions are even greater on inherently contentious issues such as the territorial disputes in the South and East China Seas. These disagreements are not surprising, given the differing security perceptions and enduring political problems among the regional countries. Nevertheless, despite these divergent interests and perspectives, progress is still possible in areas where security pressures are most commonly felt and severely affected.

In the final analysis, it must be noted that despite their expanding role in regional security, the ASEAN-led institutions are not likely to replace the decades-old US-led bilateral alliances. Indeed, the two are likely to remain co-existent, functioning side-by-side and complementing each other. Because of their different organizing modes and activity focus, the ASEAN-led institutions and the US-led alliances have, by default, functioned in a division-of-labor manner, where the former facilitates dialogues and confidence-building processes, whereas the latter constitutes deterrence and fall-back measures. Together, they have contributed to the maintenance of regional security and stability throughout the post-Cold War era. This complementarity is likely to continue in the near future.

Notes

1 I thank Wong Chee Ming for his excellent research assistantship.
2 This is adapted from the definition developed in the Introduction of this volume.
3 This definition leads us to exclude: (a) regional institutions and processes that are exclusively Southeast Asian, such as ASEAN and ASEAN-ISIS (both are dealt with in Chapter 2 of this volume); (b) regional institutions that are limited to Northeast Asian countries, such as the Trilateral Cooperation (Chapter 3); (c) regional institutions that are more oriented on Asia-Pacific than East Asian countries, that is, the APEC; (d) intra-regional cooperation such as Greater Mekong Subr-egion cooperation (Chapter 8); and (e) inter-regional cooperation such as ASEM and FEALAC (Chapter 7).
4 The members of SEATO were the USA, the UK, France, Australia, New Zealand, Pakistan, Thailand, and the Philippines. The members of FPDA were the UK, Australia, New Zealand, Malaysia, and Singapore.
5 Vietnam joined ASEAN in 1995. This was followed by Burma/Myanmar and Laos in 1997, and Cambodia in 1999. China and Russia became ASEAN's dialogue partners in 1996.

References

Acharya, Amitav. 1990. *A Survey of Military Cooperation among the ASEAN States: Bilateralism or Alliance?* Occasional Paper No. 14. Toronto: Centre for Strategic and International Studies, York University.
Acharya, Amitav. 1993. *A New Regional Order in South-East Asia: ASEAN in the Post-Cold War Era.* Adelphi Paper 279. London: Oxford University Press for IISS.
Acharya, Amitav. 1998. Culture, Security, Multilateralism: The "ASEAN Way" and Regional Order. *Contemporary Security Policy* 19 (1): 55–84.
Acharya, Amitav. 2001. *Constructing a Security Community in Southeast Asia: The Problem of Regional Order.* London: Routledge.

Acharya, Amitav and Alastair Iain Johnston, eds. 2007. *Crafting Cooperation: Regional International Institutions in Comparative Perspective.* Cambridge: Cambridge University Press.

Antolik, Michael. 1990. *ASEAN and the Diplomacy of Accommodation.* Armonk, NY: M.E. Sharpe.

ASEAN Secretariat. 1995. The ASEAN Regional Forum: A Concept Paper. http://asea nregionalforum.asean.org/files/library/Terms%20of%20References%20and%20Concept %20Papers/Concept%20Paper%20of%20ARF.pdf.

ASEAN Secretariat. n.d. ASEAN Defense Ministers' Meeting (ADMM). www.asean.org/ communities/asean-political-security-community/category/asean-defence-ministers-me eting-admm.

Ba, Alice D. 2009. *(Re)Negotiating East and Southeast Asia: Region, Regionalism, and the Association of Southeast Asian Nations.* Stanford, CA: Stanford University Press.

Ba, Alice D. 2012. ASEAN Centrality Imperiled? ASEAN Institutionalism and the Challenges of Major Power Institutionalization. In Ralf Emmers, ed., *ASEAN and the Institutionalization of East Asia.* London: Routledge, pp. 122–137.

Ball, Desmond. 2010. CSCAP's Foundation and Achievements. In Desmond Ball and Kwa Chong Guan, eds, *Assessing Track 2 Diplomacy in the Asia-Pacific Region: A CSCAP Reader.* Singapore: S. Rajaratnam School of International Studies, pp. 9–61.

Beeson, Mark. 2009. *Institutions of the Asia-Pacific: ASEAN, APEC and Beyond.* London: Routledge.

Bower, Ernest. 2010. Inaugural ASEAN Defense Ministers' Meeting + 8 in Hanoi. *Southeast Asia from the Corner of 18th and K Streets* 1 (32) October 13. http://csis.org/ files/publication/101012-southeastasia.pdf.

Buzan, Barry, and Gerald Segal. 1994. Rethinking East Asian Security. *Survival* 36(2): 3–21.

Cai, Kevin. 2001. Is a Free Trade Zone Emerging in Northeast Asia in the Wake of the Asian Financial Crisis? *Pacific Affairs* 74(1): 7–24.

Capie, David. 2013. Structures, Shocks and Norm Change: Explaining the Late Rise of Asia's Defense Diplomacy. *Contemporary Southeast Asia* 35(1): 1–26.

Capie, David and Paul Evans. 2002. *The Asia-Pacific Security Lexicon.* Singapore: Institute of Southeast Asian Studies.

Capie, David, and Paul Evans. 2007. *The Asia-Pacific Security Lexicon,* 2nd edition. Singapore: Institute of Southeast Asian Studies.

Capie, David and Brendan Taylor. 2010. The Shangri-La Dialogue and the Institutionalization of Defense Diplomacy in Asia. *The Pacific Review* 23(3): 359–376.

Chalermpalanupap, Termsak. 2005. Understanding the ASEAN Policy Making Processes. Paper presented at the Regional Conference on Civil Society Engagement in ASEAN, Bangkok, October 3–5.

Chalermpalanupap, Termsak. 2011. Carving Out a Crucial Role for ASEAN Defense Establishments in the Evolving Regional Architecture. In Bhubhindar Singh and See Seng Tan, eds, *From "Boots" to "Brogues": The Rise of Defense Diplomacy in Southeast Asia.* RSIS Monograph No. 21. Singapore: S. Rajaratnam School of International Studies, pp. 18–27.

Chalermpalanupap, Termsak. 2013. ASEAN Defense Diplomacy and the ADMM-Plus. *ISEAS Perspective* 49 (August 6).

Chin Kin Wah. 1983. *The Defense of Malaysia and Singapore: The Transformation of a Security System, 1957–1971.* Cambridge: Cambridge University Press.

Christoffersen, Gaye. 2007. Chinese and ASEAN Responses to the U.S. Regional Maritime Security Initiative. In Wu Guoguang, ed., *China Turns to Multilateralism: Foreign Policy and Regional Security.* London: Routledge, pp. 127–146.

Cohen, Benjamin. 2012. Finance and Security in East Asia. In Avery Goldstein and Edward D. Manfield, eds, *The Nexus of Economics, Security, and International Relations in East Asia.* Stanford, CA: Stanford University Press, pp. 39–65.

Cook, Malcolm. 2011. *ASEAN's Triumph.* Indo-Pacific Governance Research Centre Policy Brief No. 4. The University of Adelaide: The Indo-Pacific Governance Research Centre.

Desker, Barry. 2010. ASEAN Plus Eight Defense Cooperation: Rise of a New Player. October 15. RSIS Commentaries No. 132/2010.

Dewitt, David. 1994. Common, Comprehensive, and Cooperative Security. *The Pacific Review* 7 (1): 1–16.

Emmers, Ralf. 2003. *Cooperative Security and the Balance of Power in ASEAN and the ARF.* London: Routledge Curzon.

Emmers, Ralf and See Seng Tan. 2012. The ASEAN Regional Forum and Preventive Diplomacy: A Review Essay. In Ralf Emmers, ed., *ASEAN and the Institutionalization of East Asia.* London and New York: Routledge, pp. 89–102.

Emmers, Ralf, Joseph Liow Chinyong, and See Seng Tan. 2010. The East Asia Summit and the Regional Security Architecture. *Maryland Series in Contemporary Asian Studies* 3(1).

Foot, Rosemary. 1998. China in the ASEAN Regional Forum: Organizational Processes and Domestic Modes of Thought. *Asian Survey* 38(5): 425–440.

Friedberg, Aaron L. 1993/94. Ripe for Rivalry: Prospects for Peace in Multipolar Asia. *International Security* 18(1): 5–33.

Friedrichs, Jorg. 2012. East Asian Regional Security: What the ASEAN Family Can (Not) Do. *Asian Survey* 52(4): 754–776.

Ganesan, N. 1999. *Bilateral Tensions in Post-Cold War ASEAN.* Pacific Strategic Papers No. 9. Singapore: ISEAS.

Garofano, John. 2002. Power, Institutions, and the ASEAN Regional Forum: A Security Community for Asia? *Asian Survey* 42(3): 502–521.

Glosserman, Brad. 2010. The United States and the ASEAN Regional Forum: A Delicate Balancing Act. In Jurgen Haacke and Noel M. Morada, eds, *Cooperative Security in the Asia-Pacific: The ASEAN Regional Forum.* London and New York: Routledge, pp. 36–53.

Goh, Evelyn, and Amitav Acharya, eds. 2007. *Reassessing Security Cooperation in the Asia-Pacific: Competition, Congruence, and Transformation.* Cambridge, MA: The MIT Press.

Haacke, Jürgen. 2003. *ASEAN's Diplomatic and Security Culture: Origins, Development and Prospects.* London and New York: Routledge Curzon.

Haacke, Jürgen, and Noel M. Morada, eds. 2009. *Cooperative Security in the Asia-Pacific: The ASEAN Regional Forum.* London: Routledge.

Hemmer, Christopher, and Peter J. Katzenstein. 2002. Why is There No NATO in Asia? Collective Identity, Regionalism, and the Origins of Multilateralism. *International Organization* 56(3): 575–607.

Henderson, Jeannie. 1999. *Reassessing ASEAN.* Adelphi Paper 328. London: Oxford University Press for IISS.

Jeshurun, Chandran, ed. 1993. *China, India, Japan and the Security of Southeast Asia.* Singapore: ISEAS.

Johnston, Alastair Iain. 1999. The Myth of the ASEAN Way? Explaining the Evolution of the ASEAN Regional Forum. In Helga Haftendor, Robert O. Keohane, and Celeste

Wallander, eds, *Imperfect Unions: Security Institutions over Time and Space*. Oxford: Oxford University Press, pp. 287–324.

Jones, David Martin and Michael L. R. Smith. 2007. Making Process, Not Progress: ASEAN and the Evolving East Asian Regional Order. *International Security* 32(1): 148–184.

Kahler, Miles. 1992. Multilateralism with Small and Large Numbers. *International Organization* 46(3): 681–708.

Kassim, Yang Razali. 2010. ADMM Plus: New Twists to Old Security Issues. RSIS Commentaries. No. 133. October 19. www.rsis.edu.sg/wp-content/uploads/2014/07/CO10133.pdf.

Kerr, Pauline, and Brendan Taylor. 2013. Track-Two Diplomacy in East Asia. In Pauline Kerr and Geoffrey Wiseman, eds, *Diplomacy in a Globalizing World: Theories and Practices*. Oxford: Oxford University Press, pp. 226–243.

Khong Yuen Foong. 1995. Evolving Regional Security and Economic Institutions. *Southeast Asian Affairs 1995*. Singapore: Institute of Southeast Asian Studies, pp. 48–60.

Khong Yuen Foong. 1997. Making Bricks without Straw in the Asia-Pacific? *The Pacific Review* 10(2): 289–300.

Khong Yuen Foong. 2004. Coping with Strategic Uncertainty: The Role of Institutions and Soft Balancing in Southeast Asia's Post-Cold War Strategy. In J.J. Suh, Peter J. Katzenstein, and Allen Carlson, eds, *Rethinking Security in East Asia: Identity, Power, and Efficiency*. Stanford, CA: Stanford University Press, pp. 198–202.

Khong Yuen Foong and Helen E. S. Nesadurai. 2007. Hanging Together, Institutional Design, and Cooperation in Southeast Asia: AFTA and the ARF. In Amitav Acharya and Alastair Iain Johnston, eds, *Crafting Cooperation: Regional International Institutions in Comparative Perspective*. Cambridge: Cambridge University Press, pp. 32–82.

Komori, Yasumasa. 2009. Regional Governance in East Asia and the Asia-Pacific. *East Asia* 26(4): 321–341.

Leifer, Michael. 1989. *ASEAN and the Security of South-East Asia*. London: Routledge.

Leifer, Michael. 1996. *The ASEAN Regional Forum: Extending ASEAN's Model of Regional Security*. Adelphi Paper 302. London: Oxford University Press for IISS.

Mearsheimer, John. 1994/5. The False Promise of International Institutions. *International Security* 19(3): 5–49.

Morada, Noel M. 2010. The ASEAN Regional Forum: Origins and Evolution. In Jurgen Haacke and Noel M. Morada, eds, *Cooperative Security in the Asia-Pacific: The ASEAN Regional Forum*. London and New York: Routledge, pp. 13–35.

Roy, Denny. 1995. Assessing the Asia Pacific "Power Vacuum". *Survival* 37(3): 45–60.

Severino, Rodolfo C. 2009. *The ASEAN Regional Forum*. Singapore: ISEAS.

Simon, Sheldon W. 2002. Evaluating Track II Approaches to Security Diplomacy in the Asia-Pacific: the CSCAP Experience. *The Pacific Review* 15(2): 167–200.

Simon, Sheldon W. 2010. Evaluating Track 2 Approaches to Security Dialogue in the Asia-Pacific: The CSCAP Experience. In Desmond Ball and Kwa Chong Guan, eds, *Assessing Track 2 Diplomacy in the Asia-Pacific Region*. Singapore: S. Rajaratnam School of International Studies, Nanyang Technological University, pp. 77–111.

Simon, Sheldon W., and Donald Emmerson. 1993. *Regional Issues in Southeast Asian Security: Scenarios and Regimes*. NBR Analysis. Seattle, WA: National Bureau of Asian Research.

Singh, Bhubhindar and See Seng Tan. 2011. Introduction. In Bhubhindar Singh and See Seng Tan, eds, *From "Boots" to "Brogues": The Rise of Defense Diplomacy in Southeast Asia*. RSIS Monograph No. 21. Singapore: S. Rajaratnam School of International Studies.

Singh, Daljit. 2003. Evolution of the Security Dialogue Process in the Asia-Pacific Region. In Sharon Siddique and Sree Kumar, eds, *The 2nd ASEAN Reader*. Singapore: Institute of Southeast Asian Studies, pp. 285–288.

Storey, Ian, Ralf Emmers, and Daljit Singh, eds. 2011. *The Five Powers Defense Arrangements at Forty*. Singapore: ISEAS.

Stubbs, Richard. 2002. ASEAN Plus Three: Emerging East Asian Regionalism? *Asian Survey* 42(3): 440–455.

Sukma, Rizal. 2010. The Accidental Driver: ASEAN in the ASEAN Regional Forum. In Jurgen Haacke and Noel M. Morada, eds, *Cooperative Security in the Asia-Pacific: The ASEAN Regional Forum*. London and New York: Routledge, pp. 111–123.

Tan See Seng. 2011. From Talkshop to Workshop: ASEAN's Quest for Practical Security Cooperation Through the ADMM and ADMM-Plus Processes. In Bhubhindar Singh and See Seng Tan, eds, *From "Boots" to "Brogues": The Rise of Defense Diplomacy in Southeast Asia*. RSIS Monograph No. 21. Singapore: S. Rajaratnam School of International Studies, pp. 28–41.

Tan See Seng. 2013. Asia's Growing Defense Engagements. In Sarah Teo and Murshahid Ali, eds, *Policy Report: Strategic Engagement in the Asia Pacific – The Future of the ASEAN Defense Ministers' Meeting – Plus (ADMM-Plus)*. Singapore: S. Rajaratnam School of International Studies.

Tan Seng Chye. 2010. ADMM+8: Adding Flesh to a New Regional Architecture. RSIS Commentaries. No. 131. October 15. www.rsis.edu.sg/wp-content/uploads/2014/07/CO10131.pdf.

Taylor, Brendan. 2011. The Shangri-La Dialogue: Thriving, but Not Surviving? In Bhubhindar Singh and See Seng Tan, eds, *From "Boots" to "Brogues": The Rise of Defense Diplomacy in Southeast Asia*. RSIS Monograph No. 21. Singapore: S. Rajaratnam School of International Studies, pp. 54–62.

Tow, William, and Brendon Taylor. 2010. What is Asian Security Architecture? *Review of International Studies* 36(1): 95–116.

Valencia, Mark J. 1995. *China and the South China Sea Disputes*, Adelphi Paper 298. London: Oxford University Press for International Institute of Strategic Studies.

Wanandi, Jusuf. 2006. ASEAN ISIS and its Regional and Global Networking. In Hadi Soesastro, Clara Joewono, and Carolina G. Hernandez, eds, *Twenty-Two Years of ASEAN ISIS: Origin, Evolution and Challenges of Track Two Diplomacy*. Jakarta: Centre for Strategic and International Studies for ASEAN-ISIS, pp. 31–41.

Wu Xinbo. 2012. The Spillover Effect of ASEAN Plus Three Process on East Asian Security. In Avery Goldstein and Edward D. Mansfield, eds, *The Nexus of Economics, Security, and International Relations in East Asia*. Stanford, CA: Stanford University Press, pp. 96–119.

Yahuda, Michael. 1996. *The International Politics of the Asia-Pacific*. London: Routledge Curzon.

Yuzawa, Takeshi. 2006. The Evolution of Preventive Diplomacy in the ASEAN Regional Forum: Problems and Prospects. *Asian Survey* 46(5): 785–804.

5 Institutionalization of disaster management in Southeast Asia

Tavida Kamolvej

Introduction

Recent occurrences of more frequent and severe natural disasters have drawn greater attention of the international community to the importance of more coordinated international efforts and safety protocols. Governments around the world have taken into account the significance of comprehensive disaster management where domestic operations and international assistance coordinate effectively. The network of disaster management, at both the national and regional scale, requires a mutual understanding among all actors of coherent policies, operations, and capacities to cope with a given situation so that coordination can be conducted in a consistent manner toward the goal of saving lives and property.

Southeast Asia is prone to both large-scale disasters that could cause massive deaths and major setbacks to development, as well as recurrent small to medium disasters that could undermine national well-being and community resilience. Disasters travel across jurisdictions requiring each nation not only to be well prepared but also to forge more systematic coordination with its neighbors. Some disasters are large in scale, resulting in long and severe disruption that exceeds the capacity of a single nation to cope with the devastation. Bilateral and multilateral cooperation has been established by each nation through existing relationships that facilitate technical assistance, knowledge sharing, and integrated joint-operation exercises. However, these patterns of coordination are often fragmented and unorganized. Since the Indian Ocean tsunami in 2004, the Association of Southeast Asian Nations (ASEAN) has turned its attention to the establishment of regional collaborative disaster management. As discussed below, several mechanisms have been developed to support more effective regional collaboration.

This chapter investigates ASEAN's efforts toward institutionalizing collaborative disaster management. To institutionalize is to recognize the importance of institutional design, to strengthen collective action, and to share common resources through durable rules, protocols, standards, and mutual interests, in support of greater collaboration (Ostrom 1991: 31 and "Introduction" to this volume). This chapter examines the extent to which ASEAN's disaster-related mechanisms, such as structural arrangement, authorized codes of conduct, policies and procedures, established and authorized agency, and resource allocation, help institutionalize regional coordination. Since Southeast Asian nations share similar disaster threats and can benefit from an integrated intergovernmental network of assistance, it is vital for ASEAN members to strengthen their collaboration. Although collaborative disaster management has been prioritized in the agenda of ASEAN for many years, efforts and progress seem to fall behind the ultimate goals. Special attention is paid to identifying the obstacles, challenges, and shortfalls faced by ASEAN member countries.

The chapter argues that all stakeholders in Southeast Asia need to invest more effectively in institutionalizing disaster management within the region and beyond. Southeast Asian natural disaster risk reduction efforts should collaborate with other regional systems to benefit the wider communities in the Asia-Pacific. Such collaboration is crucial not only for strengthening human security at different levels, but also for ensuring regional resilience, development, and stability.

The threats of natural disasters to Southeast Asia

Southeast Asia is a region advantageously endowed with abundant natural resources. Various environmental conditions, however, are currently in a state of deterioration. The region is threatened by the effects of climate change and severe weather conditions, such as rising sea levels, decreasing rainfall, and the occurrence of other environmental problems. Due to the region's diverse geographic and climatic conditions, the region confronts various types of natural disasters, ranging from storms, floods, and droughts, to landslides and wildfires, and to earthquakes and volcanic eruptions. These disasters pose enormous risks to the physical, social, economic, cultural, and other existential stakes of ASEAN countries. Southeast Asia's fast changing human and developmental conditions like rapid urbanization, population growth, and various less sustainable socioeconomic activities all make it one of the more vulnerable regions to natural disasters.

The complex natural disasters have posed growing threats to Southeast Asian nations. According to a 2011 report by the United Nations Economic and Social Commission for Asia and the Pacific Environment and Disaster Statistics data (UNESCAP 2011), many more people in Southeast Asia died as a result of environmental disasters from 2001 to 2010 than during the previous decade, mainly due to two extreme events: the Indian Ocean earthquake and tsunami of 2004 and Cyclone Nargis in Myanmar in 2008 (Asian Development Bank, 2012). Disasters often affect more than one country. Asian Disaster Reduction Center (ADRC) Data Book 2009 reported that Typhoon Ketsana in 2009 alone caused 715 deaths and affected a total of more than 7.5 million people across four countries: the Philippines, Vietnam, Cambodia, and Lao PDR, with total economic damage exceeding US$1.1 billion. The World Bank estimated the economic loss to Thailand from the 2011 flood to be $45.7 billion. Similarly, the Kinetic Analysis Corp, a US-based hazard-research company, estimated the total losses after Typhoon Haiyan in the Philippines in 2013 to be somewhere between $12 billion to $15 billion, or about 5 percent of economic output.

Southeast Asia is not alone. Severe disasters have also threatened other parts of Asia. In 2010, floods in Pakistan claimed the lives of over 2,100, affected over 18 million people, and caused economic losses of US$7.4 billion. In China, earthquakes, storms, floods, landslides, and other disasters killed a total of over 7,000 people and affected 145 million people (UNESCAP 2012). In 2011, the Tohoku triple disaster in Japan left 21,000 people dead, injured, or missing, alongside an economic loss of around US$211 billion (Center for International Disaster Information, USAID 2011).

In short, natural disasters associated with climate change and other environmental hazards have presented greater threats to virtually all nations in and out of the region. While ASEAN states have focused primarily on establishing and strengthening regional collaborative disaster management, they have also sought to reach out beyond the region for more assistance toward a disaster-resilient Southeast Asia.

Conceptualizing regional disaster management

Disaster is localized, transnational, and regionalized. It usually requires assistance from non-affected or less-affected parties from within and outside the affected countries. In this respect, Southeast Asian governments and their partners have in recent years invested more energy towards a more coordinated regional response along the entire cycle of regional disaster management, namely prevention, mitigation, preparedness, response and relief, and recovery.

These components are related and mutually reinforcing. A comprehensive disaster management system with well-designed pre-disaster measures not only mitigates the consequences when disasters strike, it also helps ease response and relief operations as well as recovery efforts. Enhancing each of these components can strengthen the overall disaster management capacity of a given region and the affected individual countries, which will be better prepared, better able to respond to, and better able to recover from disasters. They are central to institutionalizing ASEAN's collaboration on disaster management.

When disasters occur, the capacity to respond varies depending on the affected country and region's preparations and economic conditions. Recent history shows that low-income countries can reduce loss of life with effective preparations against natural disasters. Cyclone Sidr in Bangladesh killed far fewer people and caused less economic damage in 2007 than did Cyclone Nargis in Myanmar a year later. To be resilient against disasters, it is crucial to enhance governance capacities at all levels, including national and community coordination with international organizations.

The idea of resilience, in essence, can be conceived of as "the capacity to cope with unanticipated dangers after they have become manifest, learning to bounce back" (Wildavsky 1988: 77). A community that is resilient would have the capacity to reorganize its physical, social, economic, and political infrastructures to mitigate risk and enhance its ability to respond to the disaster events as they occur (Haase 2006: 32). In reality, however, many countries simply do not have enough capacity to effectively respond to and recover from the disasters they confront. They thus reach out for international assistance, especially from those who possess more resources, experience, and expertise. Growing disaster threats have not only shifted the paradigm of human security, but they have also called for a more integrated collaborative disaster management at multiple levels (Sylves 2008: 195).

Natural disasters are often "transnational" because their effects transcend both local and regional jurisdictions. Disasters are the product of transnationalism, meaning "the existence of multiple and overlapping processes and transactions *outside the nation-state structure*" (Sullivan 2001: 174). A greater frequency of disasters, with a greater intensity of effects, accordingly, would prompt regional countries to improve disaster management strategies not only domestically but also internationally, through collaborative assistance within the region. Even if a given country is able to contain the situation, assistance from other countries and parties is often necessary, particularly when another country has logistical and other advantages. Given the transboundary nature and the potentially heavy damage of natural disasters, it is imperative for local, national, and international agencies to act collaboratively, both in coordinating their operations and in developing a clear understanding of shared risks. Without such understanding, it would be difficult to recognize what the impending threat constitutes and who "owns" a transboundary crisis (Comfort et al. 2010: 6). Others (Radin et al. 1996) add that multi-organizational arrangements are essential solutions for problems of this nature. Many tasks in managing states of emergency, such as evacuation, medical care, transporting victims, and recovery operations, need effective coordination across organizational sectors. A transition to cooperative multi-party organization involves engaging multiple agencies and players simultaneously to address a complex problem (Comfort 1991: 393–410). Still others (Bardach 1998: 263) highlight the potential of public agencies to work together within and across sectors as a way of adding public value. In this regard, effective mobilization of manpower, equipment, financial support, and information among the multi-level and multi-sector players is central to effective disaster management in any given region.

Nevertheless, regionalizing disaster management is difficult because it requires collaborative operation from different agencies outside the affected country to work together within another's sovereign domains. In many events, bilateral interactions prove more effective and efficient than do multinational or regional operations. On the one hand, multilayered operations may lead to chaotic situations, especially if the affected nation cannot manage the frontlines of the disaster. On the other hand, a single regional team, although united, may also lead to failure if there is a lack of proper interoperability and coherence in their operations. To avoid these issues, it is essential to exchange knowledge, information, and resources among nations at the early stages of disaster management, that is, preparation and mitigation. Scott (1995: 116) suggests that organizations confronting more complex, fragmented environments tend to develop more elaborated internal structures. In the context of disaster management in Southeast Asia, ASEAN members must be closely connected and collaborative in order to enhance regional resilience. The question lies in whether ASEAN's policies, agencies, and operations are comprehensive and coherent enough to ensure effective management of natural disaster in Southeast Asia.

Institutionalizing ASEAN's management of natural disasters

Over the past decades, ASEAN has developed a number of working groups to address natural disasters and environmental issues. However, it was not until the Indian Ocean tsunami in 2004 that ASEAN realized the need to reconsider its disaster management approach. The severe tsunami left hundreds of thousands dead across 13 nations. The devastation has alerted regional countries that they face common disaster risks and that each nation is incapable of coping with such large-scale disasters alone. Consequently, ASEAN has developed a disaster management agency, regional codes of conduct, budget provisions, and external networks to strengthen and *institutionalize* the regional management of natural disasters.

Since ASEAN's inception in 1967, disaster management and environmental matters have been overseen by the ASEAN Socio-Cultural Committee. In 1971, member countries signed the ASEAN Combined Operation Against Natural Disaster agreement, which resulted in the first meeting of the ASEAN Experts Group on Natural Disasters. Nevertheless, ASEAN cooperation in disaster management had remained minimal throughout these early decades. In August 1993, the group decided to change its name to the ASEAN Experts Group on Disaster Management (AEGDM) and to expand its tasks to cover both natural and man-made disasters. Subsequently, AEGDM restructured itself into an ASEAN Committee on Disaster Management (ACDM) to intensify its cooperation on disaster management and meet every year. This was followed by the signings of the ASEAN Agreement on Transboundary Haze Pollution in 2002, the Declaration of ASEAN Concord II in 2003, and the Declaration on Action to Strengthen Emergency Relief, Rehabilitation, Reconstruction and Prevention in the Aftermath of the Earthquake and Tsunami Disaster in 2004 (ASEAN Secretariat).

These committees, agreements, and declarations provide institutionalized frameworks for ASEAN countries to cooperate on disaster management at the regional level. Apart from the above, ASEAN developed several action plans to guide the implementation of their activities in accordance with their agreements. The progress of ASEAN's collaborative disaster management, however, was modest. It was not commensurate with the number of years it has taken to realize the aforementioned measures. At the initial phase of ASEAN's regional cooperation, the focus was on issues associated with high politics and security, such as war, communism, and military operations. Natural disasters were considered to be more technical problems. Later, researchers and experts were tasked to develop a better understanding of natural disasters. Their efforts helped to develop policies and plans under the framework of shared risks, thus laying the foundation for a regional collaborative model in disaster management. Nonetheless, coordination for disaster management was too complicated to operate at a regional level. Relief operations were the only procedures that were relatively feasible to coordinate. It was not until after the Indian Ocean tsunami that several strategies were implemented, activating a more concrete procedure for corroboratively conducting disaster management as a regional effort.

There are three pillars of collaborative actions within the ASEAN community: political-security, economic, and sociocultural. Disaster management is under the third pillar. This is perhaps due to the fact that natural disasters are regarded as a threat to human security, and that they affect mainly the sociocultural foundations of a nation. Through the concept of the sociocultural pillar, ASEAN has initiated several coordinative activities in an integrated fashion across the region. However, the question has been raised whether disaster related issues also fall under the first pillar, as environmental problems are a non-traditional form of security threat. A review of ASEAN documentation shows that several military and civilian-military operations were conducted as disaster relief and recovery measures within the emergency team.

Among the recent region-wide cooperation on disaster management are the ASEAN Agreement on Disaster Management and Emergency Response (AADMER) and the ASEAN Agreement on Disaster Management and Emergency Response Work Program (AADMERWP). The AADMER furthers reinforces the regional policy framework on disaster management through its legally binding agreement, while the AADMERWP provides guidelines to realize the implementation of activities under the AADMER. Currently, disaster management in ASEAN is generally based on AADMER and is primarily exercised through the ASEAN Committee on Disaster Management (ACDM) mechanisms. The shift from operating through ASEAN expert committees on disaster management to ACDM indicates that attention to disasters has moved away from a purely expertise-driven domain to related disaster management agencies. Each ASEAN member state will be represented in the ACDM by its national disaster management agency. With this, ACDM includes all aspects of disaster management, before–during–after, which used to be left less well attended to. Disaster management scholars and practitioners share the same principle that disaster management must be comprehensive. This switch sets a better scope of what ACDM is driving towards and a clearer translation of its policy to multi-agency implementation.

ACDM also reaches out to external parties for additional expertise and resources. This conforms to the ACDM's Term of Reference in 2003: "In case there is a need to conduct specific activities, the ACDM can establish Working Groups and/ or Project Management Committees (PMCs) to work on these endeavors. The committee can invite a country outside as an observer in the ACDM meeting." Funding for the ACDM's activities are from internal mandatory (i.e. AHA Fund) and voluntary (AADMER Fund) contributions by the ASEAN member countries, as well as external contributions from dialogue partners, donor countries, financial institutions, and international organizations. This extension helps ACDM operate as a facilitator in delegating the specific tasks for regional collaborative disaster management.

The discussion below investigates whether ACDM mechanisms are effectively institutionalized and implemented. It also examines the extent to which they support more institutionalized disaster management within and outside the region. To institutionalize collaborative regional disaster management is to infuse it with shared values and coherent policies which reflect on regional agreement, investment in the technical requirements and established agencies, and well-connected disaster management network.

Legal requirement and authorized code of conduct

The AADMER is a legally binding agreement ratified by all of ASEAN's member states. It calls on political commitment and concrete implementation from national governments to local communities within the nations. AADMER is designed to help ASEAN and national governments to conduct comprehensive disaster management processes within the region. It covers all aspects of disaster management from before, during, and after a disaster. Before a disaster, the agreement requires participants to conduct disaster risk identification, assessment, and monitoring; to establish, maintain, and periodically review their early warning systems; to develop strategies for disaster response that reduces losses caused by disasters; and to earmark assets and capacities that might support regional standby preparations for disaster relief and emergency response. During a disaster, the agreement provides details pertaining to an emergency response, including how to request, provide, and direct assistance. After a disaster, the agreement requires ASEAN member countries to coordinate in developing and implementing strategies and projects that will aid in rehabilitation. In sum, AADMER concentrates on building a nation's capacity for disaster management to help itself before requesting international assistance. As sound as these principles of disaster management might be, many countries are not prompt in systematizing risk assessment and fully providing informed reporting on their disaster response needs.

Although AADMER is equivalent to a legal requirement for all member countries to implement, its power to enforce and evaluate outcomes is limited. Still, this agreement may be the only instrument ASEAN has to create regional collaborative action and to produce the effective results as a community. "[L]aws that regulate organizational procedures more than substantive results of those procedures, and laws that provide weak enforcement mechanisms leave more room for organizational mediation" (Edelman 1992: 1532, cited in Scott 1995: 126). Voluntary contributions may be viewed as too weak and too contingent upon the capacity and priorities of each nation. The less risk-prone countries may find they have less interest in contributing to this particular fund. On the one hand, the agreement emphasizes a mutual commitment to collaborating; on the other hand, it may reflect the degree to which a country pays attention and commits to prioritizing disaster management.

In addition, the ACDM establishes working groups to lead the implementation of these measures, and it creates an ACDM chair that will supervise the working groups to ensure an efficient use of resources, a holistic implementation of the working groups, and the attainment of their expected outcomes. The working groups develop indicators for evaluating and monitoring the implementation of the activities and make recommendations and reports on technical areas of the working groups based on this information to the ACDM and the AHA Centre (ASEAN Coordinating Centre for Humanitarian Assistance on Disaster Management). According to the working groups' midterm progress reports of 2012, the working group on preparedness and response has accomplished the most, while the working group on recovery has accomplished the least. This may be understandable as preparedness and response are easy to understand and communicate to all relevant parties, and its achievement minimizes the number of deaths and losses. Meanwhile, activities led by more competent countries, Singapore and Malaysia, are more likely to succeed, while the rest of the working groups seem to be behind. For example, Thailand and Laos are leading the prevention and mitigation group, focusing on risk reduction, but this is an unfamiliar concept to both nations. The Thai government needs to invest more in education and practices on Disaster Risk Reduction. In addition, ASEAN may need to consider switching partners of each working group. This change can help the working groups to share knowledge and achieve their goals.

ASEAN's institutionalized policies, procedures, agency, and strategies

To ensure that member countries can work together effectively and efficiently before, during, and after disasters strike, AADMER has developed and institutionalized five mechanisms: the ASEAN Standby Arrangement for Disaster Relief and Emergency Response (SASOP), the ASEAN Coordinating Centre for Humanitarian Assistance on Disaster Management (AHA Centre), the ASEAN Emergency Rapid Assessment Team (ERAT), the Conference of the Parties (COP), and the ASEAN Disaster Management and Emergency Relief Fund (AADMER Fund). However, Cyclone Nargis in Myanmar, the 2011 flood in Thailand, and Typhoon Haiyan in the Philippines illustrate continued obstacles in the way of using these mechanisms.

The SASOP is a work manual that provides guides and templates for the establishment of the ASEAN Standby Arrangement for Disaster Relief and Emergency Response, the procedures for coordinating disaster relief and operations, the procedures for the facilitation and utilization of civil and military assets and capabilities, and the methodology for conducting the ASEAN Regional Disaster Emergency Response Simulation Exercises (ARDEX) to test the effectiveness of these procedures. It requires ASEAN member countries to conduct a disaster assessment to determine the nature and extent of a disaster, whether a given emergency situation arises from said disaster, and what types of assistance are needed to ensure an effective disaster relief and emergency response. The ASEAN ERAT aims to assemble and analyze findings together with governmental officials from affected countries to manage disaster response operations and provide assistance effectively. SASOP is effective at the level of regional–national relationships and coordination. It creates clearer procedures and paths to coordinate activities and operations. However, challenges remain at the level of national–local connectivity. As explained by a Thai official in an interview:

> Disaster management requires accurate decision making to deploy preemptive operations and efficient responses. Risk assessment has limitations, much like the situation in the Philippines when Typhoon Haiyan made landfall of maximum force. Underestimate[d] severity and destruction led to lack of effective countermeasures. Local authorities in Tacloban faced … a complicated and difficult situation when devastation exceeded their capacities to respond. Unfortunately, less attention and investment to the designs of preemptive national–local connectivity led to difficulties to assist affected areas. Poor logistic plans … delay[ed] … coordinat[ion of] needs assessment.
>
> (Director of Research and International Relations Bureau, Department of Disaster Prevention and Mitigation, Thailand, interviewed on May 22, 2014)

As mentioned, ERAT is an on-the-ground assistance team facilitated by the AHA center to work with domestic incident command systems. ERAT is composed of personnel from each national disaster agency who are recruited and trained to team up when an incident occurs and assistance is requested. To operate effectively, ERAT has to follow SASOP and coordinate well with local agencies. Therefore, the trained personnel of ASEAN-ERAT are very significant and instrumental to coordinating operations within their own respective national system and on-the-ground during a disaster. This may also be an effective mechanism for coordinating operations across jurisdictions for those nations that implement stricter national security mandates. According to an ERAT official:

> It was interesting when Cyclone Nargis hit Myanmar in terms of ASEAN's role. Myanmar enforced strict national security policy in order to allow the external forces to get into a country for assistance operations. Neither the United Nations nor ASEAN was trusted when discussing joint assistance operations. Thailand, instead, played a significant role in persuading and convincing Myanmar to accept assistance from other nation-states and international organizations. Bilateral relationships and trust are the most important to coordinate on-the-ground operations. Evidently, mutual agreement and familiar operations between two nations were crucial in collaborative operations across jurisdictions in the Typhoon Haiyan disaster. The United States' forces were deployed quickly when the potential of strong typhoon was advised and when emergency response was needed.
>
> (ERAT personnel, Department of Disaster Prevention and Mitigation, Thailand, interviewed on May 22, 2014)

On the one hand, the AHA center increases the importance of the community functioning as one single united body to operate and assist each other in managing disasters. Without a physical facilitation team, the workload may burden member countries to take care of all administration and facilitation on their own. On the other hand, member countries have to comply with AHA operations and its emergency assistance team. Each nation has to design its procedures to allow an ASEAN ground-team to be able to work with the Local Emergency Management Agency (LEMA) who provide the main responders to the on-the-ground operations. The incident commander of the ASEAN team will coordinate with and work under the incident commander of the affected country. In an interview conducted in 2012, an official of the UNDP stated:

> During the 2011 flood in Thailand, central and local disaster response agencies admitted that AHA center and ERAT were trying to coordinate and provide assistance systematically; however, incoherent procedures to coordinate front line operations obstructed effective results. The concept of damage-and-need assessment (DANA), used in SASOP, introduced new facets of disaster responses and relief protocols that Thailand's disaster-related agencies were not yet familiar with. It was difficult to work together because domestic procedures integrated into the ASEAN/SASOP to coordinate assistant operation on ground are unclear.
>
> (Project Coordinator, United Nations Development Program (UNDP), Thailand, interviewed on February 17, 2012)

Although the above mechanisms of AADMER are concrete and enforced, challenges and gaps remain. ASEAN needs to have a procedure to monitor and share lessons learned from each event to improve its measures. The Conference of the Parties (COP) allows AADMER to ensure effective implementation of the agreement, to consider new protocols, to contemplate, review, and adopt amendments to AADMER, and to establish the additional bodies and activities necessary to support the implementation of AADMER. The conference is a very active and effective mechanism because it keeps all activities and implementation running progressively. Evaluating and sharing information helps all parties to learn, practice, analyze, exchange ideas, design solutions, cope with challenges, and make decisions on any matter presented. Being comprised of ministers and senior officials helps administrative bodies make decisions.

To run the operations, AHA center uses a mandatory fund, paid US$30,000 annually by member countries, to manage the resources for supporting the implementation of AADMER related activities, for assisting the affected country in disaster relief and emergency response, and for use in the deployment of ERAT to the affected countries. This contribution reflects a commitment to regional collaborative operation. At the same time, Article 24 of AADMER requires ASEAN member countries to establish the ASEAN Disaster Management and Emergency Relief Fund (AADMER Fund) on a voluntary basis. Further, it allows the countries to mobilize additional resources from relevant international organizations. Setting up the AADMER Fund is the right initiative. Although regional collaboration is agreed to be mutually beneficial to all member countries, the implementation, activities, progress, and concrete delivery of services need adequate budgets to help facilitate disaster management. Because of the voluntary basis, the AADMER

Fund does not expect equal contributions from member countries. Countries with less capacity to manage disasters in their jurisdiction typically commit more and faster funding than do countries with a greater capacity to cover their disaster costs. It is not a surprise that in countries that consider disasters less of a threat, voluntary contributions will be less necessary and more of a luxury.

To what extent does ASEAN need to reach out to external agencies? Which mechanisms are best deployed to manage assistance?

ASEAN also reaches out to other nation-states and international entities for assistance in disaster management. These external collaborations include the ASEAN Plus Three (APT), the East Asia Summit (EAS), the ASEAN Regional Forum (ARF), the ASEAN-United Nations, the ASEAN-European Union, and the AADMER Partnership Group (APG). These collaborations are comprehensive because they cover all phases of disaster management including its socioeconomic and technical dimensions. They are intended to be coherent although they focus on different operations in disaster management.

Both APT and EAS allow the ASEAN community to reach assistance outside the region. APT and EAS started out in the form of an informational dialogue on disaster management. Recently, ASEAN has attempted to further the coordination utilizing expertise and resources from these partners to improve an infrastructure for regional disaster management. The APT initiative takes into account the importance of supplying necessities when disasters strike. The implementation of proper cargo management – either at the AHA center that administers and facilitates distribution or at the origin, where it is more convenient to store and then disperse to affected countries – is another challenge to optimizing the utility of these collaborations. As described by the ASEAN Secretariat:

> The ACDM+3 meeting is a platform for exploring the possible areas of cooperation between ACDM and the Plus Three Countries on disaster management. The East Asia Emergency Rice Reserve (EAERR) pilot project, an initiative of the ASEAN Ministers on Agriculture and Forestry and the Ministers of Agriculture of the People's Republic of China, Japan and the Republic of Korea (AMAF+3), is another interesting project on disaster management. It aims to establish a mutual assistance system to share rice stock among 13 member states so that they are able to provide food assistance and strengthen food security in emergencies caused by disasters and for poverty alleviation purposes.
>
> (Association of Southeast Asian Nations [ASEAN] 2009c)

After the Bali summit in 2011, ASEAN set up an emergency stockpile and logistics system in Subang, Malaysia, to coordinate and distribute all necessities to an affected area. Subang receives by far the most generous support from Japan; a total of more than US$11 million (*Jakarta Post*, December 13, 2012). Recently, Thailand has indicated interest in either another stockpile station in the region or an emergency stockpile training and exercise center. In fact, more stockpile and logistics system stations are tactically appropriate to respond to emergencies and disasters. However, operating such a system requires professional personnel and efficient accessibility techniques from host countries where capacity seems to be rare. ASEAN needs to seek technical assistance and cooperation especially from neighboring countries in Asia where logistics systems can easily be interconnected. For the greatest effectiveness in regional disaster management, the ACDM Working group should establish the linkage between the AADMER WP and the EAS Work Plan on disaster management. The Information Sharing Dialogue between the ACDM and EAS Participating Countries, Australia, China, India, Japan, New Zealand, South Korea, Russia, and the United States, allows ASEAN to address needs in technical assistance and capacity building via bilateral and multilateral cooperation.

In the past, the ARF mostly emphasized traditional security concerns and focused on military operations. Although AADMER has moved ARF's focus from traditional to non-traditional security concerns, their activities are nonetheless under a military domain, with less emphasis on civilian–military coordination practices. This aspect was reflected in the 2013 ASEAN Disaster Relief Exercises (DiREX) in Thailand, where Korea was the exercise operator and designer. DiREX is different from the ASEAN Regional Disaster Emergency Response Simulation Exercises (ARDEX), where 10 member countries operate under the same code of conduct as SASOP. DiREX is more likely to depend on a given operator, who can often be very rigid and military-like in its use of unfamiliar procedures. Additionally and surprisingly, due to the design of DiREX, the table-top exercises were primarily run by civilian agencies while all functional exercises in the field were conducted mainly by military operations. ARF, in turn, instead of mingling operations between military and civilian parties, seems to reinforce classical divisions that undermine organizational cultural diversity. ARF should instead work to narrow any division in the military–civilian network of assistance. Encouraging familiarities among personnel when they are trained together should help not only to coordinate more effectively and efficiently but also to minimize any conflict from professional differences. More integration between civilian and military parties would also have the benefit of reducing any potential discomfort with the proximity of a national military and its disaster management efforts.

ASEAN has been working with several UN agencies in disaster management. It has usually established relationships with individual UN agencies based on the specific expertise that the UN agencies have. L. N. Woods notes:

> For example, in the area of DRR, the ASEAN Secretariat signed a five-year tripartite Memorandum of Cooperation with the UN International Strategy for Disaster Reduction (UNISDR) and World Bank in 2009 to promote partnerships in order to mainstream DDR in the development processes of the ASEAN member states. The UN office of the Coordination of Humanitarian Affairs (UNOCHA) has also worked with the ACDM in joint training and exercises. The UN World Food Program (WFP) has worked closely with the ACDM on joint training in emergency logistic management.
>
> (Woods 2010)

Although the most direct and responsible agencies are supposed to be UNISDR and UNOCHA, the efforts made by UN agencies are also under several other programs such as the United Nations Development Program (UNDP), the United Nations Educational, Scientific and Cultural Organization (UNESCO), and the United Nations High Commissioner for Refugees (UNHCR). For example, the UNDP has implemented various programs providing capacity building in disaster management throughout the region. Another example is the deployment of a UNHCR emergency team to assist the Philippines government to manage internally displaced people from Typhoon Haiyan. However, support and assistance programs under the UN are usually conducted through networks of government agencies in each nation or among member countries. Co-sharing or co-managing through a national module is not easy. Government agencies responsible for disaster management have their own routines and priorities, which can hinder a collaborative process. Progress in achieving goals and desired outcomes may, as a result, fall short of the expectations of an initial plan.

Aside from such complications, ASEAN and the UN released the Joint Declaration on ASEAN-UN Collaboration in Disaster Management in 2010. The declaration has been developed based on the AADMER and the Hyogo Framework of Action 1 (HFA1). It aims to broaden and deepen the collaboration between ASEAN disaster management mechanisms and those of the UN in order to build disaster-resilient nations and safer communities in the region. The Hyogo Framework for Action itself is not simple. The framework is translated into five main tasks which the national work plan in disaster management has to implement. These include prioritizing disaster risk reduction, knowing the risk and taking action, building understanding and awareness, reducing risks, and preparing and being ready. These focuses are to be implemented under the national plan and deliver concrete results. Many countries implementing Hyogo struggle to understand both their activities under this framework as well as its capacity to maintain momentum and sustain such activities. One famous translation of the Hyogo Framework is expressed in CBDRM (the practice of Community-Based Disaster Risk Management). A CBDRM ensures capacity building among even those at the tail end of the disaster management network, namely, the local communities in each nation. However, to complete a CBDRM is time consuming and requires several key factors such as strong leadership, community understanding and self-awareness, mutual interest in motivation, and education.

The EU has been recognized for its success in sharing knowledge and experience because it has several expert teams and a range of technologies that can enhance a nation's capacity for disaster management. Choosing to promote the exchange of experience and knowledge in civilian–military cooperation on disasters through the use of AADMER is a smart move. AADMER encourages the member countries to compromise on their individual national security concerns and to accept the idea of domestic and international military teams cooperating with each other. Under SASOP, all military personnel are required to wear an ERAT uniform, thereby illustrating unity among team members while reducing differing norms and

practices across national lines. Hopefully, third party encouragement for cooperation will reduce conflicts and inconsistencies in operations.

Disaster management is multi-disciplinary so ASEAN needs many areas of
expertise which are best practiced by different types of agencies. The AADMER
Partnership Group (APG) is a consortium of international non-governmental
organizations. It consists of seven organizations, including Child Fund International, Help Age International, Mercy Malaysia, Oxfam, Plan Organization, Save
the Children, and World Vision International. "The APG aims to strengthen
ASEAN's humanitarian response and disaster risk reduction strategies through
enhancing the collaboration between civil society organizations (CSO) and
ASEAN governments on the activities under the AADMER Work Program"
(Carreon 2011). The APG looks for and facilitates further resource mobilization
to ensure the continued support for the AADMER Work Program. It fulfills the
principle of involving all stakeholders in regional disaster management and also
directly participates in ASEAN's disaster-related programs, including all meetings
of the ACDM. This initiative is very important for two reasons. First, APG has
expertise and manpower trained in specific skills dealing with specific issues.
Second, the CSO is believed to be both a primary source of assistance on special
issues that emerge during a disaster, and a secondary support partner when
needed. Thus, the provision of an organized and systematic arrangement for the
APG will help improve ASEAN operation effectiveness.

Technical assistance is an essential element in capacity building. The exchange
of knowledge and technology is usually at the heart of disaster management
assistance. Bilateral agreement is usually the most effective and efficient mechanism
in requesting and delivering assistance. Previous agreement sets proper, clearer,
and more familiar procedures for agencies on both sides to coordinate disaster
operations. Evidently, in Thailand, after the Indian Ocean tsunami in 2004, several United States agencies such as the United States Trade and Development
Agency (USTDA) and the United States Agency for International Development
(USAID) assisted the Thai government through the establishment of the National
Disaster Warning Center, the deployment of the Tsunami Deep Ocean Buoy
detection system, and training in the Incident Command System. This type of
favorable bilateral relationship was also repeated in on-ground operations following Typhoon Haiyan in the Philippines, which relied upon joint forces and
emergency teams from the United States.

Challenges

Institutionalization is a process that happens to an organization over time with a
growing convergence of values and policies among members that facilitate collaborations. To institutionalize regional disaster risk management, as the chapter has
conceptualized, is to establish regularized (as opposed to ad hoc) and harmonized
(i.e. coordinated) mechanisms, such as structural arrangement, authorized codes
of conduct, policies and procedures, established and authorized agency, and
resource allocation. There has been a lot of progress over time accomplished by

ASEAN to make disaster risk management a priority and a commitment of all member countries. However, to have all the ingredients of collaborative disaster risk management in place does not necessarily mean it is effectively institutionalized.

Moving toward an ASEAN community requires a state of stability of member countries which recently have been threatened by more frequent and severe natural disasters. Most nations are still struggling with the priority of economic development. Investing in proactive disaster management is likely to be viewed as an economic luxury because a government cannot assess the efficacy of such spending until the disaster actually occurs. However, the safer the region becomes, the more investment and economic stability there will be. Thus, taking into account the importance of setting up a regional collaboration system of disaster management, it would be ideal to create a center that can facilitate regional research, share knowledge, improve the early warning systems, assist in emergency relief, and coordinate recovery. On the one hand, it is cost-effective because such collaboration contributes to the region especially when additional assistance is needed. More systematic and organized protocols for regional collaborative assistance can help set the direction for more effective coordination. On the other hand, the broad spectrum of national practices and relief capacities of the member countries can produce varied levels of contributions and requests for additional support. Having a robust regional disaster risk management results in not only a safer ASEAN community but also can benefit the Asia-Pacific community at large. However, the challenges remain.

Southeast Asia's institutionalized cooperation on disaster management has been rapidly increased since 2004. To a large extent, this is a direct response to an increase in the number, size, and severity of the disasters occurring in the region wherein the effects have become more tangible. There are the formulations of a more concrete action plan to guide implementation of AADMER, the identification of flagship programs, the establishment of critical mechanisms to support the AADMER implementation, and the adoption of legally binding agreements. Further, the use of ASEAN mechanisms is expected to help disaster management operations become more comprehensive. The main strength of ASEAN's institutionalized disaster management is its determination and legally binding mutual agreement, namely, the AADMER that consists of the purposes and principles justifying ASEAN's instruments in support of disaster resilient nations and safer communities. This also corresponds to the HYOGO Framework for Action (HFA1) and the use of CBDRM (Community Based Disaster Risk Management). As reported in Bali Concord III:

> ASEAN resolves at the global level to 1) promote and strengthen partnership with relevant stakeholders through established ASEAN mechanisms, 2) address and ensure disaster and climate resiliency of ecosystems and communities, 3) enhance public awareness and encourage public participation in a program on community resilience to disasters, 4) improving civil–military coordination in providing effective and timely response to major natural disasters and enhance cooperation among ASEAN militaries and civilian–military in

Humanitarian Assistance and Disaster Relief (HADR), 5) facilitate regional cooperation on disaster risk reduction, and 6) strengthen cooperation between the AHA Centre as key coordinated agency and relevant regional and international organizations and agencies for ensuring prompt and smooth communication in times of disaster as well as enhancing coordination mechanisms to facilitate the flows of support in a timely manner.

(See summary of Bali Concord III at www.preventionweb.net)

This newfound institutionalized cooperation is taking place at all stages of disaster management, including before, during, and after disasters. Also, these efforts have expanded to cover both natural and man-made disasters. At some level, ASEAN expects the results of AADMER implementation will transpire through several programs, making it impossible to measure success with any single high-performing register. ASEAN has addressed disaster risk reduction as its priority, to establish more partners and stronger partnerships, and translate AADMER into several mechanisms. However, the most important goals of regional collaborative disaster management are the coordination of all parties and developing effective capacity to cope with disaster risks.

In addition, ASEAN's more proactive and institutionalized approach to disaster management is evident in the area of disaster risk reduction and climate change arrangements rather than humanitarian assistance for disaster relief and emergency response. ASEAN focuses more on community-based disaster risk reduction (CBDRR) as a way to deal with local risk patterns, to enhance disaster management capacity and to reduce the gap in disaster management capacity among the ASEAN member countries. However, the concept of risk reduction is tiresomely difficult to comprehend and translate into local practices. National agencies usually believe that they know better than the locals. The lack of mutual understanding of risk reduction can lead to either fragmented implementation or fruitless documentation from one-off community training programs.

The AADMER, though comprised of codes of conduct and enforcement for implementation among its member countries, still has problems convincing member countries to contribute more resources and to make progress in each working program. As previously mentioned, since AADMER funding is voluntary, it is to be expected that different countries will contribute at different levels according to their own capacity for disaster management. However, a contribution is also viewed as commitment to the regional collaborative effort and to ensure the continuity of not only regional operation in disaster management but also the unity of the community on one specific matter. Again, it is unsurprising that the greatest midterm progress was made by a working group on preparedness and response that Malaysia and Singapore, two of the more developed and experienced member nations, chaired together.

National capacity is another concern as much as a challenge, perhaps not only to institutionalized collaborative disaster management but also to all communal tasks within the ASEAN community perspective. ASEAN member countries are different in many dimensions including: 1) economic status, which leads to diverse capacities to contribute to regional activities and to distribute resources to the community; 2) awareness and understanding of risks and disasters, which leads to differing levels of prevention, mitigation, preparedness, response, and recovery; 3) varied knowledge and culture of communities to develop resilience against disasters; and 4) varying degrees of susceptibility to disasters among the member nations, which leads to different levels of attention and dedication to disaster management concerns. Operating on the assumption that all member states would be able to comply and make the same progress is not realistic. The dilemma is that the countries that are less able to cope with disasters are more likely to seek assistance while the more equipped nations, which have more resources to offer, are less interested in efforts to collaborate with their neighbors. Knowledge and investment are not exchanged and implemented coherently enough to optimize the potential gains to all parties.

With established agencies and authorized codes of conduct designed for more systematized operations, many difficulties arise. In its current configuration, if the AHA center operated as a hub for coordination, it would not be able to adequately facilitate and assist in satisfying the needs of all member countries should there be a disaster of large enough scale to affect all member countries at the same time. The initiative to stock rice and food to be used as back-up supplies for the affected countries within the region would fall short if such a large scale disaster were in effect. SASOP is effective at the regional to national level. However, the difficulties vary when SASOP needs to be integrated into on-the-ground operations. In one dimension, developing the same standards for conducting operations at different levels of government systems is impossible. In another dimension, SASOP is only at the beginning of its trial period, so it is difficult for each nation to develop the national–regional–local standard procedures that can be integrated into a larger ASEAN regional system. Although the ERAT program aims to create mutual understanding and agreed steps of operation, there is a lack of emphasis on assisting an individual nation to design and develop its own coherent standard operating procedures (SOPs). Hopefully, ERAT can also extend to other areas of professional assistance, such as medical and technical protocols, which require specific licenses to operate. The strict regulations on the certification of certain professionals is intended to make sure that the assistance provided is accurate; however, there is an insufficient number of search and rescue personnel at present.

National security is unlikely to become an issue when discussing disaster assistance if disaster management measures are addressed proactively during a time of normalcy, and not only during a crisis. Completing risk assessment and disaster research ahead of time is a good countermeasure to the risks a nation is already prone to. To do so, collaborative efforts have to be made across national jurisdictions. Nations will need a transboundary perspective to deploy data collecting technologies and attain interoperability among regional knowledge systems. Most often, countries are less committed to regional declarations and policies due to deeper concerns about their own internal exigencies. Additionally, from the military's perspective, there exist serious concerns regarding national security when information sharing across jurisdictions is considered. This can be viewed as a national security risk in itself. This fear of rendering a nation vulnerable through information sharing is the military's chief discomfort with military–civilian cooperation efforts.

Last but not least, there are needs for technical and structural assistance in the transferring of knowledge and hardware that ASEAN member countries cannot necessarily provide. Reaching out for collaborative assistance from external partners and allies such as the United States (through USTDA, USAID, and universities), UN agencies (though UNDP, UNISDR, and UNESCO), JICA and others are preferable and effective. All assistance projects from agencies mentioned are fragmented and not systematically integrated. This results in not only disconnects in knowledge sharing but also less understanding among agencies involved in intergovernmental relations regarding disaster management strategies at both a national and international level. Assistance can come in too many shapes, along too many channels, and at multiple levels of implementation, leading to fragmented and less effective assistance. Several programs from multiple agencies often repeat the efforts of each other and are implemented incoherently. As mentioned, government agencies who are the main responders have too much already in hand, and adding to their burden does not do any good to the achievement of the program. Also, efforts at the community level can be repetitive and overwhelm communities.

Recommendations and conclusions

The institutionalization of disaster risk management in Southeast Asia is not only about mandating collaboration within ASEAN and with relevant stakeholders; it is also about getting relevant parties to effectively execute mechanisms as regular practice, to coherently perform within the network of operation, and to ensure mutual benefit to all member countries. As indicated, all challenges faced by ASEAN are mostly to do with the implementation of its institutional design. The chapter suggests the following for more effective cooperation in the future:

1   ASEAN's implementation of disaster risk management currently relies on only ministerial committees and coordinating agencies, including the appointment of working groups designated for specific tasks. Poor communication of the regional goal toward disaster-resilient communities causes lack of participation of all involving parties. Policy, procedures, and implementable strategies at the national and local levels are still ineffective. Capacity building at the regional and national levels remains limited to conceptual goals and is in need of more directed translation and carefully designed implementation strategies. All member countries have to keep improving their capacity and capability in disaster management and invest more in future cooperation.

2   ASEAN needs to assure the international community of its commitment to achieving regional disaster coordination and national capacity building. Another problem is that ASEAN states rely on global collaborations and contributions to technical assistance and recovery aid. Consequently, its

progress in the area of disaster management is partly contingent upon the assistance it receives. Still, ASEAN could work on streamlining or improving distribution channels. Currently, the network of the World Meteorology Organization, UN agencies, US government agencies, Japanese government agencies, and other international organizations and government agencies help ASEAN improve the region's capacity for disaster resilience, but that assistance is channeled through multiple programs rather than managed systematically and organized coherently. AHA center could facilitate this by creating a database and information system that would help identify the gaps in regional efforts and assistance as well as identify the need for additional capacity building at regional and national levels.

3   Perhaps it is necessary to make the Hyogo Framework and its priorities legally binding. Regional, national, and local stakeholders must commit to the implementation, monitoring, and evaluation of the concept and the practices. All governments and stakeholders have to evaluate and develop lessons learned more concretely and effectively. There are gaps and challenges left by the end of HFA1 with lessons learned and more work to be done. These practices will create not only stronger local capacity but also more resilience against economic downturns after a disaster. Moreover, ASEAN needs to create a Knowledge Management (KM) system at the AHA Center and to determine how KM will be translated into national systems and practices. Sharing among working groups in the Work Program may help gather important lessons learned, but not in the implementation of operations on the ground. ARDEX can be tailored to support the best practices of the CBDRM program.

4   AHA Center has to invest more in the number of emergency personnel trained with the same conceptualization and well-designed SOPs. The Haiyan on-the-ground emergency response revealed the difficulties of coordinating operations among different involving agencies. The post-Haiyan Tacloban declaration, therefore, announced the statement on EAS Guidelines for Rapid Disaster Response developed and drafted by the Philippines and Australia. The guidelines provide standard operating procedures among emergency response agencies to work together effectively and efficiently. The training program can also be designed in ways that support multi-agency collaborative operation. This could allow ASEAN-ERAT to exercise not only among trained ERAT agencies, but also with international and national emergency teams; it would also test the interoperability of their Unified Incident Command System. To increase accessibility to the program, the training needs to be designed and provided within member countries by AHA representatives.

5   In order to make progress in the Work Program and in enhancing national capacity building, the practice of pairing countries as co-chairs should be strongly supported. The ACDM should also consider switching pairs, having a country with a higher level of capacity and determination pair-up with those at a lower level. A more equipped co-chair in a working group can perform as a mentor to another co-chair. These two alternate relationships help facilitate capacity building and the exchange of insights from previous lessons learned.

A mentoring dynamic can also be expanded to aid in the broader development of national SOPs to more effectively and efficiently improve regional connectivity.

6   ASEAN should provide opportunities for non-state actors like local environmental groups, civil society, or NGOs to play more proactive roles in the region's policy setting and planning networks, for example in the ASEAN subcommittee meeting and in the ASEAN Regional Program on Disaster Management teamwork. These actors could have more socio-ecological information than the member state's representatives in local environmental situations. It would also improve connectivity with other environmental networks at a global level. Incorporating civil society organizations (CSOs) into the network of assistance is a smart move; however, all parties should be able to maintain their own specific operations. First, as a primary source of assistance, these organizations should have their list of names, responsibilities, skills, resources, and logistics ready to be communicated to the AHA Center and member countries in a time of need. Second, organization networks can be a positive redundancy as they can become a fallback to regional operations. Having them assist in policy design, provide informative insight, and share in the operations of a more extensive SASOP framework helps improve policy and practice within the region.

7   ASEAN should integrate a higher degree of attention towards Disaster Risk Reduction (DRR) and more actively support the creation of shared frameworks between ASEAN and external networks, especially through APT and EAS. The initiative on emergency stockpiling is a significant development that provides mutual benefit at times of emergency. This stockpiling can be used within a host country; it can also facilitate distribution of assistance to affected countries in Southeast Asia and outside the region. While ASEAN can benefit from knowledge sharing and technical assistance from East Asian countries, they also benefit from ASEAN contributions.

The patterns of institutionalization of disaster management in Southeast Asia, as discussed above, indicate the extent to, and manner in which, ASEAN states could regularize and strengthen their policy coordination in preventing a disaster, mitigating its effects, conducting relief operations, and expediting recovery is a result of a wide range of factors. These include: the severity of a disaster, the capacity of the affected countries, organizational path-dependency and barriers, as well as the availability and scope of external assistance. Given these capability and exogenous factors, ASEAN must invest more in developing its capacity, improving institutional design, enhancing intra-ASEAN coordination, as well as strengthening its productive partnerships with external powers and international agencies.

References

ASEAN. 2005. ASEAN Committee on Disaster Management (ACDM). In *ASEAN Overview and Report*. Jakarta: ASEAN Secretariat.

Axelrod, R., and M. D. Cohen. 1999. *Harnessing Complexity: Organizational Implications of a Scientific Frontier*. New York: The Free Press.

Bardach, E. 1998. *Getting Agencies to Work Together: The Practice and Theory of Managerial Craftsmanship*. Washington, DC: Brookings Institution.

Comfort, L. K. 1991. Self-organization in Complex Systems. *Journal of Public Administration Research and Theory* 4(3): 393–410.

Comfort, L. K. 1999. *Shared Risk: Complex Systems in Seismic Response*. Oxford: Elsevier Science.

Comfort, Louise, Arjen Boin and Chris Demchack. 2010. The Rise of Resilience. In L. Comfort, A. Boin and C. Demchack, eds, *Designing Resilience*. Pittsburgh, PA: University of Pittsburgh Press, pp. 1–12.

European Commission on Humanitarian Aid and Civil Protection. 2012. ECHO Factsheet Disaster Risk Reduction in Southeast Asia.

Haase, T. 2006. *Administrative Resilience: Evaluating the Adaptive Capacity of Administrative Systems that Operate in Dynamic and Uncertain Conditions*. PhD Dissertation, Graduate School of Public and International Affairs, University of Pittsburg.

Haase, T. 2010. International Disaster Resilience: Preparing for Transnational Disasters. In L. Comfort, A. Boin and C. Demchack, eds, *Designing Resilience*. Pittsburgh, PA: University of Pittsburgh Press, pp. 220–243.

Kamolvej, T. 2005. *The Integration of Intergovernmental Coordination and Information Management in Response to Immediate Crises*. PhD Dissertation, Graduate School of Public and International Affairs, University of Pittsburg.

Kamolvej, T. 2014. Has Thailand Managed Disaster Better? *Journal of Politics and Governance* 4(2): 103–119.

Kauffman, S. A. 1993. *The Origins of Order: Self Organization and Selection in Evolution*. New York: Oxford University Press.

Kettl, D. F. 2002. *The Transformation of Governance: Public Administration for Twenty-first Century America*. Baltimore, MD: Johns Hopkins University Press.

Nathan Association Inc. 2011. ASEAN Regional Forum on Disaster Management and Regional Security Specialists, February.

Ostrom, Elinor. 1991. *Governing the Commons: The Evolution of Institutions for Collective Action. Political Economy of Institutions and Decisions*. Cambridge: Cambridge University Press.

Ostrom, E., L. Schroeder, and S. Wyne. 1993. *Institutional Incentives and Sustainable Development: Infrastructure Policies in Perspective*. Boulder, CO: Westview Press.

Radin, B. A., R. Agranoff, A. O'M. Bowman, C. G. Buntz, S. Ott, B. S. Romzek, and R. H. Wilson. 1996. *New Governance for Rural America: Creating Intergovernmental Partnership*. Lawrence, KS: University Press of Kansas.

Scott, W. R. 1995. *Organizations: Rational, Natural and Open Systems*. Englewood Cliffs, NJ: Prentice Hall.

Scott, W. R., and J. W. Meyer. 1994. *Institutional Environments and Organization: Structural Complexity and Individualism*. Thousand Oaks, CA: Sage.

Selznick, Phillip. 1953. *TVA and the Grass Roots: A Study in the Sociology of Formal Organization*. Berkeley and Los Angeles, CA: University of California Press.

Selznick, Phillip. 1957. *Leadership in Administration*. New York: Harper & Row.

Sullivan, M. P. 2001. *Theories of International Relations: Transition vs. Persistence*. New York: Palgrave.

Sylves, Richard. 2008. *Disaster Policy and Politics*. Washington, DC: CQ Press.

Wagh, W. and T. Kamolvej. 2007. Principle of Crisis Management. Unpublished Paper in Senior Crisis Management Seminar: State Department Antiterrorist Program, lecture notes. American University.

Wildavsky, A. 1988. *Searching for Safety*. New Brunswick, NJ: Transaction Books.

Electronic sources

Agranoff, R. and B. Radin. 2014. Deil Wright's Overlapping Model of Intergovernmental Relations: The Basis for Contemporary Intergovernmental Relationships. ASPA 2014 Conference. Retrieved from http://bloch.umkc.edu/cookingham/documents/symposium/Agranoff-and-Radin.pdf (accessed December 13, 2014).

ASEAN Committee on Disaster Management (ACDM). n.d. Retrieved from http://122.155.1.145/site6/download-src.php?did=5412 (accessed June 15, 2013).

ASEAN Committee on Disaster Management (ACDM). 2003. Terms of Reference. Retrieved from www.disaster.go.th/html/ricb/foreign/2006/acdm/background/acdm_tor.html (accessed December 28, 2012).

ASEAN Defense Establishments and CSO Cooperation on Non-Traditional Security. 2010. The ASEAN Partnership Group (APG): Civil Society Participation in Action. Fifth Session: SCHR and ASEAN partnership group, Bangkok. Retrieved from www.docstoc.com/docs/80658097/AADMER-Forum-in-Brunei# (accessed December 28, 2012).

Asian Development Bank (ADB). 2012. Asian Development Bank Addressing Climate Change and Migration in Asia and the Pacific. Mandaluyong City, Philippines. Retrieved from http://ipcc-wg2.gov/njlite_download2.php?id=10771 (accessed January 10, 2013).

Asian Disaster Reduction Center (ADRC). 2009. Natural Disasters Data Book 2009. Retrieved from www.adrc.asia/publications/databook/DB2009.html (accessed January 12, 2013).

Association of Southeast Asian Nations (ASEAN). n.d. ASEAN Agreement on Disaster Management and Emergency Response Work Program for 2010–2015. Retrieved from www.alnap.org/pool/files/dato-m-karmain-asean.pdf (accessed January 10, 2013).

Association of Southeast Asian Nations (ASEAN). 2005. ASEAN Agreement on Disaster Management and Emergency Response, Vientiane, 26 July 2005. Retrieved from www.asean.org/communities/asean-political-security-community/item/asean-agreement-on-disaster-management-and-emergency-response-vientiane-26-july-2005-4 (accessed January 10, 2013).

Association of Southeast Asian Nations (ASEAN). 2009a. SASOP: Standard Operating Procedures for Regional Standby Arrangement and Coordination of Joint Disaster Relief and Emergency Response Operations. Retrieved from https://www.ifrc.org/docs/IDRL/SASOP.pdf (accessed Janaury 11, 2013).

Association of Southeast Asian Nations (ASEAN). 2009b. ASEAN Plus Three Cooperation. Retrieved from www.asean.org/archive/22208.pdf (accessed December 28, 2012).

Association of Southeast Asian Nations (ASEAN). 2009c. East Asia Emergency Rice Reserve (EAERR) Pilot Project. Retrieved from www.asean.org/archive/Fact%20Sheet/AEC/2009-AEC-016.pdf (accessed December 28, 2012).

Association of Southeast Asian Nations (ASEAN). 2010. Joint Declaration on ASEAN-UN Collaboration in Disaster Management. Retrieved from www.asean.org/news/item/joint-declaration-on-asean-un-collaboration-in-disaster-management (accessed January 11, 2013).

Association of Southeast Asian Nations (ASEAN). 2011. The ASEAN-Emergency Rapid Assessment Team Dispatched to Respond to Floods in Thailand. Retrieved from www. asean.org/news/asean-secretariat-news/item/the-asean-emergency-rapid-assessment-team-dispatched-to-respond-to-floods-in-thailand (accessed January 11, 2013).

Association of Southeast Asian Nations (ASEAN). 2012a. Chairman Statement of the Second East Asia Summit Foreign Ministers' Meeting. Retrieved from www.eria.org/2012_0712_Chiarman%20Statement%20of%20the%202nd%20EAS%20Foreign%20Minis ters%20Meeting.pdf (accessed June 15, 2013).

Association of Southeast Asian Nations (ASEAN). 2012b. Co-chairs' Statement of the 19th ASEAN-EU Ministerial Meeting. Retrieved from www.consilium.europa.eu/uedocs/cm s_data/docs/pressdata/EN/foraff/129883.pdf (accessed June 15, 2013).

Association of Southeast Asian Nations (ASEAN). 2012c. Evolving Towards 2015: Annual Report 2011–2012. Retrieved from www.asean.org/images/2012/publications/annual %20report%202011-2012_2.pdf (accessed June 15, 2013).

BBC News. 2005. Malaysia Issues Tsunami Warning. Retrieved from http://news.bbc.co. uk/2/hi/asia-pacific/4241285.stm (accessed December 28, 2012).

Carreon, L. M. 2011. Working with ASEAN on Disaster Risk Reduction and Disaster Man-agement. Retrieved from www.odihpn.org/humanitarian-exchange-magazine/issue-50/working-with-asean-on-disaster-risk-reduction-and-disaster-management (accessed May 12, 2014).

Center for International Disaster Information (USAID). 2014. The Third Anniversary of Tohoku Tsunami. Retrieved from www.cidi.org/the-third-anniversary-of-tohoku-tsu nami/#.VP7tbv_9kqQ (accessed May 12, 2014).

College of Disaster Prevention and Mitigation, Department of Disaster Prevention and Mitigation, Ministry of Interior, Thailand. n.d. Collaborative Disaster Management in ASEAN. Retrieved from http://61.19.54.141/research/asean/book/ASEAN%20Disa ster%20Cop.pdf (accessed January 10, 2013).

Jakarta Post. 2012. Toward a Disaster-Resilient ASEAN Community. Retrieved from www. thejakartapost.com/news/2012/12/13/toward-a-disaster-resilient-asean-community.html (accessed May 12, 2014).

Ministry of Foreign Affairs, ASEAN Department. 2012. Disaster Management (Civilian). Retrieved from www.mfa.go.th/asean/contents/files/asean-media-center-20121218-09 5701-825006.pdf (accessed January 15, 2014].

NTS Alert. 2010. The Implementation of a Disaster Management Agreement in ASEAN: Towards Regional Preparedness. Retrieved from www3.ntu.edu.sg/rsis/nts/HTML-Ne wsletter/alert/NTS-alert-sep-1002.html (accessed January 10, 2013).

United Nations Economic and Social Commission for Asia and the Pacific (UNESCAP). 2011. Environment: Natural Disasters. In *Statistical Yearbook for Asia and the Pacific 2011.* Retrieved from www.unescap.org/stat/data/syb2011/escap-syb2011.pdf (accessed January 11, 2013).

United Nations Economic and Social Commission for Asia and the Pacific (UNESCAP). 2012. Environment: Natural Disasters. In *Statistical Yearbook for Asia and the Pacific 2012.* Retrieved from www.unescap.org/stat/data/syb2012/country-profiles/SYB2012 -Countryprofiles.pdf (accessed May 12, 2014).

United Nations Office for Disaster Risk Reduction (UNISDR). n.d. PreventionWeb. Retrieved from www.preventionweb.net (accessed January 12, 2013).

United Nations Office for Disaster Risk Reduction (UNISDR). 2010. Synthesis Report on Ten ASEAN Countries Disaster Risks Assessment. Retrieved from www.unisdr.org/files/18872_asean.pdf (accessed January 11, 2013).

Woods, L. N. 2010. Charting a New Course ASEAN-UN Post Nargis Partnership. Retrieved from www.asean.org/images/2012/publications/3.pdf (accessed January 20, 2014).

Interviews

Deputy Director of Policy and Strategic Planning Bureau, Department of Disaster Prevention and Mitigation, Thailand (Ms. Chatchadaport Boonpeeranut). Interviewed on February 16, 2013.

Director of Research and International Relations Bureau, Department of Disaster Prevention and Mitigation, Thailand (Mr. Chainarong Vasanasomsit). Interviewed on May 22, 2014.

Dispatched Emergency Coordinator, United Nations High Commission for Refugee (UNHCR), Haiyan Recovery Operation in Cebu-Tacloban, Philippines (Mr. Kannavee Suebsang). Interviewed on December 15, 2013.

Emergency Rapid Assessment Team, ASEAN ERAT personnel, Department of Disaster Prevention and Mitigation, Thailand (Mr. Arun Pinta). Interviewed on May 22, 2014.

Project Coordinator, United Nations Development Program (UNDP), Thailand (Mr. Kwanpadh Sudhidhammakit). Interviewed on February 17, 2012.

6 ASEAN's (non-)role in managing ethnic conflicts in Southeast Asia

Obstacles to institutionalization[1]

Chanintira na Thalang and Pinn Siraprapasiri

Introduction

Ethnic conflicts have long been a contentious issue for Southeast Asian states, as elsewhere in the developing world. Disparity and suppression in political, economic, and social arenas have led to discord and violence between ethnic groups. When violence turns into wars, peoples' lives are at risk. When people are at war, political, economic, and social developments are hindered. When war expands, this limits the capacity of the state to implement an effective rule of law. Moreover, war can spill over borders and can potentially change territorial borders. This makes ethnic conflict a bilateral and/or regional issue, where internal and international politics intersect.

Ethnic conflict resolution is never straightforward. Various factors such as diverse actors with conflicting goals, competing nationalisms, internal politics, and vested interests all play a part in complicating and frustrating opportunities in bringing an end to ethnic conflicts. While international organizations have become more involved in settling conflicts across the globe, there has been much reluctance among East Asian states to institutionalize a role for any regional organizations in the management of ethnic conflicts. Obstacles to institutionalization appear to be insurmountable.

By "institutionalization," this chapter adopts the conceptualization of the term proposed by the Introduction of this volume, where institutionalization refers to a process of regularizing and enhancing cooperative actions among a group of sovereign states for certain shared goals. Recent developments show that a number of ASEAN members have warmed to the idea of having a fellow ASEAN member involved in peace processes. However, external involvement is defined by the host state on an ad hoc basis as opposed to being institutionalized to regularize any set procedures.

This chapter examines two cases of armed ethnic conflicts, namely Aceh and Thailand's three southernmost provinces, from a comparative perspective. It also explores what role, if any, ASEAN or any other East Asian regional organization has played in these conflicts. Peace negotiations between the Indonesian government and the Free Aceh Movement (GAM) have resulted in the signing of the Memorandum of Understanding (MoU) in 2005 ultimately ending a three-decade long struggle for independence. In comparison, the case of Thailand's three southernmost provinces shows that the Thai government and armed groups have attempted talks for peace but without avail.

The two cases are selected for the following reasons. Firstly, they illustrate that the success and the failure of peace processes are dependent on internal configurations and not external pressure from either ASEAN as an institution or an ASEAN member state. Secondly, from a comparative perspective, this chapter explores the different ways and circumstances in which individual ASEAN member states have become involved in peace processes in the cases of Aceh and the three southernmost provinces of Thailand. In the case of Aceh, individual member states have played a role in monitoring the peace agreements of 2002–3 and again in 2005. In the case of the three southernmost provinces of Thailand, individual member states, namely Malaysia and Indonesia, have played a role in facilitating talks between the conflicting parties. Although individual ASEAN member states have been involved in settling ethnic conflicts in Southeast Asia, this is not based on institutionalized practices but: (a) is subject to the invitation of the host state; (b) is practiced on an ad hoc basis; and (c) is confined to a comparatively limited role, such as peace monitoring and facilitating. The absence of any institutionalized role for ASEAN is due to ASEAN member states' insistence on maintaining ethnic conflicts as a purely domestic matter. State sovereignty is further protected by security and cultural practices governing inter-state relations among ASEAN members emphasizing non-interference. Furthermore, it is highly questionable whether ASEAN possesses the capacity to take on such a role.

This chapter focuses on Southeast Asia to compare its cases. Thus, much of the discussion surrounds the role of ASEAN due to its existence as the only regional organization in the absence of an East Asian-wide organization. Furthermore, other East Asian regional security forums such as ASEAN Regional Forum (ARF) are to a certain degree an extension of ASEAN's security norms and practices.

Ethnic conflict management and international organizations

Many have argued that armed ethnic conflict has become one of the most significant challenges to global peace (Gurr 1993; Ryan 1995). Increasingly, international organizations (IOs) such as the European Union and the Organization for Security and Cooperation in Europe (OSCE) as well as individual governments have played various roles in different stages of conflict prevention and resolution across the globe. IOs can pressure conflicting parties to participate in peace talks or a power-sharing arrangement such as federalism or autonomy. They can act as mediators to advance accurate communication between the two parties and can foster an environment conducive to talks as well as offer alternatives (Ryan 1995: 108). Once a peace agreement has been settled, IOs can monitor peace agreements and become involved in peacekeeping.

Arguably, the United Nations (UN) remains the main institution with the legitimacy for ethnic conflict prevention. The UN has adopted various preventive measures to ensure that ethnic rights are respected rather than violated (Preece

1999: 204–206). For example, the 1966 International Covenant on Civil and Political Rights encourages states to respect minority rights, going as far as supporting autonomy though still respecting the boundaries of the existing state. The UN also promotes higher standards of living and respect for universal human rights, poverty reduction, democracy, and equitable socio-economic development as means of conflict prevention.

While the UN focuses its approach to ethnic conflict in the form of conflict prevention and minority rights protection, international interventions are conducted in a limited number of cases. Contrary to its original implications, the conception of self-determination does not guarantee the right of a nation of cultural or ethnic basis to form a separate state. Rather, self-determination became a right confined to the former colonized people under the Western rule. The idea was to allow such a right to be "exercise(d) once and for all and never again" (Heraclides 1991: 21). Efforts have also painstakingly continued to make the colonial constructed boundaries sacrosanct once most colonies were declared independent. If such a right was given to all ethnic nations, it would undoubtedly destabilize the international system given the great number of ethno-nationalistic movements. However, there have been exceptions made for circumstances perceived to be a threat to international peace and security as in the cases of the former Yugoslavia, Somalia, and more recently South Sudan, though this is a rarity rather than a norm. In many cases, international intervention is a case of selectiveness and subject to international politics and realpolitik behind the scenes.

The argument: obstacles to institutionalizing ASEAN's role in ethnic conflict resolution

While IOs have stepped up their contribution to conflict resolution and peace building, ASEAN as well as regional forums in East Asia have not followed suit. This chapter identifies three main obstacles, namely political, institutional, and operational barriers, which limit and prevent ASEAN's role in the management of ethnic conflicts in the region.

Political obstacles

Southeast Asian states remain guarded of their sovereignty; thus, the involvement of regional organizations in ethnic conflicts can create tensions on many levels. On one hand, there is the insistence by states that ethnic conflicts are purely a domestic matter. As such, the involvement of an external party can be construed as a violation of sovereignty. However, the nature of conflict itself makes it essential for the role of an external party during the various stages of a peace process such as conflict mediation and monitoring. Resolving conflict through the law of state is not a viable option as instruments of law enforcement are biased because the state and its agents such as the police and the military are a part of the conflict. Because of this, armed ethnic movements may find it hard to negotiate peace with states being the more powerful militarily. This is compounded by the high levels of mistrust between the two parties as a result of fighting.

In the past, leaders of ASEAN members, and consequently ASEAN as an institution, generally refrained from open criticism of their neighbors. There have been only a few exceptions by former Prime Minister Lee Kuan Yew and former Prime Minister Mahathir Mohamad who have voiced their concerns over issues that could destabilize the region, or during times of high bilateral tension. Other exceptions took place on less politically sensitive occasions such as Cyclone Nargis in 2008 when ASEAN Secretary-General Surin Pitsuwan called on all member states to provide urgent relief assistance through the framework of the ASEAN Agreement on Disaster Management and Emergency Response (AADMER). A deployment of an ASEAN Emergency Rapid Assessment Team (ERAT), made up of government officials, disaster management experts, and NGOs from member countries was considered a successful joint effort (Creac'h and Fan 2008). However, cases of ethnic and/or politically related conflict face much greater obstacles. As many states still struggle to claim that they have championed the universally accepted norms of democracy and human rights, they are reluctant to impose such norms on others. As seen in the past, there were no criticisms of military coups in Thailand, martial law in the Philippines, Indonesian actions in East Timor, or the use of detention without trial in Malaysia and Singapore (Funston 2000: 3).

However in recent years, a number of ASEAN members have warmed to the prospect of having a fellow ASEAN member involved in peace processes such as those in Aceh, Mindanao, and the South of Thailand, though this has been conducted based on agreements with individual states and not with ASEAN as an institution. Furthermore as the case studies of this chapter will show, the boundaries and the type of involvement of a fellow ASEAN state is dependent on what the host state is comfortable with. While this is a small step towards regional cooperation, many ASEAN member states that face challenges from ethnic conflicts still insist on protecting their sovereignty and refusing any third party involvement.

Institutional obstacles

The protection of state sovereignty is further enhanced by the principle of non-interference. Non-interference is a security and diplomatic practice not only held dear by ASEAN member states but also embraced by other East Asian security forums such as ARF. However, unlike the UN Charter, non-interference used as an ASEAN norm has never been clearly defined. In practice, ASEAN members refrain from actions ranging from criticizing a fellow member state to military intervention. This leaves very little room for ASEAN to have a role in ethnic conflict resolution, let alone conflict prevention similar to what is practiced by the UN; consequently, becoming a significant institutional obstacle. In the past, fear of instability at the domestic level was compounded by the perceived communist threat and the departure of their biggest ally, the USA after the Vietnam War that ended in 1975. Thus, during the Cold War, non-interference allowed the newly independent states of Southeast Asia that were pre-occupied with nation-building and state building to use brutal measures against their populations without the interference of their neighboring countries. Ironically, while non-interference has contributed to relative stability at the regional level, it has provided the opportunity for states to achieve stability at the domestic level through violent means.

With the Cold War over, discussion has been raised within ASEAN forums surrounding the question of ethnic conflict prevention and resolution. However, non-interference continues to be an institutional obstacle to developing regional cooperation in this area. One example would be the collaboration between ASEAN and the United Nations under the framework of the ASEAN/UN Conference on Conflict Prevention, Conflict Resolution, and Peace Building in Southeast Asia that started in 2001, which reveals mechanisms to cope with conflicts through cooperation among state agencies. This is in line with the UN's mandate as cited in the 1992 *Agenda for Peace, Preventive Diplomacy, Peace-making and Peace-keeping* to cooperate with other regional organizations across the globe to lessen the UN's burden and create a division of labor (UN 1992). In tandem with these developments, Indonesia proposed the creation of a regional peacekeeping force at the 2003 Bali Summit which was later reiterated in 2004 by Indonesia's foreign minister, Hassan Wirajuda. Indonesian support for such proposals is in line with Indonesia's acceptance of international mediation and peace monitoring on its own soil. As part of the peace agreement that ended three decades of conflict in Aceh, the Aceh Monitoring Mission (AMM) was established to monitor the agreement and support the demobilization process that started in 2005. The AMM consisted of officials from the European Union (EU) and individual ASEAN member states. However, other ASEAN member states were opposed to the idea, citing that having a peacekeeping force would go against the principle of non-interference (Pitsuwan 2011).

Another obstacle is persuading member states to see that these initiatives can be implemented without threatening state sovereignty. Many have maintained that ethnic conflicts are purely a domestic matter and continue to use military means to maintain control over their peoples, resources, and territories. Thus, the challenge is to convince ASEAN member states to see the benefits of non-violent means to resolving conflicts and peacekeeping. However, any peacekeeping force should be utilized as a means to preserve regional peace and stability as opposed to a military tool to threaten one another. It should be made clear that a peacekeeping force would conform with the three guiding principles for UN peacekeeping, namely consent of the parties, impartiality, and non-use of force unless in self-defense, which would serve to respect state sovereignty rather than violating it (UN 2014).

Not only is non-interference an obstacle to establishing a peacekeeping force, it also hinders cooperation in terms of conflict prevention. The ASEAN Intergovernmental Commission on Human Rights (AICHR), inaugurated in 2009 as a consultative body tasked with the mission of promoting human rights in the region, could potentially be developed to enhance the protection of minority rights. However ASEAN member states have stopped short of providing AICHR with any investigative and monitoring powers, rendering AICHR as a toothless body that lacks any authority to address human right violations in the region. Though there have been some developments including the establishment of the ASEAN Intergovernmental Commission on the Protection of the Rights of Women and Children and the ASEAN Committee on the Implementation of the ASEAN Declaration of the Protection of the Rights of Migrant Workers, AICHR has yet to explicitly mention the rights of minorities in its mandate.

Operational obstacles

While a peacekeeping force could significantly enhance regional cooperation in the area of ethnic conflict resolution, ASEAN may suffer from various operational obstacles. Reluctance to collectively intervene to stop the violence in East Timor in 1999 led ASEAN to establish the ASEAN Troika in 2000, enabling "ASEAN to address in a timely manner urgent and important regional political and security issues and situations of common concern likely to disturb regional peace and harmony" (ASEAN 2003). However, failure to respond to security situations post-2000 has not only illustrated ASEAN's reluctance but also its limited capacity. ASEAN did not react to inter-state conflicts between Thai and Burmese troops in 2001; and between Thai and Cambodian forces in 2009 as well as intra-state conflicts such as Aceh. While many ASEAN member states (Indonesia, Malaysia, Philippines, Brunei, Cambodia, and Thailand) have been involved in UN peace-keeping operations (UN 2014), many other states lack the experience, and in some cases, the political will, to engage in such activities at the regional level. If such initiatives are to be materialized and institutionalized, this would greatly enhance political and military cooperation within the region. So far, cooperation in the area of conflict prevention and peace building goes as far as establishing the ASEAN Institute for Peace and Reconciliation (AIPR) based on discussions from the November Summit in 2011. Most members envisioned that the center would take on a more research-focused role as opposed to taking on a more practical one with activities including research, capacity building, network building, and information dissemination (ASEAN 2013). AIPR would also help enhance cooperation among ASEAN think-tanks. While such initiatives are a good start, it still remains to be seen how ASEAN can achieve such goals and transform them into concrete and effective measures. Another cooperation is ASEAN Peacekeeping Centers Network (APCN), proposed by Indonesia in 2003 with the hope to help assist in the settlement of internal disputes such as the conflicts in Aceh and the southern Philippines. APCN came into effect in 2011, with its first meeting held in Kuala Lumpur in September 2012 and the second meeting in Bogor in September 2013 (Thayer 2014). Among its many objectives, APCN aims to utilize existing and planned national peacekeeping centers in ASEAN member states to establish regional arrangements for maintaining peace and stability. This initiative is still in its nascent state with only countries with national peacekeeping centers participating.

Precisely because political, institutional, and operational obstacles leave very little space for any ASEAN involvement, ethnic conflict resolution is a result of favorable domestic configurations rather than ASEAN or individual member states pressuring the two conflicting parties to negotiate. Conditions conducive to peace mediation and negotiations are never standard. Peace talks occur when there is a combination of opportunities as well as the ability and political will to seize the moment. Often, pure luck including a change of government and a ripe situation on the ground are crucial factors in bringing conflicting parties to the negotiating table. The comparison between the cases of conflict in Aceh and Thailand's three southernmost provinces exemplifies two contrasting examples. *Reformasi* post-Suharto has paved the way for more democratic means in resolving the conflict in Aceh, including peace negotiations. The Indonesian government has been relatively more open to third party involvement including the support of ASEAN individual member states in monitoring peace agreements in Aceh at various junctures. In comparison, the Thai government has been largely uncomfortable with any form of third party involvement. Thus, third party involvement has been limited to facilitating talks between the conflicting parties rather than mediating negotiations in search of a long-term solution to the conflict. The two cases illustrate that it is up to the host state to define the boundaries of any third party involvement. However, any third party involvement regarding a fellow ASEAN member state is conducted on a state-to-state basis and not with ASEAN as an institution or by existing institutionalized practices among ASEAN member states whether formal or informal.

The case studies

Based on the above discussion, this section will explore two cases of protracted ethnic conflicts in Southeast Asia in a comparative perspective. It will then examine what roles ASEAN member states have played in each of the conflicts.

The case of Aceh

The role of a fellow ASEAN member state in Aceh's peace process was minimal to begin with. However, as democracy began to flourish, Jakarta gradually became more accepting of an increased role for external parties in ethnic conflict resolution. In turn, various ASEAN member states have been involved in monitoring Aceh's peace process at various junctures. However, any involvement of an ASEAN member state was subject to what Jakarta deemed as acceptable.

The success of the 2005 Helsinki Peace Process in Aceh highlights favorable domestic conditions that helped foster a peace agreement. Firstly, Aceh had one prominent armed group, the Free Aceh Movement (GAM). Furthermore in 2005, Indonesia had a strong and more unified government. As such, there was no formidable opposition, not even from the military, when peace negotiations occurred. Secondly, at the time negotiations were being conducted, Indonesia enjoyed considerable political and economic stability. National stability enabled the political elites to focus without having their attention diverted by problems at the national level. Thirdly, the peace talks in 2005 were fortunate enough to have been brokered by a strong mediator.

There were no calls for the independence of Aceh until Dr. Teungku Hasan Muhammad di Tiro, a prominent businessman and aristocrat, founded the GAM in 1976. As a region rich in natural resources, perceptions of economic exploitation played a crucial role in igniting a sense of ethnic discontent towards Indonesian rule. Furthermore as a region ruled by a long line of Sultans, Aceh was promised autonomy in the 1950s; however, this never materialized. Soon after Suharto rose to power, hopes for autonomy diminished as Suharto's New Order consolidated and became more centralized. During the Suharto period (1967–1998), Jakarta responded to the conflict solely through military force. Initial support for GAM was marginal but gradually increased in the late 1980s due to mass human rights abuses that were committed on a wide scale. The sustained use of force by the state brought together a community that suffered common grievances under Jakarta's rule. By the mid-1990s, support had expanded to areas of Pidie, North Aceh and East Aceh (Sulistiyanto 2001: 441).

The unraveling of Suharto's regime in 1998 and subsequent democratization changed the way Jakarta dealt with the conflict in Aceh. While the use of force still remained in the early post-Suharto years, there was no doubt that democratization and reform at the national level encouraged more peaceful means of resolving the conflict. Not only were there peace talks but there were also talks of implementing some form of autonomy arrangement in Aceh as a means of managing ethnic relations. Altogether there were three attempts at resolving the conflict through peace talks. While the first two failed, the third produced a peace deal in 2005 which still stands today.

The first attempt to negotiate with GAM happened in 2000 under President Abdurraman Wahid (1999–2001). There was little involvement from either ASEAN as an institution or any of ASEAN's individual member states, mainly attributed to the effects of the Asian Financial Crisis of 1997–1998. ASEAN was suffering from growing irrelevance in the light of the crisis and its individual member states were coping with its aftermath. Hit with economic and social tensions, Southeast Asian states individually sought help from other governments, international agencies, creditors, and banks, as ASEAN provided no financial or monetary cushions for its member states. At this juncture, bilateralism with extra-regional institutions reigned over regional multilateralism.

Instead, talks were mediated by the Geneva-based Henri Dunant Center (HDC), a relatively young NGO that was established in 1999 by a group of humanitarian workers formerly associated with the International Committee of the Red Cross. By May 2000, the parties agreed on a Joint Understanding on a Humanitarian Pause which aimed to act as a means for confidence building measures and to open access for humanitarian aid. Subsequently, joint committees were set up to look after various aspects of the agreement. These committees consisted of representatives of the Indonesian government and GAM.

However, the Humanitarian Pause was short-lived and crumbled in 2001 amidst attacks against ExxonMobil's liquefied natural gas facilities. The government was quick to blame GAM (Jakarta Post 2000). The main obstacle to peace was that both sides were adamant about their objectives. On one hand, GAM insisted that it would not settle for anything less than independence. Furthermore, though the Acehnese had little confidence in Jakarta's promises, participating in negotiations that were mediated by an external party seemed like a good opportunity for GAM to internationalize the conflict. On the other hand, even though President Wahid initiated talks, there was much opposition from the political elites in Jakarta. No major political party supported the president's initiatives in Aceh and the Indonesian military was especially opposed to the potential destruction of national unity. They asserted that any agreement could only be based on the unitary state of Indonesia. There was also insistence that the offer of autonomy was the starting point of negotiations (Wiryono Sastrohandoyo, interview with author, Jakarta, June 24, 2005). However, the costs of participating in the peace deal seemed low enough for both sides to take the risk (Huber 2004: 18). Failure to gain the military's backing would later cause disruptions and collapse in 2001 and again in 2003 (during Megawati's presidency). Though talks went ahead, clashes on the ground continued. Despite Wahid being a key advocate for reconciliation with the Acehnese, the impeachment case against him, which began in the first half of 2001, overshadowed the peace process. Soon Wahid lost control of his government as it became increasingly disunited. This provided the space for the Indonesian military to take more coercive measures against GAM (McGibbon 2004: 40; Aguswandi 2004: 387). Subsequently, the peace process came to an end.

In 2002, Megawati Sukarnoputri's (2001–2004) efforts to initiate peace in Aceh started with granting the province "special autonomy" while the HDC brokered further peace negotiations. Other forms of international involvement included a group of "wise men" which consisted of foreign dignitaries and former diplomats including the former Secretary General of ASEAN, Dr. Surin Pitsuwan.[2] The wise men were selected for their expertise as well as international stature and connections to crucial states (Huber 2004: xi). Also recognizing the pitfalls of the Humanitarian Pause, the Joint Security Committee (JSC) was established to monitor the situation. The JSC comprised of representatives from GAM, the Indonesian military, and a neutral third party including unarmed military personnel from Thailand and the Philippines who were asked to serve as representatives of HDC and not their respective governments (Aspinall and Crouch 2003: 33). The JSC, headed by Thai Major General Tanongsuk Tuvinun and his deputy Philippine Brigadier General Nogomora Lomodag, stationed monitoring teams across Aceh.

Unfortunately, there were unfavorable factors that made this round more prone to failure than the previous one. Almost immediately the deal began to come apart. Special autonomy was never fully implemented and the manner in which it was imposed on Aceh with the absence of any consultation was immediately rejected by GAM. The Indonesian military were not supportive of the agreement. When both sides began violating the ceasefire, the JSC lacked the capacity to investigate and stop them. The JSC's capacity was limited to what was deemed acceptable to Jakarta. As it was, the government felt it had already made major concessions by allowing international monitors a role in the peace process.

Another factor was that Megawati's nationalistic views brought her closer to the military than her predecessor (Sukma 2003: 175). As one senior official had noted, Megawati had acted as "Bung Karno's daughter rather than a president" (confidential interview with author, June 15, 2005). Megawati felt that GAM's goal for independence was destroying the Indonesian nation or what her father, Sukarno, Indonesian nationalist hero, helped to create.

As the government favored a more military approach, the international environment post 9/11 encouraged it. Because of anti-terrorist rhetoric, governments were placing a great deal of importance on state security. At this juncture, the Indonesian government sought to take advantage of the changing context by labeling GAM as a terrorist organization. Parliamentarians began to lobby for more coercive means that gradually led to the imposition of martial law on May 19, 2003, which was extended again in November for an additional six months.

The third attempt to negotiate happened under Megawati's successor, Susilo Bambang Yudhoyono (SBY, 2004–2014), though Vice President Jusuf Kalla was the main proponent of the talks. The tsunami of December 26, 2004 shattered a region already mourning the daily loss of lives in the conflicts with the Indonesian military. Many media reports suggested that the Boxing Day tsunami was the determining factor that brought the two sides back to the negotiating table (BBC 2005). While the human catastrophe prompted the two sides to rethink their positions and re-open negotiations, steps to resurrect negotiations had started before the tsunami occurred. The post-tsunami context provided both sides with an opportunity to push for peace negotiations especially for those in the government supporting a peaceful resolution to the conflict. Both the military and GAM agreed to suspend hostilities to allow humanitarian aid to reach the territory devastated by the tsunami. The Indonesian military was also reassigned to assist with relief efforts. This differed from the previous talks where fighting occurred while negotiations were taking place. International interest was renewed in promoting a peaceful resolution to the conflict (Aspinall 2005: 20). The context enabled SBY and his deputy Jusuf Kalla to present the talks as a humanitarian response to the Boxing Day tsunami as opposed to a concession (Aspinall 2005: 21). As a result, both sides would not lose face.

On the whole, peace in Aceh could not occur without a number of factors. Firstly, both sides were more committed to the peace process than in previous attempts. On GAM's side, this had much to do with battle fatigue. Martial law in 2003 under the Megawati presidency, which was followed by civil emergency status, reduced GAM's capacity in combat. The military also implemented a number of limitations on the movement such as placing restrictions on printing facilities, postal services, and telecommunications (Jakarta Post 2003). Furthermore, rallies were held almost every day for Acehnese to repent their disloyalty to Jakarta, pledge their support for the state ideology, *Pancasila* and the 1945 Constitution, sing the national anthem and other patriotic songs as well as fly the Indonesian flag. A number of senior GAM personalities had been captured or killed. With the military gaining ground, GAM fighters were deeply demoralized. GAM capacity was reduced not only because of martial law but also because of its own actions. In order to fund the conflict, GAM had been involved in taxing the people which alienated pockets of the population. However, in areas that did support GAM, the people could not fully support the guerrillas and were limited by martial law. Because GAM needed the population for its guerrilla warfare, this ultimately deprived GAM of its crucial source of food, supplies, and intelligence (ICG 2005b: 4).

On the government's side, there was a strong and capable state that had the ability to appease key stakeholders and make the peace deal attractive to all winners and losers of the conflict. It was Vice President Jusuf Kalla who had a personal interest in reviving a peace deal with the Acehnese, though the initiative was not without opposition from some of the political elite. However, the wider population which formerly supported a military approach in resolving the conflict now deemed such measures politically incorrect (Sukma 2006: 219).

Secondly, there were smoother civil-military relations. Peace negotiations during the administrations of Wahid and Megawati were disrupted by the military. Another difference was that both Wahid and Megawati needed the military for their political survival. In comparison, SBY-Kalla defied any opposition and were more prepared to defend their policies. This was due to Kalla's relatively strong position within the Indonesian polity. First of all, the SBY-Kalla government had more control over the military. Secondly, Kalla is also a chairperson of Golkar, the leading party of the 2004 legislative elections. Hardliners were becoming less influential in the government (Sukma 2006: 219–220).

The military's disruptions to peace processes had much to do with the vested interests the military had in areas of conflict. Because the military receives only 30 per cent of its operating expenses from the national government, it needs to finance the remaining 70 per cent from other sources. As the government does not provide the military with sufficient resources, military enterprises include illegal logging, drug production and trafficking, and prostitution, as well as "security" payments viewed by many as extortion. Though figures are exaggerated, it has been widely believed among security personnel that when they "come to Aceh with an M16, they leave with 16 M" (million rupiah) (Large 2008: 64). This notion stems from the military's involvement in illegitimate business which is a known "secret" that is generally accepted by the public (Bradford 2004). As the Indonesian military had a stake in the Acehnese conflict, SBY sidelined the conservative generals who were obstacles to peace. Furthermore, SBY allocated a 526 billion rupiah package to the military. This in turn convinced the military that the peace deal was economically advantageous to them (Mietzner 2006: 51).

Thirdly, peace in Aceh would not occur without a strong mediator. The Crisis Management Initiative (CMI) was an independent and non-profit organization that would not have succeeded in bringing peace to Aceh if it was not for its Chairman, the former Finnish President Martti Ahtisaari. Both CMI and Ahtisaari kept the process unofficial and independent which suited the Indonesian government as it did not want to internationalize the conflict. Based on the experience of failed attempts (under the administrations of Presidents Wahid and Megawati) at peace mediating and monitoring in Aceh, many supported the idea of bringing in a body with more diplomatic and political clout. It was because of these short-comings of the previous attempts at peace, GAM had strongly supported the idea of having an international peacekeeping force. Naturally, this was strongly rejected by the Indonesian state. Eventually, the parties decided to compromise by accepting the creation of the AMM. Though some AMM personnel consisted of serving military officers, it was a civilian body with the purpose of monitoring the situation in Aceh post-MoU.

Originally, the Indonesian state had wanted the AMM to consist of staff from only ASEAN member countries as in the previous peace process in 2002–3. However, GAM had insisted on the EU's involvement. Finally, the EU was not only involved in monitoring the peace process but it predominantly managed the AMM. In comparison, the authority of AMM was greater than the previous body, the JSC (Aspinall 2005: 46).[3] It was a relatively short term mission of six months from September 2005 to March 2006. Thereafter, the presence of monitors gra-dually reduced until the mission ended at around the time of the December 2006 elections. AMM was charged with overseeing the demobilization that had helped to reduce the distrust between GAM and the military (ICG 2005c: 1–2). The AMM was also empowered to rule on disputes between the conflicting parties. While a few incidents of violence occurred, AMM was able to resolve and handle these well (ICG 2005b: 7). On the whole, AMM has been credited for its role in peace monitoring in Aceh.

While the AMM consisted of personnel from EU member states and some ASEAN member countries, ASEAN as an institution had very little to do with AMM. Rather, individual ASEAN member states including Thailand, the Phi-lippines, Malaysia, Singapore, and Brunei were involved in coordinating and fielding monitors. The reasons behind this are two-fold. Firstly, the principle of non-interference prevented any involvement in what was considered as Indonesia's domestic concern. Rather, ASEAN's role along with the involvement of the EU and CMI was defined upon invitation by the Indonesian government. The scope of authority and duration of the external parties involved was set by the peace agreement which was heavily influenced by the Indonesian government. Secondly, it was doubtful that the EU would have allowed the participation of other ASEAN states especially the CLMV countries that were perceived to have very little regard for human rights abuses in their own countries. In the past, EU–ASEAN and US–ASEAN relations have suffered due to differences over Myanmar. In 1996, when ASEAN granted Myanmar observer status, it was faced with opposition from the United States, Canada, and the EU. In 1997, the western disapproval of ASEAN's handling of Myanmar's human rights violations and anti-democratic stance became louder when the EU refused to attend the EU–ASEAN summit unless Myanmar was only a "passive observer" (Peterson Institute for International Eco-nomics 2014). In 1998, the USA could not host the 14th ASEAN–US Dialogue meeting because it would not issue visas to Myanmar delegates, while the EU excluded Myanmar from participating in the second Asia–Europe meeting held in London (Chalermpalanupap 1999). As well as a series of trade bans and visa restrictions, the EU and the USA punished Myanmar and its "accomplice" by boycotting ASEAN-led forums after incidents of unrest such as the 2003 pro-democracy crackdown and the 2007 Saffron Uprising. Thus, ASEAN as an institution could not be made responsible for the coordination and management of peacekeepers. Instead, individual member states of ASEAN with an "acceptable" record on human rights sent their own personnel.

While ASEAN member states made a valuable contribution to peace monitoring after a peace deal was signed in 2005, the main factors that ended the conflict were predominantly internal as opposed to external. Essentially, the conflict could not have ended without a stable government and a strong mediator. Most importantly, the peace deal had to be attractive enough to both parties in the conflict. Peace talks began with clear action plans and reasonable offers, including amnesty for GAM, decommissioning, concrete economic programs, and most importantly, an autonomy package that was labeled as "self-government."[4] Self-government meant Aceh would exercise authority in all sectors except for foreign affairs, external defense, national security, monetary and fiscal matters, justice, and freedom of religion. The new Aceh Governing Law (LoGA, Law 11/2006) devolved additional fiscal and economic powers to the province. As a result, Aceh retained 70 percent of "all current and future hydrocarbon deposits and natural resources in Aceh as well as in the territorial sea surrounding Aceh" (MoU article 1.3.4). In terms of devolving political powers, the LoGA provides for the direct election of the Provincial Governor and District Heads (*Bupatis*); while subdistrict heads (*Camats*) are still appointed by the Bupati.

Since the signing of the peace deal in 2005 in Aceh, the people have enjoyed relative peace. Generous funds from the international community have helped spur local development. Though imperfect, the progress of reconciliation, governance, and democracy has contributed to the transition towards peace.

The case of the three southernmost provinces of Thailand

In comparison to the Aceh peace process, the case of Thailand's three southernmost provinces illustrates limited involvement from a fellow ASEAN member state. While the Indonesian government invited a few ASEAN member states to monitor the Aceh peace processes in 2002–3 and 2005, only Malaysia and Indonesia have been involved in facilitating talks among the conflicting parties in Thailand's three southernmost provinces. The term "facilitator" refers to a third party's role in open-ended dialogue without the authority to conclude an agreement or a resolution to the conflict. Talks conducted at various junctures are predominately secretive and not necessarily sanctioned by the Thai state. These talks can at best be described as confidence building measures as they do not go as far as negotiating terms of a peace agreement, unlike the case of Aceh. This can be attributed to the Thai government's stance on international involvement of what it perceives is a purely domestic matter which should be handled internally. Furthermore, many prominent Thai political elite believe that negotiations would upgrade the status of the armed groups operating in Thailand's southernmost provinces level with the state. However, the bigger challenge lies within the nature of the conflict itself. Firstly, a multiplicity of actors involved in the conflict posed a major difficulty. Unlike Aceh where there is one dominant armed ethnic group, there is a multiplicity of armed groups that rarely cooperate with each other. Secondly, Thailand's governments have been fraught with divisions and instability since 2006 which has diverted the attention of policy makers from resolving the conflict.

The three southernmost provinces of Thailand, namely Pattani, Narathiwat, and Yala, are home to 1.3 million Malay Muslims. This is equivalent to 80 percent of the population of the three provinces, but only accounts for 3 percent of Thailand's total population which is predominantly Buddhist (McCargo 2012: 217). Malay Muslims only form a small group within the wider Muslim population in Thailand. From time to time, the conflict has affected neighborly relations between Thailand and Malaysia. The complexity of the problem does not only lie within historical, cultural, ethnic, and linguistic ties with northern Malaysia but also the fact that up to 200,000 people hold dual citizenship (Thai and Malaysian). Although irredentist or separatist aims were supported by the local population in neighboring Kelantan (in northern Malaysia), this development neither transcended into a significant security challenge nor did it have an effect on bilateral relations in any way. During the Cold War, the ASEAN bond and the external security threat had kept Malaysia on Thailand's side.

Since its formal incorporation into the Thai state in 1909, policies towards managing the three border provinces have aimed to assimilate the Malay Muslim population. These policies included forcing them to take Thai names, outlawing the traditional Malay dress, and banning the use of the Malay language, a slow destruction of Malay culture. As a result, these policies exacerbated the longstanding opposition and resistance to Siamese rule.

As assimilation policies continued, mounting discontent was gradually transformed into armed resistance in the 1960s up to the early 1980s. Unlike other armed ethnic movements in the region such as the former GAM, the conflict in the south consisted of a multiplicity of armed groups, some of which have separatist underpinnings but many of which still lack clear goals. As many as 60 armed groups were operating at the time, some of which had political goals while others were purely criminal groups capitalizing on the situation. These groups rarely cooperated (ICG 2005a: 6). This generation of fighters includes groups such as *Barisan Revolusi National* (BRN), Patani United Liberation Organization (PULO) and the National Patani Liberation Front (BNPP) (ICG 2005a: 6–8).

The situation changed in the 1980s when the Thai state began implementing policies with a good degree of accommodation. The Prem Tinsulanonda administration (1980–1988) began pursuing economic development and an offer of increased political participation and broad amnesty to the insurgents. Most significantly, there were some institutional arrangements which provided a channel for local participation. The government oversaw the creation of the Southern Border Provinces Administrative Centre (SBPAC) which has been credited with maintaining good relations with community leaders and giving the locals a sense of ownership over certain local matters. Another achievement was the joint civilian-military-police (CPM 43) which has been instrumental in forming intelligence links with community leaders. As a result of these accommodative counter-insurgency measures, a number of groups disbanded while some began to splinter. Thereafter, violence gradually subsided.

However, relative calm was short-lived and hostilities re-emerged in 2001 in the form of small sporadic incidents. In January 2004, the conflict resurfaced in the form of well-coordinated attacks on the army camp in Narathiwat. These attacks were followed by two other major incidents including the shootings at the historical mosque of Krue-Ze and the demonstrations at Tak Bai. Both incidents resulted in a considerable loss of lives. Dismissing the perpetrators as common bandits, the Thaksin administration's (2001–2006) response was heavy-handed and included extra-judicial killings. At the time Thaksin came to power, his closest advisors were bound to the task of pleasing him as opposed to finding a long-lasting solution to the conflict. Unfortunately for the south, most of these advisors endorsed hawkish approaches (Pathmanand 2006: 83). Furthermore, Thaksin dismantled SBPAC and CPM 43 in 2002 and transferred operations from the military to the police. His ill-advised decision not only brought an end to a delicate balance between state officials and the locals, essentially disrupting local governance, but it also further exacerbated inter-agency rivalry between the police and the local military.

Since the re-emergence of the conflict in 2004, militarization of the area has happened at an alarming rate, which reflects the state's prioritization of security over conciliatory measures. From January 2004–April 2014, there were 6,097 conflict-related deaths. According to statistics, the majority of deaths were Muslim (Jitpiromsri 2014). Moreover, the planning and the precision of the attacks carried out by the insurgency groups have become more sophisticated.

In tandem with the government's military responses to conflict, there have been some attempts to manage the conflict through a more peaceful means. Dialogue initiatives with the insurgents in Thailand's three southernmost provinces started in 2005 with some degree of involvement from a fellow ASEAN member state, although as in the case of Aceh, involvement was conducted by individual ASEAN member states and not through ASEAN's multilateral structures. While ASEAN member states have been involved in monitoring peace in Aceh in 2002–3 and 2005, involvement in Thailand's southernmost provinces has come in the form of facilitating talks. As outlined above, "facilitator" refers to a third party that brings conflicting parties together to engage in a dialogue which is open-ended and a facilitator does not have the authority to conclude an agreement or seek a resolution to conflicts. This differs from a mediator who is entrusted with the authority to help foster communication between the parties in a search for a favorable outcome, such as occurred in Aceh.

However, facilitating dialogue was not always carried out with formal endorsement by the Thai government. Throughout the decades, talks have taken place in various secret locations around the world. Only at the recent 2013 talks has the government openly acknowledged talks. Since the re-emergence of violence in the 2000s, two ASEAN member states have attempted to resolve the conflict in Thailand's three southernmost provinces. However, most of these meetings were initiated by various state agencies with very little coordination, with other relevant state agencies or stakeholders in the conflict reflecting a deeply polarized and fragmented Thai state. One example would be the talks facilitated by Malaysia. In October 2005, former Malaysia leader Mahathir Mohamad had arranged meetings between Thai officials and Muslim leaders from Thailand's south with the aim of brokering a ceasefire. Mahathir emphasized that he was conducting talks in the capacity of head of a non-government organization, Putrajaya-based Perdana Global Peace Organization (PGPO), to avoid any tension that might affect bilateral relations. The talks were held in Langkawi after Mahathir had consulted former Thai Prime Minister Anand Panyarachun though Prime Minister Thaksin Shinawatra at the time refused to endorse the process. Thaksin's aggressive approach to the conflict would not only prove to be a significant obstacle to talks but also to regional relations. The Tak Bai incident almost endangered ASEAN's unity as Thaksin threatened to walk out of ASEAN's summit held in Vientiane if any member brought up the issue for discussion (*The Nation*, November 27, 2004). His confrontational approach also created a wedge between the Thai and Malaysian governments where bilateral relations reached an all-time low. Consequently, the conditions imposed on the talks made it impossible to achieve any favorable results.

Several insurgent groups known as the old-guard leaders that were active during the 1980s attended the meetings, while the Thai government was represented by Armed Forces' Security Centre chief Lieutenant-General Vaipot Srinual and General Winai Pathiyakul of the National Security Council, though in unofficial capacity (*The Nation*, October 8, 2006). This suggested that the Thai state at the very least acknowledged the talks. However, it was questionable how much authority, if any at all, the Thai representatives were given. It was reported that an agreement known as the Joint Peace and Development Plan for South Thailand, was produced as a result but was never ratified by the Thai government (*The Nation*, October 12, 2006). This was not surprising due to Thaksin's opposition to talks at the time. All in all, talks could at best be described as a confidence building exercise.

Later attempts in late 2008 in Bogor (Indonesia) were made, only this time talks were moderated by the then Vice President of Indonesia Yusuf Kalla, who was credited with the peace deal in Aceh (*Antara News Agency*, September 22, 2008). While Presidential spokesman Dino Patti Djalal was quick to claim success (Khalik and Nurhayati 2008), the Thai Foreign Ministry immediately announced that the government had not formally supported the talks (*Bangkok Post*, September 27, 2008). While news reports suggested that a number of groups were present, the violence that continued was evidence that those at the talks had very little control over the situation on the ground (*The Strait Times*, September 27, 2008). Consequently, the 2008 peace talks failed to produce any agreement of substance (*Asia Sentinel*, October 18, 2006).

Attempts to resume the peace process occurred again when Thailand's former Prime Minister-in-exile Thaksin Shinawatra in collaboration with Malaysia's Premier Najib Razak jump-started a new process. Thaksin's involvement in the process has aroused suspicion from many sides, especially his political opponents, who hold him at least partly responsible for the dramatic escalation of the insurgency during his period as prime minister. Some believe that the peace talks are an attempt to rehabilitate Thaksin's image (McCargo 2013). Najib Razak was also keen to see a deal concluded, especially after UMNO's poor showing in the previous 2008 and 2013 elections (McCargo 2014: 8). Favorable coverage would hopefully give his party a boost in Kelantan, a stronghold of the opposition party, Pan Malaysian Islamic Party (PAS) (Wheeler 2014). PAS members sympathize with the Malay Muslims across the border and have criticized Thailand's policies in suppressing separatism.

On February 28, 2013, the National Security Council (NSC) and Hasan Taib, the "liaison" for the BRN, signed an agreement in Kuala Lumpur to hold talks. Each side, respectively the Thai government and the insurgency groups, were represented by a delegation of 15 people. The Thai government's team, headed by Lt. Gen Paradorn Pattanathabutr (secretary general of the NSC), consisted of high ranking officials, representatives from security agencies, university academics, and religious leaders from the Southern provinces (*Bangkok Post*, March 27, 2013). Prior to the second round of talks, the BRN went public on YouTube to lay out demands which included the recognition of the BRN as representatives of the Patani Malays; upgrading Malaysia's role to mediator; involvement of external parties such as ASEAN in the process; the establishment of a special administrative arrangement; and the release of all detained fighters. In turn, the insurgents were asked to prove to the Thai government that they were capable of controlling the situation on the ground. However, signs were not encouraging. Violence increased and attacks became more dramatic and daring. One example is a bomb attack on April 5, 2013 which killed Yala deputy governor Issara Thongthawat and an assistant governor in Yala's Bannang Sata district. Furthermore, banners bearing messages opposing talks were also found (Harai 2013). The locals believe that the perpetrators are state-backed officials opposed to the talks (Wheeler 2014). However some seem to suggest that the spoilers of peace are the insurgents themselves aiming to show their opposition to various aspects of the peace process (confidential interview with NGO worker, January 24, 2014). It had been widely reported that Malaysia's Special Branch Police had forcibly brought the exiled separatist leaders to the table (Davis 2013; ICG 2012: 21). As such, they did not have the blessing of the *Dewan Pimpinan Party*, or DPP, the highest decision-making body of the BRN. As violence increased, the BRN called for their five demands to be ratified by the Thai parliament as a condition for continued talks (Pathan 2013). Unfortunately, the Thai government's response came too late as Hassan posted a clip on YouTube on December 1, 2013 referring to himself as a "former" BRN delegate. Talks were suspended at the end of 2013.

Though this is the first time Bangkok has publicly acknowledged the peace process (previous attempts at talks were conducted in secret), it is questionable whether the government is really committed to resolving the conflict with an actual peace deal. To date, the government has not offered any incentives attractive enough for the insurgency groups to stop their fight. Consequently, there is little suggestion that the Thai government has any inclination to upgrade the status of peace talks from a confidence building exercise to negotiation for a more long lasting peace deal. Towards the end of 2013, the Yingluck Shinawatra government passed an amnesty bill aimed at clearing Thaksin's conviction for corruption and abuse of power. The move ignited large-scale protests, led by former Democrat Party deputy leader Suthep Thaugsuban, which eventually paved the way for a military coup in May 2014. While the coup has brought about national stability, divisions within the Thai polity still remain. Though in 2014 the coup leaders met with Malaysia's leaders in an attempt to revive the defunct peace process, one of the biggest challenges to peace is domestic, rooted in national instability and a fragmented insurgency movement.

The conflict in Thailand's three southernmost provinces consists of a multiplicity of insurgency groups with various demands. This affects talks because it is not clear if leaders can control the situation on the ground. Many analysts indicate that the militant movements form a leaderless rebellion or a network without a core (McCargo 2008: 10). As one report suggests, insurgency groups in the south operate autonomously in small cells consisting of roughly 10 or more militants known as the *juwae* (deriving from *pejuangan*, a Malay term for struggle). It is also believed that there is no knowledge of people outside one's cell, though communication between cells can be conducted through symbols or codes (ICG 2008). This is to prevent a compromise of overall operations if one of the *juwae* is captured (confidential interview with author, April 15, 2009). The vast majority of the *juwae* are most likely linked with the BRN. Although this connection must not be construed as organized in a strict hierarchical order, some analysts believe that there is some level of command and control over the militants on the ground (Pathan 2015). This loose coalition intentionally makes recruitment, organization, and mobilization difficult to detect. BRN also commands influence over a network of Islamic schools believed to be a crucial recruiting ground for the insurgency.

PULO operates on a much smaller scale than the BRN. However it is far from united, with three different people claiming to be its leader (*The Nation*, November 26, 2013). Other active groups include *Permuda*, under the influence of BRN, Pattani Islamic Mujahideen Movement (GMIP) vying for an independent Islamic state, and PULO which aims for a secular independent state (ICG 2005a, i). The multiplicity of groups is further complicated by the lack of coordination between them. Because the insurgency groups remain divided over goals which vary from seeking outright independence, autonomy, or justice as well as the means of achieving these goals, the structure of the insurgency in the south will remain fluid (Liow and Pathan 2010: 8). Though lacking a hierarchical command, some degree of coordination has existed in past attacks such as the January 4, 2004 raid by armed groups on Narathiwat's army camp.

While the multiplicity of armed groups with various different demands and little knowledge of who they are is an obstacle to peace talks, it remains questionable how serious the successive governments have been about such talks. When talks do occur, the government seems to lack an offer serious enough to entice the insurgents to give up their cause. Many analysts have suggested a form of decentralization or autonomy arrangement but Bangkok is still reluctant to go that step further (McCargo 2008). In the past, the reluctance to start talks or initiate some degree of autonomy has had much to do with the Thai public's fear that autonomy is a step away from independence. However, since 2008, Thailand has experienced vigorous debate on autonomy as a means of managing the conflict in Thailand's three southernmost provinces. Prior to 2008, decentralizing governance was a taboo subject. Consequently, there was very little serious dialogue about something seen as a threat to a unitary kingdom (Jitpiromsri and McCargo 2008: 407). One of the forerunners of recent debates is the well-respected social critic, Dr. Prawase Wasi, who advocated nationwide devolution in the form of "monthon" in 2008. Leading academics Srisompob Jitpiromsri and Duncan McCargo (2008: 414–418) suggest creating an administrative body equivalent to a *thabuang* or minor ministry that would come under the direct supervision of the Office of the Prime Minister to prevent it from being captured by military and bureaucratic interests. They also propose agencies to oversee cultural and judicial matters. General Chavalit Yongchaiyudh proposed Pattani City – covering Pattani, Narathiwat, and Yala – in 2009, but Abhisit was against the idea (Satha-Anand 2012: 146).

The source of the problem is not a shortage of suggestions, but Thailand's overly centralized governance structure. Apart from Bangkok, governors of Thailand's 76 provinces are directly appointed by the Ministry of Interior. Governorships in the three southernmost provinces are considered as undesirable posts usually reserved for punishing incapable officials or sidelining political opponents. Furthermore, most Thai military leaders are largely uncomfortable with peace talks as they perceive the whole process as a step towards international intervention and eventual partition (ICG 2012: 20). Part of the problem is that the responsibility of talking to the insurgents has shifted from civilian agencies to the military ever since General Prayuth Chan-Ocha took power in 2014 (Pathan 2015). The increasing military budget may be an incentive for the military to continue its presence and prominence over Thailand's three southernmost provinces and its opposition to talks. From 2004 to 2014, the Thai government spent 206 billion baht (US$6.2 billion) on counter-insurgency measures (Deep South Watch 2014).

Political instability at the national level has compounded the problem. Since 2006, Thai politics has been polarized by intense divisions and violence. Political tensions have also manifested in the form of mass movements, often disrupting the functioning of the government of the day. Various tactics have included seizing government buildings and at one point setting fire to one of Bangkok's major department stores and occupying Bangkok's main airports, Don Mueng and Suwannabhumi. National instability has affected the conflict in the South in two ways. Firstly, instability at the national level diverts the attention of policy makers. An issue such as a remote conflict in the South evidently becomes secondary. Likewise, political uncertainty in Bangkok is also a disincentive for insurgents to take peace initiatives such as talks seriously.

Secondly, showing disapproval of governments through street protests rather than via elections means a discontinuity of policies as well as talks. As such, throughout the post-2006 period, there has been a clumsy mixture of military and conciliatory measures. These policies are rarely coordinated and most importantly, lack cohesive long-term initiatives in resolving the conflict. Successive Thai governments have been preoccupied with mass street protests which at various junctures have not only turned violent but have brought governments to a standstill. The fight for political survival not only puts the conflict on the back burner but also discourages more permanent and cohesive measures for conflict resolution. On the other hand, it is highly questionable how interested the past governments have been in the matter itself. Various initiatives in the past few years have been contradictory, often reflecting the conflicting parties at the national level. As such, it is not surprising that there has been a limited role for ASEAN member states in Thailand's southern conflict. Since 2005, Malaysia and Indonesia have been the only two ASEAN member states involved in facilitating talks both with and without endorsement from the Thai government. As such, roles have been limited in comparison to the involvement of individual ASEAN states in the peace process in Aceh in 2005. The 2013 talks mark the first time Bangkok has acknowledged talks, implying that the Thai government has conceded the fact it cannot resolve the conflict without Malaysia's help. From time to time, the conflict has been a sticky issue for Thailand's relations with Malaysia. Malaysia has approached the southern problem with caution and sympathy (Funston 2006). Apart from ethnic affinities that the population of Thailand's southernmost provinces shares with northern Malaysia, dual citizenship facilitates cross-border movement. While Malaysia has openly acknowledged meetings organized by Thailand's insurgents and has allowed them to reside in Malaysia, it has maintained that it will not allow any armed activity against the Thai state (Liow and Pathan 2010: 77). Malaysia cannot seem to be too hawkish in its approach for fear of a domestic backlash. At the same time, Malaysia has a stake in securing a peaceful border between the two countries. It has been willing to help but Thailand refuses to view Malaysia as an honest broker. Because the conflict is intertwined on many levels with Malaysia, Thailand cannot avoid Malaysia's involvement in any conflict resolution process. However, the problem is not so much Malaysia's involvement as it is the lack of any incentives attractive enough for the insurgency groups to cease their struggle. To resolve the conflict Bangkok needs to shift from talking to negotiating a peace deal. That also means expanding the role of the third party from facilitator to mediator.

Conclusion: ASEAN's (non-)role in settling ethnic conflicts

What role can regional organizations like ASEAN play in the management of ethnic conflicts? Are there any set procedures that allow fellow member states to become involved in settling ethnic conflicts in Southeast Asia? This chapter has identified key barriers that hinder the institutionalization of any regional cooperation in this area.

To begin with, Southeast Asian states remain guarded of their sovereignty, which has proven to be a significant political obstacle to advancing any procedures in regards to settling ethnic conflicts. While it has been argued there are no institutionalized practices for ASEAN as an institution to have a role in settling ethnic conflict, some ASEAN member states have been involved in various stages of conflict resolution and management. However this has been conducted on a bilateral basis and upon invitation rather than being proceeded by ASEAN through intervention. Thus, the host states retain the authority to define the boundaries of any role played by a fellow ASEAN member state. The two cases examined show the different roles played by different ASEAN member states in the respective conflicts. At different junctures, the Thai government has allowed a fellow ASEAN member state to play a comparatively limited role as a facilitator in the conflict in Thailand's southernmost provinces. This can be attributed to the Thai military's fear of foreign intervention in what it perceives to be purely a domestic issue.

On the other hand, Indonesia has displayed a more open attitude towards third party involvement. Individual ASEAN member states have contributed to monitoring peace agreements. As the case of Aceh shows, a few ASEAN states have supported peace monitoring in 2002–3 and again in 2005, though this was conducted within the confines of what the Indonesian government was comfortable with. However, the two cases show that the success or failure of conflict resolution is dependent on domestic factors rather than the role of third party involvement. For the case of Thailand, failure to resolve the conflict can be attributed to a lack of stability at the national level. There also is a multiplicity of groups operating in Thailand's south which makes it even harder to resolve the conflict should the Thai government decide to upgrade talks to negotiations. Most importantly, a highly centralized Thai state makes it difficult to introduce a form of decentralization as a means of resolving the conflict. Talks that have occurred in the recent years could at best be described as a confidence building exercise but the Thai government has yet to offer something more substantial to entice the insurgents to give up their fight for independence.

The case of Aceh provides a counterpoint to the Thai situation. Favorable internal conditions contributed to the success of peace talks in Aceh in 2005. One of the main differences between the conflicts in Aceh and Thailand's three southernmost provinces is the number of actors in the respective conflicts and unity amongst actors. The only armed group challenging the Indonesian state in Aceh was GAM. This is not to deny some divisions within GAM and other non-armed groups operating in Aceh but it was clear who was in command. The SBY government experienced political and economic calm and strong standing in the polls at the time of the 2005 negotiations which enhanced the government's capacity to see the peace deal through. Furthermore, Aceh had a strong third party mediator. Mediators are essential because of the high levels of mistrust between the two parties that have been locked in armed conflict for decades. However, third party involvement tends to be successful only when they possess credible sanctions. With the case of Aceh in 2005, the AMM, which was a combined effort between the EU and a few ASEAN member states, helped enhance the credibility of the process. This is important, as an NGO cannot possess enough leverage to induce the two parties to stop fighting, especially when one party is a state. Getting international organizations involved such as the EU increases the stakes for the conflicting parties should they violate any terms of the peace accord. However, the success of the actual negotiation must be attributed to the CMI and its Chairman, former Finnish President Ahtisaari. Most importantly, the Indonesian government was willing to negotiate an autonomy package which was attractive enough for GAM to cease armed opposition to the state.

Such political obstacles are further compounded by institutional obstacles, namely the principle of non-interference. Non-interference was introduced to create a strong region based on strong states, not strong regional institutions during the Cold War. To strengthen the state at the expense of creating a strong institution meant the protection of state sovereignty. However, as times change and new challenges are brought to the fore, maybe it is time to re-think the norms and principles that ASEAN once upheld. Since 2000, there has been more discussion about various roles ASEAN should play in settling ethnic conflicts including Indonesia's proposal for a regional peacekeeping force. However this was immediately rejected by fellow ASEAN member states citing the principle of non-interference. Paradoxically, many ASEAN member states are involved in UN peacekeeping operations but refuse to introduce such activities in their own backyard. Based on the same UN principles for UN peacekeeping including consent of all conflicting parties, an ASEAN peacekeeping force could ensure peace and security within the region while respecting the principle of non-interference as opposed to violating it. Thirdly, while turning these proposals into reality would greatly enhance cooperation and deepen integration on both political and military levels, it is highly questionable whether ASEAN possesses the capacity to perform such tasks. As mentioned, only a few member states contribute to UN peacekeeping operations while others might not be open to the idea or may lack the capacity to do so.

Notes

1 The authors would like to thank the editors of this volume and Duncan McCargo for their insightful comments and suggestions.
2 Apart from Dr. Surin Pitsuwan, the group of wise men includes US Marine General Anthony Zinni, former ambassador Budimir Loncar, former Swedish Diplomat Bengt Soderberg, and Sir Eric Avebury as an advisor.
3 Monitoring mechanisms are more formalized, both the Indonesian government and GAM are not allowed to veto decisions and decisions made by the AMM are binding to both parties.
4 "Autonomy" had negative connotations associated with past failed promises made by the Indonesian government.

References

Aguswandi. 2004. Civil Society: The Missing Piece in Peace Building in Aceh. In Annelies Heijmans, Nicola Simmonds, and Hans van de Veen, eds, *Searching for Peace in Asia Pacific: An Overview of Conflict Prevention and Peacebuilding Activities.* Boulder, CO: Lynne Rienner Publishers, pp. 381–398.

Antara News Agency. 2008. President Receives South Thailand Delegation to Bogor Peace Talks. September 22. www.indonesia-ottawa.org/information/details.php?type=news_copy&id=5356 (accessed September 30, 2013).

ASEAN. 2003. *Handbook on Selected ASEAN Political Documents*, www.asean.org/archi ve/pdf/HBPDR.pdf (accessed October 22, 2015).

ASEAN. 2013. ASEAN Institute for Peace and Reconciliation Kicks Off in Jakarta. www.asea n.org/news/asean-secretariat-news/item/asean-institute-for-peace-and-reconciliation-kick s-off-in-jakarta (accessed December 10, 2013).

Aspinall, Edward. 2005. *The Helsinki Agreement: A More Promising Basis for Peace in Aceh?* Washington, DC: East-West Centre Washington.

Aspinall, Edward and Harold Crouch. 2003. *The Aceh Peace Process: Why it Failed.* Washington, DC: East-West Centre Washington.

Bangkok Post. 2008. Govt "Not Party" To Peace Talks. September 22. www.bangkokpost. com/220908_News/22Sep2008_news03.php (accessed September 30, 2013).

Bangkok Post. 2013. Nine Separatist Groups to Join Malaysia Talks 15-delegate Panels on Both Sides Confirmed. March 27. www.bangkokpost.com/news/security/342511/ nine-separatist-groups-to-join-malaysia-talks (accessed March 31, 2013).

BBC Online. 2005. Aceh Rebels Sign Peace Agreement. http://news.bbc.co.uk/2/hi/asia -pacific/4151980.stm (accessed August 15, 2013).

Bradford, John F. 2004. The Indonesian Military as a Professional Organization: Criteria and Ramifications for Reform. *Explorations in Southeast Asian Studies* 5(2). http:// scholarspace.manoa.hawaii.edu/bitstream/handle/10125/2824/John%20F.%20Bradford% 20-%20The%20Indonesian%20Military%20as%20a%20Professional.pdf?sequence=1 (accessed October 22, 2015).

Chalermpalanupap, Termsak. 1999. ASEAN-10: Meeting the Challenges. www.asean.org/ resources/item/asean-10-meeting-the-challenges-by-termsak-chalermpalanupap (accessed November 30, 2014).

Creac'h, Yves-Kim and Lilianne Fan. 2008. ASEAN's Role in the Cyclone Nargis Response: Implications, Lessons and Opportunities. Humanitarian Practice Network, Issue 41. www.odihpn.org/humanitarian-exchange-magazine/issue-41/aseans-role-in-the-cyclon e-nargis-response-implications-lessons-and-opportunities (accessed February 4, 2014).

Davis, Anthony. 2013. No Peace Tomorrow for South Thailand. *Asia Times Online*, July 12. www.atimes.com/atimes/Southeast_Asia/SEA-01-120713.html (accessed July 31, 2013).

Deep South Watch. 2014. http://deepsouthwatch.org/deepnumber (accessed December 11, 2014).

Funston, John. 2000. ASEAN and the Principle of Non-Intervention-Practice and Pro- spect. A paper presented at a Council of Security Cooperation in the Asia Pacific 7th Comprehensive Security Working Group Meeting in Seoul, on December 1-2, 1999. Institute of Southeast Asian Studies. www.kysd.org/ngosplatform/wp-content/uploa ds/2012/12/002-12-Asean-and-the-Principle-of-Non-Intervention-Pratice-and-Prospe cts-www.iseas_.edu_.sg_.pdf (accessed January 5, 2014).

Funston, John. 2006. Thailand's Southern Fires: The Malaysia Factor. A substantially revised version of a paper prepared for the Academy of the Social Sciences in Australia/ UNESCO/University of New England. Workshop on Migration Challenges in the Asia- Pacific in the 21st Century. November 28–29, 2006, University of New England, Armidale. www.une.edu.au/asiacentre/PDF/No26.pdf (accessed July 31, 2013).

Gurr, Robert Ted. 1993. *Minorities at Risk: a Global View of Ethnopolitical Conflicts.* Washington, DC: U.S. Institute of Peace.

Harai, Waedao. 2013. Anti-peace Sign Put Up in Narathiwat. *Bangkok Post*, April 16. www.bangkokpost.com/news/security/345583/banner-opposing-peace-talks-malaysia n-flags-erected-overnight-in-narathiwat (accessed May 31, 2013).

Heraclides, Alexis. 1991. *The Self-Determination of Minorities in International Politics*. London: Frank Cass.

Huber, Konrad. 2004. *The HDC in Aceh: Promises and Pitfalls of NGO Mediation and Implementation*. Washington, DC: East-West Center.

International Crisis Group (ICG). 2005a. Southern Thailand: Insurgency, Not Jihad. Policy Briefing No. 98.

International Crisis Group (ICG). 2005b. Aceh: A New Chance for Peace? Asia Briefing No. 40.

International Crisis Group (ICG). 2005c. Aceh: So Far, So Good. Crisis Group Asia Briefing No. 22.

International Crisis Group (ICG). 2008. Thailand: Political Turmoil and the Southern Insurgency. Policy Briefing No. 80.

International Crisis Group (ICG). 2012. Thailand: The Evolving Conflict in the South. Policy Briefing No. 241.

Jakarta Post. 2000. Security Forces to Guard State Facilities in Troubled Aceh. November 1. www.thejakartapost.com/news/2000/11/01/security-forces-guard-state-facilities-trou bled-aceh.html (accessed July 31, 2013).

Jakarta Post. 2003. Covering Both Sides a Tough Challenge in Aceh War. May 23. www. thejakartapost.com/news/2003/05/23/covering-both-sides-tough-challenge-aceh-war .html (accessed July 31, 2013).

Jitpiromsri, Srisompob. 2014. An Inconvenient Truth about the Deep South Violent Conflict: A Decade of Chaotic, Constrained Realities and Uncertain Resolution. www. deepsouthwatch.org/node/5904 (accessed October 22, 2015).

Jitpiromsri, Srisompob and Duncan McCargo. 2008. A Ministry for the South? New Governance Proposals for the Thailand's Troubled South. *Contemporary Southeast Asia* 30(3): 403–428.

Khalik, Abdul and Desy Nurhayati. 2008. Thailand: Govt and Muslims Agree to End Southern Conflict. *Jakarta Post*, September 22. www.thejakartapost.com/news/2008/ 09/22/thai-govt-muslims-agree-end-conflict.html (accessed September 30, 2013).

Large, Judith. 2008. The Challenge of Hidden Economies and Predation for Profit. *Accord* 20: 64–5. www.c-r.org/downloads/20_Indonesia.pdf (accessed June 2, 2014).

Liow, Joseph Chinyong and Don Pathan. 2010. Confronting Ghosts: Thailand's Shapeless Southern Insurgency. Lowy Institute. www.voltairenet.org/IMG/pdf/Thailand_south ern_insurgency.pdf (accessed September 2, 2013).

McCargo, Duncan. 2008. *Tearing Apart the Land: Islam and Legitimacy in Southern Thailand*. Ithaca, NY: Cornell University Press.

McCargo, Duncan. 2012. Southern Thailand: The Trouble with Autonomy. In Michelle Ann Miller, ed., *Autonomy and Armed Separatism in South and Southeast Asia*. Singapore: ISEAS, pp. 217–234.

McCargo, Duncan. 2013. Understanding the Southern Thai Peace Talks. Asia Peacebuilding Initiatives, June 27. http://peacebuilding.asia/understanding-the-southern-tha i-peace-talks (accessed July 31, 2013).

McCargo, Duncan. 2014. Southern Thailand: From Conflict to Negotiations? Lowy Institute. www.lowyinstitute.org/files/mccargo_southern-thailand_0.pdf (accessed September 2, 2014).

McGibbon, Rodd. 2004. *Secessionist Challenges in Aceh and Papua: Is Special Autonomy the Solution?* Washington, DC: East-West Center.

Mietzner, Marcus. 2006. *The Politics of Military Reform in Post-Suharto Indonesia: Elite Conflict, Nationalism, and Institutional Resistance.* Washington DC: East-West Center.

Pathan, Don. 2015. Educating the BRN for the Sake of Peace in Deep South. *The Nation*, February 18. www.nationalmultimedia.com/opinion/Educating-the-BRN-for-the-sake-of-peace-in-deep-so-30254288.html (accessed November 1, 2015).

Pathan, Don. 2013. Ball Now in Govt's Court as BRN Peace Talks Look to Be Over. *The Nation*, August 10. www.nationmultimedia.com/opinion/Ball-now-in-govts-court-a s-BRN-peace-talks-look-to-30212321.html (accessed August 12, 2013).

Pathmanand, Ukrist. 2006. Thaksin's Achilles' Heel: The Failure of Hawkish Approaches in the Thai South. *Critical Asian Studies* 38(1): 73–93.

Peterson Institute for International Economics. 2014. Case Studies in Sanctions and Terrorisms. www.iie.com/research/topics/sanctions/myanmar.cfm (accessed December 2, 2014).

Pitsuwan, Fuadi. 2011. Time for an ASEAN Peacekeeping Force. *The Diplomat*, May 2. http://thediplomat.com/2011/05/02/time-for-asean-peacekeeping-force (accessed July 31, 2013).

Preece, Jennifer Jackson. 1999. Self-Determination and Minority Rights. In Ho-Won Jeong, ed., *The New Agenda for Peace Research*. Aldershot: Ashgate, pp. 179–210.

Ryan, Stephen. 1995. *Ethnic Conflict and International Relations.* Aldershot: Dartmouth.

Satha-Anand, Chaiwat. 2012. When Autonomy is not an Option?: Governing Violence in Southern Thailand. In Rajat Ganguly, ed., *Autonomy and Ethnic Conflict in South and Southeast Asia*. New York: Routledge, pp. 138–155.

Sukma, Rizal. 2003. Secessionist Challenge in Aceh Problems and Prospects. In Hadi Soesastro, Anthony L. Smith and Han Mui Ling, eds, *Governance in Indonesia Challenges Facing the Megawati Presidency*. Singapore: Institute of Southeast Asian Studies, pp. 165–181.

Sukma, Rizal. 2006. Indonesia and the Tsunami: Responses and Foreign Policy Implications. *Australian Journal of International Affairs* 60(2): 213–228.

Sulistiyanto, Priyambudi. 2001. Whither Aceh? *Third World Quarterly* 22(3): 437–452.

Thayer, Carl. 2014. ASEAN and UN Peacekeeping. *The Diplomat*, April 25. http://thediplomat.com/2014/04/asean-and-un-peacekeeping (accessed April 30, 2014).

United Nations (UN). 1992. *An Agenda for Peace, Preventive Diplomacy, Peacemaking and Peace-keeping.* (accessed September 16, 2015) www.unrol.org/files/A_47_277.pdf.

United Nations (UN). 2014. What is Peacekeeping? www.un.org/en/peacekeeping/operations/peacekeeping.shtml (accessed April 1, 2014).

Wheeler, Matthew. 2014. Thailand's Southern Insurgency. *Southeast Asian Affairs* 2014 (1): 319–335.

Part 3

Levels of cooperation

7 Institutionalization of sub-regional cooperation

The case of the Greater Mekong Sub-region

Nguyen Quoc Viet

Introduction

In the early 1990s, Southeast Asia saw the emergence of sub-regional cooperation initiatives that cut across national boundaries. Three important programs were adopted: the Greater Mekong Sub-region (GMS), the Indonesia-Malaysia-Thailand Growth Triangle (IMT-GT), and the Brunei Darussalam-Indonesia-Malaysia-Philippines East ASEAN Growth Area (BIMP-EAGA). Indeed, sub-regionalism is a growing phenomenon in East Asia today, as manifested in the rapid emergence of sub-regional growth triangles and transnational economic areas that encompass geographically contiguous countries and subnational areas. It is expected that these sub-regional initiatives promote the advantages of geographical proximity and economic complementarity. Since border restrictions have been eased in East Asia with the end of the Cold War, political and economic reforms in socialist countries, and trade and investment liberalization among market economies, the GMS Program and similar sub-regional programs can potentially be an effective framework for narrowing the development gap in the region.

This chapter considers, in particular, cooperation within the Greater Mekong Sub-region (GMS), a region of 2.6 million km^2, a population of over 255 million people, and one that is rich in natural and human resources (Krongkaew 2004). While challenges remain, GMS cooperation initiatives and its related programs can also be seen as a successful case of sub-regional cooperation. This chapter thus takes up some key questions offered in the introduction of this volume. Specifically, if "institutionalization" is the process of regularizing and harmonizing behavior among a group of sovereign actors, to what extent can we say that Mekong sub-region cooperation has contributed to new "institutions" of durable rules, expectations, and interests? What drives and constrains cooperation? How does it relate to or affect more multilateral institutionalization processes as those in ASEAN? And to what effect for regional relations and its political geography?

Evolution of Greater Mekong Sub-region as sub-regional institutionalization

In the early 1990s, the GMS countries recognized the importance of cooperation for economic development, drawing the attention of many politicians, donors, policy makers, and researchers, in the region as well as other countries in the world (ADB 2004, 2010a; Thang, 2005; King 2002; Mehtonen et al. 2008). Facing a series of challenges, such as poverty and national infrastructure limitations in terms of transport, energy, telecommunications, health, and education, GMS governments have been aware that enhancing cooperation among them can over-come these difficulties. However, the question is how to develop effective mechanisms given sub-regional states' limited development and resources. Coop-eration offers one way to facilitate sub-regional development. Aided by interna-tional organizations and donors, especially the Asian Development Bank (ADB), the Greater Mekong Sub-region Economic Cooperation Program – or GMS Program – was started in 1992, with the participation of five Southeast Asian states (Cambodia, Lao People's Democratic Republic (Lao PDR), Myanmar, Thailand, and Vietnam) and Yunnan province in China (Dosch and Hensengerth 2005). In 2004, Guanxi-Zhuang also joined the program. The creation of the GMS Program in 1992 can be seen as providing an important initial step towards the creation of an institutional setting for greater cooperation.

The purpose of the GMS Program is to improve infrastructure and expand the scale of trade and investment among the countries in the sub-region (Bhattachar-yay 2009). Supported by the ADB, GMS's members believe that the GMS Pro-gram and projects will provide the foundation for enhanced connectivity and promote economic relations between the countries in the sub-region (ADB 2012). Practical developments in cross-border trade, as well as intra-regional trading, investment, cooperation in electricity system development, exploitation and use of the water resources of the Mekong River, and the development of tourism both contribute to and confirm the success of GMS cooperation. The program has helped member countries implement high priority sub-regional pro-jects and initiatives, and foster financial support from development partners and other important stakeholders. In addition, projects also facilitate and contribute to cooperation not just among the countries in the GMS sub-region, but also between them and other regions in Asia and elsewhere in the world (Krongkaew 2004). The acceleration of the GMS Program has brought concrete results and contributed to the shared vision of a prosperous, integrated, and harmonious area.

In December 2002, demand for greater sub-regional cooperation was addi-tionally evidenced by the holding of the GMS's first summit in Phnom Penh, Cambodia, celebrating 10 years of sub-regional cooperation. Particularly notable was the full participation of the Chinese government, not just the representatives of Yunnan as had been initially the case. Such commitment from government leaders has been very important and indicative of a high level of political commit-ment. At that meeting, leaders unanimously adopted 11 key programs of the GMS Program of ADB, which focuses on eight areas, namely infrastructure, transportation, energy, telecommunications, tourism, trade and investment, human resources and environment. At that 2002 summit, states also conducted ministerial meetings in transport, telecommunications, energy, tourism, environment, human resource development, trade and investment, and control of drug trafficking (ADB 2004). Their agreement on a strategic framework (GMS-SF) for GMS cooperation for the period of 2002–2012 and also the Phnom Penh Plan for Development Management (PPP) can be seen as milestones in terms of GMS cooperation.

Of GMS initiatives, the agreement on cross-border transportation (CBTA) may be the most important and successful sub-regional institutional arrangement among GMS countries (ADB 2004, 2008, 2012). This project is based on agreed-upon general principles of cooperation, namely, economic equality and mutual respect, shared prosperity and aspiration to a commonwealth of the region, and joint pursuit of common goals. Its aim is to facilitate trade, unity on financing, and the implementation of a North–South economic corridor. The 13th ministerial summit in 2003 agreed to develop a strategic framework based on "3C" strategies of the GMS, namely, enhancing connectivity, improving competitiveness, and creating a greater sense of community.

In the same year, GMS cross-border transportation agreements (CBTA) took effect in all six countries. The CBTA is now constituted by 16 annexes and three protocols, as agreed by the Member Countries on March 20, 2007. The CBTA also includes a number of bilateral MOUs which comprise CBTA annexes. Figure 7.1 details the institutional structure of CBTA.

Although there are questions about the efficacy of the CBTA and its MOUs, the development of GMS economic corridors (the East–West, North–South, and

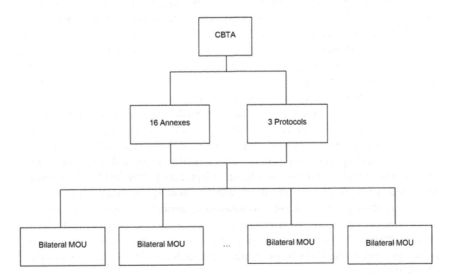

Figure 7.1 GMS cross-border transportation agreements chart
Source: ADB 2002, cited in Ishida 2008: 125.

Southern corridors) has been especially notable. First introduced at the 7th GMS ministerial meeting in 1998, these economic corridors are good illustrations of the sub-regional cooperation taking place. The creation of a network of roads connecting the sub-region will also reduce the cost of transporting goods and people from one corner of the region to the other (ADB 2008, 2012).

With regard to the transport sector, the main objectives include: (i) developing priority transport corridors linking each sub-region and promoting trade and investment, (ii) reducing the intangible barriers in people travel, and movement of goods and services, and (iii) developing and coordinating strategies to ensure that the development of transport corridors leads to the diversification of agriculture, industrialization, and the creation of employment opportunities (Bhattacharyay 2009). In addition, states have taken efforts to (i) improve the major transport links in the East–West Economic Corridor (EWEC), North–South Economic Corridor (NSEC), and Southern Economic Corridor (SEC); (ii) build, negotiate, adopt, and implement cross-border transport agreements (CBTAs) in the GMS countries; and (iii) convert the three economic corridors into official corridors.

In March 2006, the 10th session of the Sub-regional Transport Forum (STF) adopted the GMS Transport Sector Strategy Study (TSSS) (Stone and Strutt 2010). This was followed by the adoption of a plan of action at the STF conference at Bangkok on May 8–9, 2007. From that conference, some efforts have been implemented to put the plan into action, including investment research and establishing a Corridor GMS–BF Consulting Committee of EWEC in 2006. In addition, there are plans for the broader economic and social development of other priority GMS corridors.

Perhaps the second most successful example of GMS sub-regional cooperation is the 2004 Strategic Framework for Action on Trade Facilitation and Investment (SFA–TFI), which aims to energize GMS cooperation on trade and investment. SFA–TFI was endorsed by the 2nd GMS Summit, identifying goals, guiding principles, motivation strategies, and priority areas in trade and investment. The SFA–TFI has created a fundamental platform for the reality of the second strategic thrust of the current GMS Strategic Framework and involves promoting and facilitating intra- and extra-GMS trade, investment, and tourism.

Under the strategic framework related to trade and investment promotion is also cooperation in agriculture. The GMS Program has helped member countries to build strategies in sub-regional cooperation in agriculture, as well as enabling the formation, funding, and operation of issues linked to expanded cross-border trade in agrifood products and climate change adaptation (ADB 2011). According to the GMS Strategic framework, there will be cross sub-regional cooperation in agriculture through the first pillar to modernize agriculture, trade and investment in the context of sub-regional linkages and infrastructure development (Bhattacharyay 2009). The sub-regional cooperation in agriculture is expected to help reduce poverty in the GMS by promoting sustainable livelihoods and food security (ADB 2004).

As regards energy, cooperation has focused in three main areas: (i) promoting the development of commerce in the GMS to assist in the full development and use of the potential energy of the sub-region, (ii) facilitating the development of an infrastructure grid connected through transmission lines built to connect various electrical systems among GMS countries, and (iii) promoting private sector investment in GMS electricity projects (ADB 2004). A fourth area was added after the sharp increase in oil prices in the 2005–2006 period. This is the expansion of cooperation including the development of alternative and renewable energy sources, energy efficiency, and energy security.

In 2004, the GMS countries took another step in institutionalizing sub-regional cooperation. At their 13th Ministerial Summit in China, they adopted a plan of action (POA) for the 2004–2008 period towards ensuring the effective implementation of priority programs under the GMS-SF. For each sector of cooperation, this POA identifies necessary measures, the corresponding outputs expected, and time frame of implementation. The POA has provided a useful management tool to monitor and evaluate the progress of implementation of the GMS-SF.

The 2nd GMS Summit in China in July 2005 and 3rd GMS Summit in Laos in March 2008 took additional steps towards institutionalizing sub-regional cooperation with new governmental commitments in four main areas: development of common infrastructure, improvement of the trade and investment environment, improvement of social equality and environmental protection, and strengthened partnership cooperation. Under the banner of "Strengthening partnership for the prosperity of the common wealth," senior leaders attending the 3rd GMS Summit confirmed the continued promotion of the cooperation program. At the 4th GMS Summit in 2011, leaders and policy makers solidified 20 years of GMS cooperation with a new GMS-SF for 2012–2022. The new GMS-SF builds on the commitment and institutional arrangement that all member countries should integrate GMS priorities into their national development plans towards promoting regional development and encouraging greater GMS integration as part of a broader process of further integration within the ASEAN region.

In 2005, the GMS countries launched GMS Core Environment (CEP) which is a response to growing concern about the environmental impacts of rapid economic development. Administered by ADB and also by the governments of six countries, the Working group on Environment was founded to address the environmental challenges of the sub-region with a strong mission given by the GMS Ministerial Conference environmental in Shanghai in May 2005 and then by the GMS leaders at the 2nd GMS Summit in Kunming, Yunnan, China in 2005. CEP is intended to: (i) guarantee important ecosystems and the environmental quality of GMS economic corridors; (ii) ensure that investments in critical sectors such as hydropower, transport, and tourism are sustainable; (iii) conserve biodiversity and provide a protected areas corridor; (iv) identify and implement sustainable financing strategies and market mechanisms to preserve the natural systems of the GMS region; (v) integrate environmental issues into national and sub-regional plans, and develop and apply environmental indicators to measure progress towards a sustainable path to development; and (vi) establish a secretariat to provide full-time support in the implementation of the Sub-regional Working Group on Environment (WGE).

Sub-regional cooperation on environmental issues in the GMS provides a good example of close cooperation between agencies, national environmental organizations and international areas. A tradition of such partnerships developed from the start of the program and sub-regional cooperation has been generally maintained since then. In this regard, organizations such as the United Nations Environment Program, the Mekong River Commission (MRC), the International Union for the Conservation of Nature (IUCN), World Wildlife Fund (WWF), and ADB have been working closely with the environmental agencies of GMS countries on a number of sub-regional projects implemented by WGE.

As mentioned above, the GMS Program has been successful in maintaining a collaborative approach for sub-regional cooperation and institutionalization for more than 20 years. The viability of its sub-regional approach to common challenges is evidenced in both new cooperative activities and the provision of public goods and services experienced by states in the Mekong sub-region.

Box 7.1 Key ADB-GMS flagship programs and principles

The GMS has implemented, through various projects, the following 11 flagship programs:

1 The North–South Economic Corridor
2 The East–West Economic Corridor
3 The Southern Economic Corridor
4 The telecommunications backbone
5 Regional power interconnection and trading arrangements
6 Facilitation of cross-border trade and investment
7 Enhancement of private sector participation and competitiveness
8 Development of human resources and skills competencies
9 A strategic environment framework
10 Flood control and water resource management
11 GMS tourism development

The selection of the 11 key GMS flagship projects is on the basis of the following six principles:

1 Programs and projects should reflect a balance between economic growth, human resource development, poverty reduction, and environmental protection.
2 The project can attract a number of countries in the sub-region, not necessarily including the six GMS members.
3 The renovation and restoration of existing facilities are a higher priority than the construction of new facilities.
4 Funding should be encouraged for capital projects from both government and private sources.

5   Regular meetings and exchange of information by stakeholders is essential and is the driving force for the development cooperation.
6   The cooperation projects should be selected and designed to not harm the interests of any other country, whether in the present or future.
Sources: ADB (2011) – GMS EC framework 2012–2022, and ADB (2005).

Institutional arrangements of GMS cooperation

As for the institutional structure of the GMS, the sub-regional arrangement shares some common features with more broadly regional frameworks covered in earlier chapters. For example, the GMS is not a rules-based organization, and many of its sub-regional units such as the Mekong Tourism Coordination Office and the Environment Operations Center have no legal standing or sustainable funding arrangements (ADB 2008, 2010b). But while the GMS may not display institutionalization in the sense of formal and legal structure, it is still illustrative of institutionalization processes if we consider the regularization and normalization of both sub-regional and more broadly regional cooperation and integration efforts. This is evidenced, for example, in its comprehensive cooperation institutional arrangements and programs (ADB 2010b; Bhattacharyay 2010). Via a relatively flexible and activities-based approach comprised of specific development projects, hundreds of projects have been designed and implemented under the GMS Program over the last 20 years. These include the GMS Program of ADB, the Mekong River Commission (MRC), ASEAN–Mekong Basin Development Cooperation (AMBDC), the Summit ACMECS (Ayeyawady, Chao Phraya, Mekong Economic Cooperation Strategy), the GMS Business Forum (GMS–BF), and the triangular development cooperation mechanism and programs. These mechanisms and programs also take place at multiple levels of cooperation.

Initially, the main activities of the GMS cooperation were conducted via annual ministerial meetings, which were supported by senior official meetings. These GMS Program Ministerial Conferences provide the sub-region's first and most important regional institutional mechanism for sub-regional cooperation. Held annually since 1992, the Ministerial Conferences have been responsible for discussing and adopting, for example, the ADB's Initiative Cooperation of Greater Mekong Sub-region (GMS Program) and other key projects.

As noted above, in 2002, GMS cooperation gained another important mechanism – namely, the GMS Summit involving the heads of government, such as Prime Minister or deputy Prime Minister. At that summit, the six original participants (again, Cambodia, Laos, Myanmar, Thailand, Vietnam, and Yunnan province in China) were joined by Guangxi Province, China. GMS cooperation thus receives attention from the highest level. The GMS Summit of Leaders is normally held every three years, in contrast to the Ministerial Conferences which are held annually, though there may also be extraordinary meetings of leaders and senior officials. Normally, the GMS Summit of Leaders involves decisions on common policies, agreements, and commitments to the action plan of the GMS Program. Figure 7.2 shows the management arrangements of the GMS Program.

Underneath the Summit of Leaders and Ministerial Conferences, the participating GMS countries have also established national coordinating committees of GMS cooperation that also involve leaders and members of related collaborative industries. Those committees are responsible for advising their governments on the related issues of sub-regional cooperation and development. In addition, industry forums, working groups, specialized consultancies or specialized task-forces are also formed in preparation for higher-level conferences and meetings. Sector working groups organized by member countries and the ADB provide additional cooperative venues. So far, nine working groups have been established under this cooperation mechanism (see Box 7.2).

Box 7.2 List of GMS working groups

1   GMS Sub-regional Transportation Forum (STF)
2   Sub-regional Telecommunication Forum (STCF)
3   Electric Power Forum (EPF)
4   GMS Working Group on Human Resource Development (WGHRD)
5   Sub-regional Working Group on Environment (WGE)
6   GMS Business Forum (GMS-BF)
7   Sub-regional Investment Working Group (SIWG)
8   GMS Tourism Working Group (TWG)
9   Working Group on Agriculture (AGA)

(Ishida 2008: 117)

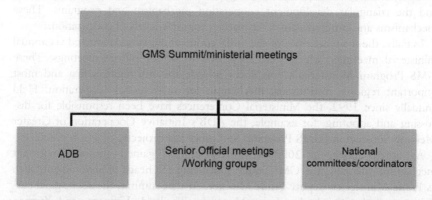

Figure 7.2 Management arrangement chart of the GMS Program
Source: Author drawing from ADB (2012).

The most important institutional arrangement for the GMS Program is the development of inter-government commitments and agreements which are in the form of multilateral agreements to implement the GMS-SF. During the last 20 years, many GMS commitments and agreements have been established such as: the Greater Mekong Sub-region Economic Cooperation Program (GMS-ECP), Agreement on Cross-Border Transportation (CBTA), Strategic Framework for Action on Trade Facilitation and Investment (SFA-TFI), The Phnom Penh Development Plan (PPP), and so on (ADB 2008, 2010a, 2012). Vietnam's agreements and institutional activity under the GMS framework provide an illustration of the kind of cooperation pursued (see Box 7.3).

Box 7.3 List of GMS institutional arrangements/framework: Vietnam

1 The formulation, negotiation, and finalization of the GMS Cross Border Transport Agreement (CBTA)
2 The formulation of a Strategic Framework for Action on Trade Facilitation and Investment (SFA-TFI)
3 Study on a Regional Indicative Master Plan on Power Interconnection in the GMS
4 Facilitation of regional power trade coordination and development, and environmentally sustainable electricity infrastructure in the GMS
5 Prevention of HIV/AIDS among Mobile Populations and promotion of Regional Communicable Diseases Control
6 Capacity building program for GMS officials under the Phnom Penh Plan for Development Management (Phases 1–4)
7 Formulation of, and agreement on, a Strategic Environment Framework and development and implementation of the Core Environment Program and Biodiversity Conservation Corridor Initiative
8 Prevention of Trafficking of Women and Children and Promoting Safe Migration in the GMS
9 Promotion of agriculture sector cooperation
10 Poverty reduction and environmental management in remote watersheds and critical wetlands in the GMS
11 Development of Cross-Border Economic Zones between PRC and Vietnam
12 Accelerating the implementation of the Core Agriculture Support Program
13 Improving Farmers' Livelihood through Rice Information Technology
14 Improving Farmers' Livelihood through Post Harvest Technology
15 Trans boundary Animal Disease Control for Poverty Reduction in the GMS (Phases 1 and 2)
16 Expansion of Sub-regional Cooperation in Agriculture in the GMS
17 Integrating Human Trafficking and Safe Migration Concerns for Women and Children into Regional Cooperation
18 HIV/AIDS Prevention and the Infrastructure Sector; HIV Prevention and Infrastructure: Mitigating Risk in the GMS

19   Strengthening Human Resource Development (HRD) Cooperation in the GMS
20   Implementation of the GMS HRD Strategic Framework and Action Plan
21   Strengthening the Coordination of the Greater Mekong Sub-region
22   Support for Implementing Action Plan for Transport and Trade Facilitation in the Greater Mekong Sub-region.

(ADB (2011): Vietnam in GMS Program)

As suggested, GMS cooperation has also involved a network of international donors and partners, whose participation has been integral to GMS cooperation. Of these, the ADB has provided around $5 billion in loans and grants for GMS projects. Other development partners have provided around $4.6 billion, and the GMS governments themselves have provided $4.3 billion. In addition, ADB and other development partners have supported 172 technical assistance projects with a total cost of $233 million for project preparation, capacity development, economic and sector work, and coordination and secretariat assistance. The ADB has played the role of lead development partner, coordinator, and honest broker in the GMS Program (ADB 2011). ADB has also approved a total of 203 regional technical assistance (RETA) projects, amounting to $231.4 million for project preparation, capacity building, policy advice and studies on various areas of GMS cooperation. ADB provided $100.1 million of its own funds, with other development partners providing co-financing totaling $111.6 million and GMS governments, $19.7 million (ADB 2012).

Clearly, the ADB institutional arrangement plays a critically important part in the development of GMS sub-regional cooperation programs. Partly this stems from the ADB Charter, which mandates it to promote economic growth and cooperation in the Asia and Pacific region by supporting the growth of developing member countries (DMCs). As per its establishing agreement in 1966, the ADB should give "priority to those regional, sub regional, as well as national projects and programs which will contribute most effectively to the harmonious growth of the region as a whole."

Besides the GMS Program, GMS sub-regional cooperation also takes the form of other formal or informal institutional arrangements, which can be among all of the six countries or a smaller group of member states. These arrangements may be bilateral among GMS countries. They may also be more localized, for example, between provinces, regions, or localities of different GMS countries. One example is the Triangle development programs. These development programs cover 10 provinces in the border areas of the three member countries of Vietnam, Laos, and Cambodia, which includes eight main areas of cooperation. Another example is the Golden Triangle Cooperation Program that was supported by the Thai and Chinese governments. In fact, there were many golden triangle programs formed between Thailand and other GMS countries in which the main purpose has been to develop the transport network upstream in the Mekong Delta.

An additional institutionalized mechanism of cooperation is the Mekong River Commission (MRC), which was set up in April 1995 between four representatives of member countries of Cambodia, Laos, Vietnam, and Thailand under their Agreement on Sustainable Development of the Mekong Delta. The main concern of the MRC is sustainable and equitable use of water and other resources, and the protection of the ecological environment of the Mekong River Basin. The different program activities pursued include plans for basin development, the introduction of general principles and procedures regulating the use of water resources, the maintenance of water quality and quantity, and assessment of environmental impact in the use of water resources (Dosch and Hensengerth 2005). The main limitation of MRC projects, however, lies in the fact that only four of the six GMS countries participate in the commission. More specifically, the absence of the two upstream countries (namely China and Myanmar) greatly limits the efficacy of MRC projects, since the source of the problems is often upstream. This is despite efforts to promote implementation mechanisms and dialogue with those two states.

While the MRC is illustrative of a smaller cooperative enterprise within the Mekong sub-regional framework (a kind of sub-sub-regional cooperative mechanism), the ASEAN-Mekong Basin Development Cooperation (AMBDC) illustrates a more broadly regional one. On the initiative of Malaysia, the AMBDC was launched at the ASEAN Summit held in Bangkok in December 1995. The first Conference of Ministers of the AMBDC was held in Kuala Lumpur in June 1996 with the participation of 10 ASEAN countries and China. As reflective of its broader regional mandate, the cooperation pursued also extends beyond the Mekong sub-region. A good example is the development of the railway system, namely, the Trans-Asia railway from Singapore to Kunming.

Even more broadly regional, GMS cooperation also takes place within established institutional "ASEAN plus" frameworks – for example, ASEAN+1 and ASEAN+3. Especially active has been Japan, which has demonstrated its interest and support through such initiatives as the ASEAN Economic Ministers (AEM)-MITI Japan Economic and Industrial Cooperation Committee (AMEICC). The purpose of this mechanism is to bridge the gap between old and new ASEAN countries and to help those new members better integrate into ASEAN. This mechanism also helps to increase the attractiveness and competitiveness of the participating countries. The first AMEICC meeting was held in Bangkok in November 1998. In addition, the cooperation mechanisms such as the Mekong-Ganga Cooperation (MGC), and MMAEC (Mekong-Menam-Irrawady Economic Cooperation) have contributed to the strengthening of cooperation in the GMS region.

Lastly, GMS cooperation is also supported by private business and industry. As noted above, industry leaders have played advisory and consultative roles in working groups and national coordinating committees. In recent years, initiatives have been taken to energize the promotion and participation of the private sector in the GMS, the most notable of which is the establishment of the GMS Business Forum (GMS-BF) in 2000 and the adoption of SFA-TFI in 2005. GMS-BF is an independent, non-governmental organization that was founded to support the business activities of enterprises in the region and to strengthen the relationship between government and the private sector. Activities of GMS-BF include organizing events to encourage business – such as organizing group tours, fairs, exhibitions, conferences, seminars – offering business consulting, and providing information on trade and business opportunities for local businesses.

Meanwhile, the business initiatives of the Chamber of Commerce of the six GMS countries have played a role in facilitating and regularizing the participation of the private sector in the sub-region. Additionally, the GMS Program currently has the potential to serve an important role in promoting, facilitating, and catalyzing cross-border investors, as well as investment by "third countries" in the GMS. While continuing the GMS Program, other organizations and the private sector also target forums and conferences within GMS-BF that can further enhance its advocacy role of policy and regulation reforms in the region.

The success and challenges of institutionalization of GMS cooperation

As analyzed in the previous section, the GMS cooperation and institutionalization process has achieved considerable success, especially within the overall framework of the GMS Program developed by ADB. The overarching achievement of the GMS cooperation programs, including their objectives, outputs and outcomes, which can be summarized in the GMS results framework, Appendix 1, has helped accelerate the process of regional and international integration of all member countries (ADB 2004, 2010b, 2012).

As noted, the two most important and successful sub-regional institutional arrangements among GMS countries have been the GMS's Cross Border Transportation Agreement (CBTA) and the Strategic Framework for Action on Trade Facilitation and Investment (SFA-TFI). Under these agreements, the GMS region now benefits from improved infrastructure, including transport systems, electricity, and telecommunications, among GMS countries and with other ASEAN members. This process has significantly contributed to reducing the transportation costs of implementing trade and investment, and increasing connectivity between local and external GMS regions.

The GMS Program has helped create favorable conditions for sub-regional trade and investment. This step of the GMS Strategic Framework (GMS-SF) involves promoting and facilitating intra-GMS (among GMS countries) and outside the GMS (GMS remaining and the world trade, investment and tourism). The GMS has set up the Trade Facilitation Working Group (TFWG) and GMS Working Group and Sub-regional Investors (SIWG) that are coordinating sub-regional cooperation activities in trade and investment (ADB 2004). The 2nd GMS Summit in 2005 adopted the Strategic Framework for Action on Trade Facilitation and Investment (SFA-TFI), identifying goals, guiding principles, motivation strategies, and priority areas to promote trade and investment in GMS region.

The GMS-SF also aims to ensure environmental issues are satisfactorily resolved in cross-border initiatives and properly integrated into the sub-region's economic development efforts. To achieve this goal, a number of program activities are supported by the sub-regional technical assistance of ADB in the region from 1994 to 2004, including: (i) state information and environmental monitoring systems (semi-final) stage I and II; (ii) strategic environmental framework first phase; (iii) Sub-regional Environmental Training and Institutional Strengthening (SETIS); (iv) poverty reduction and environmental management in remote GMS watersheds; and (v) management and protection of important wetlands in the Lower Mekong Basin.

GMS is also implementing a successful program of human resource development within the sub-region. It is also displaying greater interest in protecting the environment and ecosystems in the sub-region. The Phnom Penh Plan for Management Development (PPP) has developed and implemented a strong program to build the capacity of GMS government officials, especially as regards strengthening their capacity for managing regional economic integration (REI) and the transition towards a more open economy. Besides learning a wide range of analytical, management, and leadership skills, about 900 civil servants have trained under PPP, with the opportunity to develop a professional network and be exposed to views on the latest issues of development management. PPP also provides the opportunity for continuous learning and networking managers' GMS development. The relative success of the PPP is also due to the enhanced financial support from various sources. Phase I had a budget of $1.15 million, contributed by ADB jointly funded with the New Zealand Agency for International Development. The program was able to raise $4.1 million for Phase II, with additional funding from the government of China and France.

In these ways, it can also be argued that GMS projects have made inroads in poverty reduction. The leaders of GMS countries have thus reaffirmed their commitment to the Millennium Development Goals (MDGs) in the first and second summits (ADB 2010a; Dosch and Hensengerth 2005; Krongkaew 2004). GMS countries could successfully lower poverty levels by improving economic growth and development. The GMS strategy of developing an economic corridor is thus an important part of the effort to reduce poverty and inequality, and is supported by empirical evidence on sustainable economic growth in developing countries (ADB 2010b). At the same time, more quantitative assessments of how Mekong sub-regional projects and integration serve poverty reduction would be useful.

Another area that has also benefitted from GMS initiatives has been the tourism industry, which has helped to put GMS firmly on the world tourism map (ADB 2012). Though a working group, sub-regional cooperation in the GMS tourism sector since 1993 has been indicative of close cooperation between several partners. The task force is one of the most dynamic sectors under the GMS Program. The program has a secretariat, the Agency Coordinating Mekong Tourism Activities or AMTA. In addition, the Mekong Tourism Coordination (MTCO) began in 2005 supported by contributions from each GMS country. The French government also agreed to assist in coordinating the MTCO and its priority projects under the GMS Transport Sector Strategy Study (TSSS) starting in 2007. Such progress in sub-regional cooperation in tourism has been greatly facilitated by the working group's success in creating corporate support through Ministry of Tourism meetings and the senior officials meetings (SOM).

As noted, current GMS arrangements rely very much on international and external donors and investors. Through the GMS, the Mekong sub-region has been able to benefit from more regularized funding avenues from different international organizations and international investors. At the same time, the heavy dependence on external financing is also the biggest drawback of the current GMS cooperation (Than and Abonyi 2001). Typically, donors are more interested in projects covering the whole GMS region, or a majority of the member states. The funding resources for projects involving two or three member states, such as the construction and infrastructure projects involving traffic in the Eastern Economic Corridor North–South, depend mainly on the concerned countries. The constrained financial capacity of the participating countries limits the progress of that project.

Similarly, while the GMS has established some important links and connections with private business and industry, the activities of the private sector are still quite slow, according to many researchers (Bhattacharyay, 2010; Xiong and Wen, 2009). The GMS Business Forum (GMS-BF) has kicked off, but the relationship between the businesses remains limited to information exchange. If these connections in investment and production are to be made more dependable, GMS countries need to tackle issues related to software infrastructure, including skilled human resources, policy coordination to create a business environment that is more open, and expanded cooperation in production.

The challenge is thus not the exchange method, but that of consistency. Again, these relationships would benefit from an updated information system as regards states, industry, and business. To solve this problem, trained manpower and funding resources are required if cooperation and advances are to be sustained. Such funding challenges can affect such basic operations as the operating costs of the Mekong Tourism Coordination Office. Similarly, the GMS Working Group on Agriculture would benefit from more established linkages with GMS forums and working groups. The Core Agriculture Support Program has a direct interface and relationship with other sectors and areas of cooperation in the GMS – for example, in trade (cross-border trade in agricultural products, bio-safety and food standards), and facilitating transport across the border (transporting agricultural commodities, especially perishable goods, and quarantine inspection of live animals in accordance with the CBTA) – but it also needs logistical support (for example, warehousing), energy (renewable energy, biofuels, and rural electrification), telecommunications (ICT application to agricultural supply chain management, capacity building, extension services, and research), and human resource development (impact of cross-border animal and plant diseases on the health of the population of the GMS, capacity building, training and skills related to agriculture).

The GMS and ASEAN

Last but not least, it is significant that the GMS countries are located within ASEAN and the cooperative trade and investment context created by ASEAN.

Being connected to both ASEAN as an organization and other ASEAN economies, for example, improves the attractiveness of the GMS as a target for trade and investment. GMS economies benefit from the ASEAN economic zone, which provides a platform for developing strategies of sub-regional cooperation (Arip and Hong 2011). They also benefit from investment and trade from individual ASEAN members (ADB 2012). The competitiveness of both GMS and ASEAN as a whole should benefit from liberalization, restructuring, and efforts to harmonize the trade and investment regimes in ASEAN (Verbiest 2013; ADB 2010a). ASEAN's commitment to accelerating the establishment of the ASEAN Community in 2015 indicates the potential benefits that can be obtained from the GMS economic integration into ASEAN.

The sub-region of GMS is thus in a position to broaden cooperation efforts – not just at the sub-regional levels, but also regional and international. This includes expanded economic relations with ASEAN, North Asia, and South Asia. In this vein, the construction of the ASEAN-China Free Trade Area (ACFTA) has had a positive influence on GMS development. To strengthen the multi-faceted relationship between ASEAN and China, the implementation of ACFTA not only requires participating countries to gradually reduce tariff barriers and non-tariff trade, but also to develop comprehensive economic cooperation. In their 2002 Framework Agreement on Comprehensive Economic Cooperation, ASEAN states and China specified information technology, agriculture, investment, human resources, and development of the Mekong River Basin as key areas of cooperation. In this way, the GMS can also be seen as supportive of larger integration efforts through both ASEAN and ACFTA. According to some researchers (Arip and Hong 2011), focusing on the GMS might be a good first step in support of a successful ACFTA.

Conclusion and future prospects of institutionalization of GMS cooperation

While different sectors may vary in funding avenues, rule-based arrangements, and legal structures, it is also clear that GMS cooperation has been regularized and normalized in some important respects. As this chapter makes clear, this is not to say that GMS cooperation does not have its share of challenges. In particular, countries in the GMS region are keenly aware of the importance of relations with partners – the private sector, international organizations, social as well as academic institutions, particularly the ADB – in mobilizing resources necessary for the development of sub-regional cooperation. Also, while GMS mechanisms share similar objectives and activities, they can also diverge in how they prioritize their efforts. Thus, as regards this volume's interest in institutionalized cooperation, it may be said that both GMS cooperation and its linkages to international funding sources have been made more durable and regular in some very important ways, but they are not as harmonized as they might be. There also still remain some uncertainties about future funding.

In addition, trade and investment liberalization commitments in ASEAN, APEC, ACFTA, and WTO pose some large challenges for lesser developed GMS

Table 7.1 GMS Program results framework

Main Objective	Main Outcomes	Main Outputs	Main Activities
Increased economic growth, reduced poverty, and environmental sustainability across the GMS	-Increased cross-border flows: investment, traffic, labor migration, with reduced human trafficking	-Economic corridors established -All GMS countries connected to a GMS rail network -Enhanced labor migration management systems and social protection for migrant workers	-Promotion of development of economic corridors and trade facilitation institutions -Sub-regional transport infrastructure and systems planning -Promotion of regional cooperation in education and skills development
	-Increased use of energy by all sectors and communities, particularly the poor	-Increased generation of energy from indigenous, low carbon, and renewable sources -Increased connection of GMS country power systems and functioning of regional power market	-Promotion of environmentally sustainable regional power trade planning
	-Increased access to information and communications	-Improved telecommunication linkages among GMS countries	-Capacity building and promotion of information and communication technology, especially for rural dwellers
	-Increased tourism with reduced negative impacts	-Improved tourism infrastructure (pro-poor, pro-women, and environmentally friendly)	-Capacity building and training of government officials, and tourism and hospitality enterprises -Upgrading of tourism training facilities
	-Increased sustainable agricultural production	-Increased resilience of agriculture to climate change	-Drafting of science-based, harmonized good agricultural practices and food safety standards
	-Increased conservation of nature	-Strengthened protected area network	-Strengthening Working Group on environment and national support units -Environment Operations Center functions as GMS environmental referral and service center

Source: ADB 2010b, 2012.

economies. For GMS economies, intra-regional inequality and development gaps also remain concerning. Across the region, GMS has the advantage of cheap labor, but member states still can compare unfavorably to neighboring countries that have the advantage of scale and/or more established economies. This issue impacts on the smaller GMS economies' ability to attract foreign investment from other member states, which, in turn, affects their ability to diversify their industries. Currently, Cambodia is heavily dependent on the garment industry and Laos and Myanmar still have very limited access to the world's FDI. At the same time, Thailand and Vietnam also face different kinds of challenges as regards human resources especially as regards the major deficiency of skilled labor at present (in Thailand) and in future (in Vietnam).

Nevertheless, GMS cooperation is being implemented in a new developmental context. That context is characterized by economic globalization trends. GMS governments are aware that in order to benefit from this process, important adjustments have to be made. They also know that strengthening regional integration offers one way to mitigate otherwise increasing economic disparities between countries, as well as internal disparities within each country. Regional integration can help minimize the negative impacts of globalization.

Such demands thus require increasing cooperation of the GMS member countries. To better integrate into regional and global economies, GMS cannot help but take advantage of incentives that ASEAN has won for the new member states, and cannot help but strengthen cooperation if they are going to be able to effectively and sustainably exploit their advantages in natural and human resources. The benefits resulting from implementation of the GMS Program, such as improved infrastructure, electricity supply, telecommunications network, trade, investment, and tourism, technical support and training of human resources, now provide driving forces and incentives for greater regional cooperation. Even Myanmar, whose trade regime is relatively more closed than the other member countries, now advocates border trade as a key mechanism for promoting bilateral trade relations not only with the remaining members of the GMS, but also with other countries in the region.

References

ADB. 2004. *Building on Success: A Strategic Framework for the Next Ten Years of the Greater Mekong Sub-region Economic Cooperation Program*. Manila: ADB.

ADB. 2008. Greater Mekong Sub-region: Maturing and Moving Forward. Regional Cooperation Assistance Program Evaluation, Reference Number: CAP: REG 2008–2073, December 2008.

ADB. 2010a. *Institutions for Regional Integration: Toward an Asian Economic Community.* Manila: ADB.

ADB. 2010b. *Strategy and Action Plan for the Greater Mekong Sub-region East–West Economic Corridor.* Mandaluyong City, Philippines: ADB.

ADB. 2011. *The Greater Mekong Subregion Economic Cooperation Program Strategic Framework 2012–2022.* Manila, Philippines: Asian Development Bank.

ADB. 2012. The Greater Mekong Subregion at 20: Progress and Prospect. www.adb.org/p
ublications/greater-mekong-subregion-20-progress-and-prospects (accessed September
18, 2015).

Arip, M. A., and P. C. Hong. 2011. Trade Interdependence of Greater Mekong Sub-region
countries. Paper presented at the Business, Engineering and Industrial Applications
(ISBEIA), 2011 IEEE Symposium.

Bhattacharyay, B. N. 2009. Infrastructure Development for ASEAN Economic Integration.
ADBI working paper series.

Bhattacharyay, B. N. 2010. Institutions for Asian Connectivity. *Journal of International
Commerce, Economics and Policy* 1(2): 309–335.

Commons, J. R. (2003). Institutional Economics. *Revista de Economía Institucional* 5(8):
191–201.

Dosch, J., and O. Hensengerth. 2005. Sub-regional Cooperation in Southeast Asia: The
Mekong Basin. *European Journal of East Asian Studies* 4(2): 263–286.

Ishida, M. 2008. GMS Economic Cooperation and Its Impact on CLMV Development. In
C. Sotharith, ed., *Development Strategy for CLMV in the Age of Economic Integration,
ERIA Research Project Report 2007.* Chiba: IDE-JETRO, pp. 115–140.

King, R. 2002. Development Opportunities in the Greater Mekong Sub-region. Perth,
Australia (kingintedservs@bigpond.com).

Krongkaew, M. 2004. The Development of the Greater Mekong Subregion (GMS): Real
Promise or False Hope? *Journal of Asian Economics* 15(5): 977–998.

Mehtonen, K., M. Keskinen, and O. Varis. 2008. *The Mekong: IWRM and Institutions
Management of Transboundary Rivers and Lakes.* New York: Springer.

Stone, S., and A. Strutt. 2010. Transport Infrastructure and Trade Facilitation in the
Greater Mekong Subregion. In D. H. Brooks and S. F. Stone, eds, *Trade Facilitation
and Regional Cooperation in Asia.* Cheltenham: Edward Elgar, pp. 156–191.

Than, M., and G. Abonyi. 2001. The Greater Mekong Subregion: Co-operation in Infrastructure and Finance. ASEAN Enlargement: Impacts and Implications. Papers originally
presented at the ASEAN Transitional Economies Roundtable, Singapore, November 20–21,
1997.

Thang, N. X. 2005. GMS Regional Cooperation: Initiatives, Development and Priorities.
The World Economic Issues, 12(116): 6. (Vietnamese journal, see: http://imbd.edu.vn/
tainguyen/nhung-van-de-kinh-te-va-chinh-tri-the-gioi/5158/.)

Verbiest, J. P. A. 2013. Regional Cooperation and Integration in the Mekong Region.
Asian Economic Policy Review 8(1): 148–164.

Xiong, B., and S. Wen. 2009. Towards a Better Understanding of the Political Economy of
Regional Integration in the GMS: Stakeholder Coordination and Consultation for Sub-
regional Trade Facilitation in China. Asia-Pacific Research and Training Network on
Trade Working Paper Series (77).

8 The institutionalization of inter-regional cooperation

The case of ASEM and FEALAC

Yulius P. Hermawan

Introduction

The Asia-Europe Meeting (ASEM) and the Forum for East Asia-Latin America Cooperation (FEALAC) are two major examples of the relatively few inter-regional institutions. Despite their different geographical scopes and memberships, the two forums perform a similar function: establishing links and institutionalizing cooperation between East Asia and a geographically distant region: ASEM with Europe; FEALAC with Latin America.

The two institutions were created in the 1990s in the post-Cold War context of interdependence, when deepening globalization and burgeoning regionalization went hand-in-hand in many parts of the world. ASEM was established in 1996, while FEALAC began its activities in 1999. The advocates envisaged the two institutions as serving as platforms for dialogue between regions, so that nations from the respective regions could develop a common understanding, forge cooperation, and pursue their shared interests. This inter-regional platform was developed as a complementary approach to the existing bilateral channels and the various intra-regional institutions (as discussed in Chapters 1–4 of this volume), and sub-regional mechanisms (Chapter 7) in post-Cold War Asia. Notwithstanding their different levels of cooperation and membership, these institutions share at least one thing in common: they are all ASEAN-initiated, and arguably, ASEAN-centered. The centrality of ASEAN as a driving force is evident especially in the formation stage, when leaders discussed the agenda and membership choice of each forum. At the time of their foundations, ASEM's Asian memberships consisted of ASEAN Plus Three (APT, i.e. ASEAN plus China, Japan, South Korea), while FEALAC's Asian memberships comprised of ASEAN plus five (ASEAN plus China, Japan, South Korea, Australia, and New Zealand).[1]

At the outset, it is pertinent to note that since the creations of ASEM and FEALAC, there has been criticism that the two forums are nothing more than mere talk shops, because no concrete action has been taken to follow up the forums' decisions and no tangible results have been generated (Olivet 2005; Spyros 2011). Despite such skepticism, the two organizations have survived, and indeed, expanded. More members have joined ASEM and FEALAC; and more agendas for dialogues have been included in the two forums. Perhaps more

importantly, there are signs that the member countries have sought to institutionalize more collaborative activities and mechanisms, raising hope that the forums
may produce more tangible and concrete benefits over time.

This chapter examines the pace and patterns of institutionalization of ASEM
and FEALAC as two exemplary inter-regional forums in the contemporary international system. Following the conceptualization developed in the Introduction of
this volume, the chapter defines "institutionalization" as an ongoing process in
which member states agree to forge, regularize, and strengthen their collaborative
endeavors by establishing and expanding a set of durable rules, norms, and
mechanisms, for the ultimate goal of pursuing certain shared goals and collective
preferences. Depending on the scope and substance of the respective inter-states'
collaborative endeavors, different pace and patterns of institutionalization processes
of different inter-regional forums may have differing impacts on the mapping and
reconfiguring of East Asia's cooperation with the outside world.

In performing the above task, the chapter pays particular attention to the drivers
and effects of the institutionalization processes of ASEM and FEALAC. Specifically, it seeks to address the following questions: How has the institutionalization
process of the two forums taken place since their inceptions in the 1990s? What
drives and limits the process? What norms and principles have prevailed in the
institutionalization process? To what extent have the existing regional arrangements
facilitated or limited the institutionalization of the inter-regional cooperative activities?

To this end, the chapter is organized into four sections. The first part discusses
two contrasting perspectives in understanding the dynamics of institutionalization
of inter-regional institutions, namely the rationalist and reflectivist approaches.
The second and third parts trace the patterns of institutionalization of ASEM and
FEALAC, respectively. The fourth and final part concludes by summing up the
findings.

Theorizing inter-regional cooperation: perspectives of rationalism and reflectivism

There are two major perspectives to understand the drivers and effects of the institutionalization of inter-regional arrangements, namely: rationalism and reflectivism
(Keohane 1988; Smith 2000; Acharya 2012).

Rationalism emphasizes that states are utility maximizing actors which are concerned about relative and absolute gains while forging international cooperation.
According to this perspective, states form international institutions to facilitate
mutually beneficial agreements so that they can reduce uncertainty and alter the
cost of never negligible transactions "since it is always difficult to communicate, to
monitor performance and especially to enforce compliance with rules" (Keohane
1988: 386–387). Accordingly, the institutionalization of inter-regional organizations is seen as a strategic means on the part of participating actors to maximize
gains while reducing uncertainty and transaction cost. The gains are measured in
material terms: the extent to which an institutionalized cooperation could deliver
tangible benefits to member states. Member states are likely to formalize,

institutionalize, and regularize their cooperative arrangements so long as there is a strong material incentive for the states to do so: that is, greater institutionalization of collaborative transactions promises greater benefits and expected utility.

In contrast, reflectivism suggests that the impetus behind inter-regional arrangements is not always materialistic interests, and that the institutionalization process is not necessarily driven by a rational calculation of maximizing benefits. Rather, the reflectivist approach highlights the role of social forces and the influence of the cultural practices, norms, and values, which are not based on the calculation of interests. Instead, it emphasizes the importance of the development of shared social values and norms, alongside the need for the regularization of formal and informal interactions among actors as embedded components of the institutionalization process. Institutionalization, therefore, is regarded as a social learning process that values inter-subjective meanings, rather than the *structuration* of materialistic oriented activities or a utility maximization strategy. Actors learn from each other through their interactions, and the result of the learning process affects the future direction of the arrangement, including whether the participating countries will maintain and expand inter-regional arrangements. Legitimacy of the institution is very important in this context, so that inter-regional cooperation can maintain social incentives. In this respect, legitimacy is based on normative consideration rather than material forces (Acharya 2012). The institutionalization of the inter-regional cooperation should confirm the legitimacy of the arrangement to pursue collective actions.

These perspectives have provided two contending frameworks of analysis for scholars working on international institutions, including those who focus on inter-regional cooperation such as ASEM and FEALAC. The majority of the existing scholarly works have departed from the rationalist approach, viewing the two inter-regional platforms as a strategic means on the part of rational states to cope with the challenges of deepening globalization and interdependence. From this perspective, the two inter-regional organizations help the Asian countries to maximize benefits while reducing the cost of globalization with a collective effort.

Dent (2004), for instance, analyzes the establishment of ASEM as an endeavor to deal with the widening gap between two sets of inter-regional dynamics which have become the world's triadic political economies: North America, Europe, and Asia. The trans-Atlantic relationship between Europe and North America has been strong, and so has the trans-Pacific relationship between North American countries and the Asia Pacific. In Dent's view, ASEM serves material interests: by expanding the scale of the relationship between Europe and Asia, the participating countries have been able to maximize their respective and collective gains. The institutionalization of ASEM is thus seen as a rational means to gain benefits through expanding inter-regional cooperation. It serves multiple purposes: managing economic and political relations in a fast growing region (Gilson 2005), while lessening the tense rivalry between Japan and China by bringing the two longtime rivals together in the same forum (Gilson 2002, 2007). Doidge (2007) examines the economic and non-economic benefits of ASEM and further suggests that inter-regionalism reinforces regional development process.

Kollner (2000) perceives that on one hand, ASEM is one example of the bandwagoning behavior where the European Union has a very strong interest to develop the relationship with remarkable emerging Asian economies. The rise of the Asian century was the main motive behind the EU's interest to maintain the growth of European countries through investment. On the other hand, Asian economies have very strong interests to maintain their access to the European market amidst the successful process of European market integration. In the perspective of Asian countries, ASEM can help to alleviate their panic about the emergence of a "Fortress Europe" (Kollner 2000).

Lluc Lopez i Vidal (2008) similarly notes geopolitical reasons behind the inception of ASEM. In the European perspective, the formation of ASEM was driven by the increasing American influence in Asia, as demonstrated by the rise of the Asia Pacific Economic Cooperation (APEC). The increase of American influence in the region can be a vehicle to increase its influence in global politics and thus lessen European power in the world's decision-making process. For Asian countries, ASEM can help them to ensure that the United States keeps its commitment to multilateralism. From this vantage point, ASEM represents a collective strategy to keep the balance of influence between the United States and Europe in their relationship with Asia.

Many scholars see the formation of FEALAC in a similar perspective. The FEALAC was established to serve the economic interests of nations in East Asia as well as Latin America. Hence, it seems reasonable to measure the value of the Forum particularly in terms of economic benefits, including the growth rate, the increase of investment in the regions, and the increase of inter-regional trade volume. Olivet (2005), however, suggests that there is skepticism whether FEALAC will be able to achieve real outcomes in the short and medium term. Spyros (2011) is also skeptical whether the FEALAC can deliver tangible results because there is only little will from the leaders of both regions. Other scholars have taken a comparative approach in studying the inter-regional institutions. Avila (1999), for example, compares APEC and ASEM through the institutionalist perspective and suggests that APEC can learn from ASEM how to develop political dialogue.

This chapter adopts a reflectivist perspective. We hold that ASEM and FEALAC are exemplary of the normative-based institutions, as both emphasize the ideational vision to promote a common understanding among countries in different regions.

It is true that some of the impetus for the two inter-regional arrangements does include some aspects of rationalist thinking such as "to promote greater trade and investment between Asia and Europe" (ASEM Chairman's Statement 1996). This rationalist impetus, however, does not deny the centrality of norm infusion and social learning process in the inter-regional arrangements. Both ASEM and FEALAC were established as a collective effort to recognize the idea that there is a missing link between East Asia and the two regions, and hence there is a need for fostering dialogue and cultivating a common understanding to bridge the inter-regional gaps. This normative consideration provides the basis for linking and configuring collaborative arrangements between the respective regions. At the heart of a forum of inter-regional cooperation is a "dialogue" activity, through which the formal and informal norms are discussed, agreed, and to some extent, internalized. Dialogue activity means in essence an exchange of ideas and information between the participating states. The dialogue can be sustained if the channels for communication are institutionalized and expanded.

The institutionalization of the inter-regional arrangement thus refers to the process of regularizing dialogue activities and harmonizing behavior among different groups of sovereign actors from different regions. It results in the shared rules, norms, and mechanisms that all participating members should comply with. Institutionalization involves the working structure and agencies such as political leaders, official representatives, social agencies, and individuals from different regions. It requires both formal and informal media of communication. The formal media may include the formal meetings of governmental officials, ranging from heads of state to senior officials. The informal media may include informal gatherings, seminars, and conferences where state and non-state actors can get together and engage in extensive interactions on specific concerns. Both formal and informal media of communications should be institutionalized to ensure the strengthening of common understanding between participants in the process. To be more specific, the institutionalization of a forum of dialogue should cover the efforts to keep the meetings sustainable and the members' compliance with the agreed rules and norms. It thus requires the regularization of both extensive and intensive meetings.

The active engagement of the participating states in the dialogue constitutes another determining element to guarantee the sustainability of the institutions. It denotes a social learning process rather than rigid structure of communication. The participating actors should be open minded and prepared to welcome any ideas even if they totally disagree with the ideas presented by their dialogue counterparts. The social learning process is very important here. The institutionalization of the forum of dialogue refers to the Deutschian conception of social transactions (Deutsch 1953). The conception underpins the significance of the extensive and intensive interactions within and between regional organizations or arrangements. Unless there is a development of intensive and extensive interactions, there will be no "*we feeling*," a feeling of being part of a community of values.

Recognition of the importance of a social learning process leads us to define the institutionalization of the forum of inter-regional dialogue as an evolutionary process. It depends on the existing nesting of the actors involved and the substance of the dialogue process. Participants will learn from others, and this social learning can proceed in either fast or slow motion. The function of institutions is mainly to ensure that the process does not end in a social vacuum and should not be measured by the ability to generate tangible benefits. Whatever the situation and achievement reached at a dialogue (for instance, harmony, the agreement to disagree, the failed consensus), another dialogue should be pursued by the participating actors. Participants should keep their commitment to continuing the dialogue and strive to keep the dialogue on course.

Political commitment is another important element for this institutionalization of the inter-regional dialogue. The initiative to build inter-regional arrangements may be presented by any actor, but the political leaders' commitment will be the determinant to making the arrangement legitimate and thus durable. Leaders can agree or disagree on some issues, but once they agree they can authorize officials to follow up and create a political guarantee that the states will keep their commitment. Political leaders' responsibilities include setting up the institutionalized channel of communications, and an agenda to be put on the communication tables, as well as providing political guidance and spaces for broad participation among their citizens.

Box 8.1 Elements of the institutionalization of the forum for inter-regional dialogue

1   Channels of communication including informal and formal media, and official and unofficial forums, regularized meetings.
2   Structured working methods or procedures.
3   Active engagement and commitment by the participating members to host or to attend meetings.
4   Social learning process at different levels: the multilateral, regional, and sub-regional institutions involved, and the linkages between those institutions.
5   Legitimate normative considerations on the origin of existence (*raison d'être*) and the political commitment by leaders to make the process durable.
6   Shared norms and principles including the inter-regionally balanced responsibility, flexibility, open-mindedness, accommodativeness, informality, flexibility, and openness for other eligible participants.

(Compiled by author)

Furthermore, shared norms and principles of institutionalization of these inter-regional arrangements constitute elements that shape (or even constrain) standard behavior of the participating countries. The participating members of a dialogue should first agree on particular norms and will remain respectful to the adopted norms. Since the dialogue is an open learning process, the process should not be based on a rigid contractual form. There should be open and greater opportunity for the participants to build dialogue on the shared norms and principles, and if necessary agree on the introduction of new norms and principles. Thus, the norms and principles at the end are not in any way dogmatic and rigid, but open for amendment, so long as the participating members agree.

Based on this conceptualization of the institutionalization of inter-regional arrangement, the following sections will further discuss how the institutionalization of the ASEM process and FEALAC has evolved over time.

Institutionalizing ASEM

The origin of ASEM can be easily understood when put in the historical and sociological reflective perspective. The initiators were leaders of Singapore and France who met in 1994 and shared their view of the importance of inter-regional cooperation to build a missing link between Europe and Asia. Singapore's proposal explicitly highlighted the importance of inter-regional dialogue between Asia and Europe, arguing that it could help to build common understanding. The simple idea behind the initiative was that through dialogue, Asians would become better informed about Europe and so would Europeans about Asia. At the core of the process is of course the idea that the forum should provide opportunity for interaction between nations from the two different regions.

Both Singaporean and French leaders agreed that the forum should be institutionalized at the highest level of leadership. The two countries accordingly proposed a summit to be the forum's institutionalized mechanism. Leaders of the two regions should be engaged actively in the forum, giving stronger political commitment to ensure the working process of the forum. Most leaders of the 25 states and the President of the European Commission attended the inaugural meeting in Bangkok (Annex I 1996). Leaders agreed on the responsibility of the forum "*in building greater understanding between the peoples of both regions through closer people-to-people contacts*" (ASEM Chairman's Statement 1996).

The formation of ASEM could also be seen as a reflection of the new reality in the post-Cold War context and this constitutes a new model in the twenty-first century's international relations. The relationship reflects a natural demand in the new global context following the end of the Cold War. First it is recognized that globalization has led to the increase of the interdependence between nations. It provides opportunities and challenges as well as a certain degree of sensitivity, vulnerability, and uncertainty. At the London summit, ASEM leaders clearly recognized the significance of ASEM in the context of growing interdependence: "*They reaffirmed, in a highly interdependent world, the role of ASEM in reinforcing the partnership between Europe and Asia in the political, economic, cultural and other areas of co-operation*" (ASEM Chairman's Statement 1998). This statement is then reaffirmed repeatedly in the outcome documents of the following ASEM summits.

How has the inter-regional cooperation evolved institutionally since its inception in Bangkok in 1996? The following pages describe the institutional development of ASEM as being indicated by the adoption of norms and principles of working methods, the making of channels for communication, mechanisms of the recruitment of new participating countries in the forum for dialogue and self-evaluation of past working processes.

The institutional foundations

The 1st Summit in Bangkok laid down the basic institutional foundation of the formation of the forum. Leaders agreed that ASEM is an informal forum to ensure flexibility. However leaders also emphasized the importance of the institutionalization of the informal forum so that ASEM could achieve its vision and carry out a bridging role to strengthen the partnership between Europe and Asia. At the second summit in London, leaders concurred with an agreement on the principles of the institutionalization of the ASEM process. They adopted *equal partnership, mutual respect*, and *mutual benefit* as three basic values of ASEM. Cooperation should value equality in building partnerships among Asian and European nations. They should also respect each other despite differences found among Asian and European nations. ASEM should also bring balanced benefits for nations from both regions. This norm highlights shared responsibility in organizing the meetings and running various activities, so that the benefit can be shared by both nations.

ASEM leaders also took on several principles of institutionalization of the ASEM process ranging from the tenet of open and evolutionary process to the networking of broad multi-stakeholders. Box 8.2 summarizes eight principles of the institutionalization of the ASEM process.

Box 8.2 Principles of the institutionalization of the ASEM process (As agreed at the ASEM London Summit, 1998)

1   Ensure an open and evolutionary process
2   Enlargement should be conducted on the basis of consensus by the heads of state and government
3   Enhance mutual understanding and awareness through a process of dialogue leading to cooperation concerning the identification of priorities for concerted and supportive action
4   Carry forward the three key dimensions with the same impetus: fostering political dialogue, reinforcing economic co-operation and promoting co-cooperation in other areas
5   ASEM is an informal process
6   It should stimulate and facilitate progress in other forums
7   Go beyond governments in order to promote dialogue and co-operation between the business/private sectors of the two regions and, no less importantly, between the peoples of the two regions
8   ASEM should also encourage the co-operative activities of think-tanks and research groups of both regions

(Chair's Statement, ASEM London Summit, 1998)

At the First ASEM Summit, leaders reached a consensus about the formation of necessary channels of communication. The structure of the ASEM working process was further strengthened at the ASEM's 10th commemorative year Summit in Helsinki where leaders adopted the ASEM working method and institutional mechanism which were based on the ASEM best practices in the last decade.

The working method includes official means of communication, their functions and authoritative relationship. At the highest level is the summit of leaders. The summit ensures that heads of governments or states of ASEM members come to share political commitment. Leaders meet biannually to formulate the key priority agenda and major political guidance. The Foreign Ministers' Meeting (FMM) will then formulate strategies to follow-up the agenda and to coordinate various meetings in the forum so that the priorities can be carried out well by relevant instruments. ASEM also has other ministerial meetings to promote specific areas of cooperation such as finance, labor, culture and education, environment, and transportation as agreed by the leaders at the summit (Annex to Helsinki Declaration 2006). Leaders also agreed on the appointment of ASEM coordinators in order to deepen regional coordination. The European Commission and the EU Presidency carry out their role as European coordinators. Asian coordination consists of one selected coordinator representing ASEAN and another representing non-ASEAN members from Asian counterparts. The Asian coordinators are selected once every two years. Table 8.1 shows various channels of communication through which leaders and other governmental officials can exchange their views extensively and intensively.

To ensure that the selected agenda is discussed intensively in the ASEM process, ASEM set up working groups. The working groups are usually attached to the work of particular ministerial meetings and senior official meetings. This procedure is particularly established to follow up certain strategic decisions made at the ministerial and senior official forums.

Another channel of communication is the ASEM's virtual secretariat whose main tasks are to support the role of the coordinator and information sharing. The secretariat is also responsible for facilitating the circulation of the information about the agenda, program, and activities and for building an institutional memory.

How are the channels of communication functioning to ensure the realization of the ASEM's vision? ASEM has a very tight schedule of meetings. More than 50 meetings at various levels are held every year. The meetings cover very broad issues including finance, trade, education and culture, disaster management and mitigation, human rights, food security, development, employment, and support for global governance. This proves ASEM to be a multidimensional institution where various issues that gain concerns from Asian and European members are put on the discussion table.

ASEM has held summits once every two years which take place alternately in European countries and Asian countries. This reflects a balanced and shared responsibility and ownership. Summits generate outcome documents consisting of the ASEM priority agenda for the next two years to be followed up by representatives of the governments and other stakeholders. The host has the privilege to set specific issues of interest that need to gain support from other ASEM members. The chosen issues are discussed intensively by the leaders. The results are adopted in the so-called thematic outcome document.

The selection of topics for dialogue at the summit levels shows the flexibility and inclusiveness of the ASEM process. This is in accordance with the principles of

Table 8.1 The channels of communication between governmental representatives

No.	Channels of Communication	Function
1	Summit	Forum of leaders to set up the priority agenda and political agenda
2	Foreign Ministers' Meetings	Forum of foreign ministers to formulate workable strategies to execute leaders' decisions at the Summit
3	Other relevant ministerial meetings	Forum of other authoritative ministries to promote particular cooperation in the area of politics, economy, and others
4	Regional Coordinators: the European Commission, President of the EU; one selected from ASEAN members, one selected from non ASEAN members	To deepen regional coordination between ASEM members to ensure the balanced and shared responsibility
5	Senior Official Meetings	To prepare for the FMM and other particular ministerial meetings, including drafts of outcome documents
6	Working Groups	To prepare for setting up details of priorities agreed by Foreign or other particular Ministerial Meetings; to ensure that specific issues are discussed intensively
7	Supporting Groups	To support the work of the ASEM chairmanship to carry out his or her main responsibilities effectively and efficiently
8	Virtual Secretariat	To facilitate the circulation of information, program, and activities, to keep the institutional memory; to support the Regional Coordinators' work
9	Jointly organized informal meetings such as seminars, conferences, workshops	Forum of government officials, societal groups and individuals to talk about specific issues such as human rights, climate change, and so on

Source: ASEM Chairman's Statement, Bangkok March 2, 1996, and Chairman's Statement of the 10th ASEM Summit, Helsinki, 2006.

the institutionalization of the ASEM process. ASEM gives priority to the three clusters of issues to be put in the dialogue: strengthening political dialogue, economic cooperation, and the promotion of cooperation in other fields. The third cluster implies that ASEM can touch issues other than political and economic agendas.

At the ministerial levels, schedules of meetings are also extensive to follow up the agenda agreed at the summits. Ministries of foreign affairs, ministries of finance, and ministries of immigration are involved extensively in the inter-regional ministerial dialogues. Other officials that have been actively participating at the ministerial meetings are ministries of trade and industry, those of labor and employment, the environment, education, transport, science and technology, small and medium enterprises, and energy. The inter-regional ministerial meetings generate chair's statements, declarations, and action plans on the specific authoritative agendas.

To support the working process of the ministerial meetings, Senior Official Meetings (SOMs) were held to bring together senior officials from ministries relevant to the agenda being discussed. The SOMs are responsible for preparing the next meeting of their ministers. Their main task is to prepare drafts of outcome documents to be discussed and agreed on by ministers at the ministerial meetings. ASEM also forms working groups in specific fields and support groups as being mandated by leaders at the summits, FMM, or other ministerial meetings. In the working group, the authorities can share best practices in public policies, so the procedures could be more efficient to facilitate relationship between Asia and Europe.

People-to-people contacts

Since the first ASEM Summit, leaders have recognized the important role of people-to-people contacts in building greater understanding between the people of the two regions involved. ASEM is thus not only an intergovernmental forum where governmental representatives come and talk, but also a people-to-people forum where members of parliament (MPs), CSOs, think-tanks, journalists, research groups, universities, business professionals, and various sectors of society from the two regions can meet and enhance intellectual and cultural exchange.

Several forums have been established to facilitate the people-to-people contacts. The forums include the Asia-Europe Business Forum (AEBF), the Asia-Europe Parliamentary Partnership (ASEP), the Asia-Europe People's Forum (AEPF), the ASEM SMEs Eco-Innovation Center (ASEIC), and the Asia-Europe Environment Forum (ENVforum). These forums reflect the human dimension of the ASEM process where multiple stakeholders can share their views and promote understanding between them. These transnational forums provide space for different nations to meet their counterparts from different regions. They should not be restricted by national and regional sentiments that frequently dominate the intergovernmental forums.

Some people-to-people forums were created through a top-down mechanism, being based on the leaders' declarations, and initiated or sponsored by certain governments. However, these forums can retain independence in expressing their ideas and promoting an exchange of human interests. It is hoped that the people-to-people contact forums can strengthen the ASEM intergovernmental process. There will be a balance between G-to-G meetings and P-to-P meetings; the second would also complement the first, mutually strengthening each other. The fact is that a forum such as the ENVforum can perform its role as a facilitator and act as a bottom-up promoter of wide ranging initiatives, contributing to the formulation of sound political decisions which have implications for environmental protection.

The AEBF is a forum which brings together business professionals and economic actors from the two regions. The first meeting was held in Paris in October

1996 as a follow-up of the agreement between leaders at the ASEM 1st Summit in Bangkok. Similar to the ASEM forum, the AEBF promotes a spirit of balance. The meeting is held in alternate countries between Asia and Europe. The host of the meeting chairs the forum. The agenda runs parallel with the one of the ASEM summit in that year.

Other channels of people-to-people contact are worth noting briefly. The ASEP is a forum for members of parliament from Asia and Europe whose objective is to promote understanding on parliamentary issues between members of parliament. The ASEP meetings are held once every two years prior to the ASEM meetings. The AEPF is an inter-regional network of civil society and social movements from Asia and Europe. Since the first AEPF meeting which was held in Bangkok in 1996, the network holds meetings biannually which take place alongside the ASEM Summit. It discusses various issues which also become concerns of the leaders at the ASEM, identifies strategies, and articulates common concerns shared by the people from the two regions. The ASEIC was formed by ASEM leaders at the summit in Brussels, Belgium in 2010. The ASEIC serves the function of being an international platform for facilitating constructive discussions among the government, business world and individuals in promoting international cooperation and exploring the opportunities of green business.

The ENVforum was formed in 2003 to follow up the leaders' agreement at the seventh summit in Beijing, particularly following the second and third environmental ministers' meetings. This forum provides a place for people across the two regions to share their knowledge and views on climate change as a contemporary threat to society. Leaders hope that the Asia-Europe forum can support the work of the United Nations Environment Programme (UNEP) in facilitating dialogue on Sustainable Development Goals (SDGs).

The broadening of participants

One important element of the institutionalization of the ASEM process is inclusiveness in terms of being open for eligible countries to be participants in the inter-regional dialogue. In this respect, ASEM proves that enlargement of the membership is an important part of the institutionalization. Quantitatively, the membership of ASEM has increased from time to time, bringing more Asians and Europeans to the inter-regional cooperation boards. In the 1st Summit, there were 26 founding member-states. In 2004, 10 new EU member states and three new ASEAN member states joined the Forum. This made ASEM amount to 39 members at the 4th Summit in Hanoi, Vietnam. In 2008, two new EU member states acceded to the forum together with the accession of the ASEAN Secretariat and three Asian countries, namely India, Mongolia, and Pakistan. In total, 45 members officially attended the 7th Summit in Beijing, China in 2008.

Two years later, ASEM welcomed Australia, New Zealand, and Russia as new members at the 8th Summit in Brussels, Belgium. In 2012, Norway, Switzerland, and Bangladesh joined the forum at the 9th ASEM Summit. This addition made ASEM the largest inter-regional forum, bringing 20 Asian countries and 31

European countries to stand on the same footing, sit at the same table, and uphold shared principles. The expansion is likely to continue in the next summits.

It is interesting to further analyze the enlargement process. The initiators and founding members of ASEM since the beginning agreed that the forum should be inclusive, being open to eligible countries to participate as members in the inter-regional arrangement. The enlargement indeed proves that ASEM is inclusive in terms of membership, and this is a very important pillar of the inter-regional dialogue. As a consequence of the envisaged role of the forum, ASEM should bring as many Asian and European countries on board as possible. The institutional mechanism for the recruitment of new members is not overly rigid, but flexible. As long as leaders can come up with consensus among themselves, a new candidate can soon join the forum. ASEM is apparently flexible in defining the meaning of Asia and Europe as regions and is open to thinking beyond rigid regionalism. ASEM membership is not limited to eligible countries in Western Europe or East Asia centric from a geographical perspective. The accession of Australia, New Zealand, and Russia can be seen as a value added to the ASEM's inclusiveness. Russia has been part of the European history of relationships, while Australia and New Zealand have developed good partnership with East Asian countries.

Reflecting on the ASEM process

Despite its extensive achievement in quantitative indicators, recently critical questions emerged about the extent to which ASEM has been able to deliver tangible benefits for all members of ASEM. The question was particularly raised by India, host of the 11th Foreign Ministers' Meeting in November 2013. India then called for the ministers to exchange their views on ways of making ASEM able to generate "tangible outcomes." In response to the call, ASEM foreign ministers recognized that "the dynamism of the ASEM partners should find expression in tangible result-oriented initiatives amongst ASEM partners" (ASEM FMM Chair's Statement 2013). The ministerial meeting then came with an identification of the members' shared interests on these tangible initiatives.

How should the latest development be understood? The concern is understandable as a response to a critique saying that ASEM is merely "a talk shop." This critique is something logical in the rationalist perspective that argues for materialist results as determinant factors to sustain international cooperation. Many see that ASEM has political economic modalities to move beyond the idea of being merely a forum of dialogue. ASEM represents 60 percent of the world population, half of the world GDP and almost 70 percent of the world's total trade. Having these modalities, ASEM has potential resources to achieve rationalist materialist benefits. India's concern about the slow progress of the Forum in delivering concrete results may highlight ASEM's reflection on its *raison d'être* and achievement. The initiatives make the ASEM process more deliverable yet strengthen the ASEM's existing working practices: members are invited to express their views on iconic projects and be committed to realize tangible projects.

However, it should be acknowledged that the institutional development of ASEM is lagging far behind the materialist market-driven impetus. The focus of the ASEM process in the last decade and a half of its existence has been to establish regular dialogues and to ensure that these channels of communication work to bring Asians and Europeans to the same table extensively. Accordingly, ASEM may not be able to deliver very concrete tangible results from the materialist perspective. ASEM's institutional development has strengthened its function as a forum of dialogue, but has not developed the capability of the institution as a "delivering agency."

Institutionalizing FEALAC

The FEALAC has a similar *raison d'être* to ASEM: how to build the missing inter-regional link between East Asia and Latin America. The objective of the forum was formulated at the first FMM in 2001: "*to promote better understanding, political and economic dialogue and cooperation in all areas so as to achieve more effective and fruitful relations and closer cooperation between the two regions.*"

The Forum set up three key specific objectives, namely: (1) to increase and promote common understanding, trust, political dialogue, and friendly cooperation, which is important for enriching and sharing knowledge and supporting the partnership; (2) to provide a forum for developing potential multidisciplinary cooperation in the field of economy, investment, trade, finance, culture, tourism, science and technology, environmental protection, and *people-to-people exchange*; and (3) to broaden common interest and positions on the international political economic cooperation in various multilateral forums. The document also suggests that the forum eschews a multidisciplinary approach and brings active involvement of both the public and private sectors. How has the Forum developed institutionally over the years?

FEALAC's norms and channels of communication

Following the first Senior Official Meetings in Singapore, foreign ministers held the first ministerial meeting in Santiago, Chile in 2001 with an agenda to approve framework documents. The FMM also agreed to rename the EALAF to FEALAC. The forum adopts key principles of voluntarism, informality, and flexibility in its working procedures. It has five principles as a code of conduct to follow in developing the inter-regional cooperation: "*respect for each other's sovereignty and territorial integrity; non-interference in each other's internal affairs; equally, mutual benefit and the common goal of development; respect for each other's unique cultures and social values; and decision-making by consensus*" (FEALAC FMM 2001).

In addition, the framework also highlights two other norms: the members' individual capacity and balanced responsibility. Every member participates in its national capacities, as suggested in the framework document. ASEAN members hold autonomy to express their view in the FEALAC. Latin American countries have the same position even though they are members of either Mercosur or the Organization of American States (OAS).

> **Box 8.3 The principles of FEALAC**
>
> 1   Respect for each other's sovereignty and territorial integrity
> 2   Non-interference in each other's internal affairs
> 3   Equally, mutual benefit and common goal of development
> 4   Respect for each other's unique culture and social values
> 5   Decision-making by consensus
>
> (Framework for a Forum for Dialogue and Cooperation between East Asia
> and Latin America, 2001)

The FEALAC upholds the principle of balanced responsibility. This can mean practical responsibility for hosting the meetings which should be held alternately in East Asia and Latin America. It should build consensus in choosing the host of the meetings. This can also be intended more substantively, suggesting that both East Asia and Latin America share reliability and trustworthiness in promoting inter-regional cooperation. The activities of the Forum depend much on the commitment of the members. Unless every member shows initiatives for specific projects that cover the two regions, there is no progress in increasing awareness and better understanding between East Asia and Latin America. The initiator should implement the project at a certain time and is also responsible for providing funding for the project's implementation.

The *FEALAC Framework Document* (2001) also affirms three levels of meetings as channels of communication: FMMs, SOMs, and working groups. FMMs are held biannually and are responsible for formulating the objectives of the FEALAC, selecting major projects, adopting and approving official documents, and approving new members. SOMs are held annually and are responsible for preparing details of the agenda for FMMs, drafts of decisions and, if relevant, drafts of declarations, providing some recommendations to gain approval from the FMM. SOMs also make appraisals of new members and provide recommendation about candidacies for the FEALAC FMM. SOMs also discuss various new initiatives such as the formation of the institutional mechanism, working groups, and committees, which are proposed by members. SOMs monitor the working groups' activities, and appoint the co-chair of the working groups. In this respect, SOMs constitute the core processes of the FEALAC.

Another channel of inter-regional communication is the working group. The FEALAC has four working groups, each established to focus on specific issues, and to strengthen dialogue and cooperation in particular FEALAC projects. The working groups were initially set up at the 1st FMM, but there was slight change in terms of their specific responsibility at the 6th FMM. Working Group 1 deals

192 Yulius P. Hermawan

with social and political cooperation and sustainable development. Previously, this working group was also responsible for disaster management, but not sustainable development. Working Group 2 is responsible for trade, investment, tourism, and micro, small, and medium enterprises (previously also for sustainable development, but not for tourism). Working Group 3 focuses on culture, youth and gender, and sport (previously, it also focused on cooperation in the field of tourism). Working Group 4 deals with science and technology, innovation, and education. Working groups are led by co-chairs, each representing a different region. The co-chair is elected by members of forums and will carry out his or her responsibility for the next three-year term. The Forum does not have a permanent secretariat, but to facilitate communication, the Forum set up a cyber secretariat which was managed by the Republic of Korea.

To ensure the function of regional representation and the effectiveness of the FMMs, SOMs, and working groups, the FEALAC has two regional coordinators. Their main role is to become focal points of contact in between formal meetings of the officials and ministers. Each is elected based on a consensus reached among members in each region. The regional coordinators' term is two years. To ensure the continuity of the FEALAC process, the Forum also has two deputy coordinators. The deputies are appointed to replace the regional coordinators at the end of the two-year term.

The FEALAC also facilitates forums which bring in non-state actors, including journalists, business professionals, and young members of parliament from the two regions. The Forum holds seminars on terrorism, trade, and so on. Yet the forums are not strongly institutionalized in terms of regularity as part of the FEALAC working procedures.

Enlarging the participants

Similar to ASEM, the FEALAC is an inclusive forum which is open for new members to join as long as they share recognition of the importance of bi-regional cooperation between Asia and Latin America. New membership is accepted based on consensus among the existing members. The Forum has expanded its membership by recruiting more countries from East Asia and Latin America. When it began its first SOM in 1999, 27 member-states attended the meeting. Fifteen members were from Asia; 12 from Latin America. The first enlargement took place at the first Foreign Ministers' Meeting, bringing three more Latin American countries to the inter-regional cooperation: Costa Rica, El Salvador, and Cuba. The second enlargement occurred five years later in 2007, welcoming the membership of Guatemala and Nicaragua. Mongolia and the Republic of Dominica joined in 2010. A year later, Honduras and Suriname officially joined the Forum. This enlargement indicates the increase of enthusiasm among Asian and Latin American states to be part of the inter-regional dynamism. There are now a total of 36 members: 16 from East Asia (including 10 ASEAN members) and 20 from Latin America. The non-ASEAN members are Australia, China, Japan, New Zealand, Korea, and Mongolia.

Reflecting on the past

FEALAC's institutional development is evolutionary, similar to the institutionalization of the ASEM process. There is also a kind of social learning in the FEALAC process. Ministers have spent time evaluating the Forum's past achievement. For instance, at the 4th FMM in Japan, the foreign ministers made an assessment of the Forum's past ten-year performance and recognized that FEALAC should be more focused and systematic in running its activities. There should be better coordination with more effective management. A year later, ministers agreed to establish the FEALAC Vision Group whose task was to formulate a long-term vision and workable strategies in regard to the FEALAC mechanism. The Group proposed the guidelines and the future direction of the FMM as well as a roadmap to achieve their goal. It then formulated strategies of specific cooperation and technical means to promote development of the FEALAC. The Group's task also includes a monitoring and evaluation system to support the decision-making process, continuity and effectiveness of the Forum activities.

The Vision Group's report was submitted to the 10th SOM in Bali, in 2013. The report recommended an overarching vision: *"FEALAC should move forward to become the premier Forum for inter-regional dialogue and understanding and to enhance connectivity and nurture further cooperation between member countries from the two regions"* (FEALAC Vision Group 2013). FEALAC should focus on iconic projects to enhance its visibility and deepening impact. The project should involve broad sectors of society including academics, youth and private business sectors, and media to support people-to-people contact. The Vision Group also recommended the strengthening of its institutions and the increasing of the effectiveness and efficiency of FEALAC's mechanisms by the establishment of the permanent secretariat, reorganizing of the working groups and convening of a summit.

The Vision Group's reflection shows that FEALAC remains a very loose inter-regional arrangement. Institutional development is very slow.

Experimental inter-regional cooperation?

The previous sections show both commonalities and differences in the institutionalization of ASEM and FEALAC. The formation of both ASEM and FEALAC departed from the reflectivist ideal of the importance of inter-regional cooperation to build the missing link between different regions. To bridge the regions, the two inter-regional arrangements serve their function as forums of dialogue where leaders and peoples have opportunities to develop common understanding of various shared concerns. To serve this function, both ASEM and FEALAC have institutionalized the process to ensure continuity and institutional capability. Leaders agreed on the shared norms and principles to be upheld as a code of conduct in pursuing this inter-regional cooperation. Leaders built consensus on the working methods where official representatives at different levels are equipped with certain tasks and authorities to collaborate with their counterparts from different regions in a series of meetings. Leaders set up people-to-people forums where common understanding between different communities can be enhanced through knowledge-sharing activities.

Both forums adopt informality and flexibility into the institutionalization process. They are informal because no rigid institutional blueprint to follow was adopted at the very beginning of their inceptions in the 1990s. Decisions are less binding. Flexibility opens the possibility of an adaptation to the development of the issues discussed at the meetings. The decisions on the formation of supporting or working groups to strengthen the institutionalization that were made at previous meetings remain open for modification in the following meetings.

Both ASEM and FEALAC are member-driven forums. The two forums encourage every single member to have their initiatives for the specific projects covering two regions. The ASEM activities and continuities thus depend very much on the initiatives of the members. The implementation of these initiatives depends on the commitment of the members who initiated the activities and others who share similar interests. The extensiveness and frequency of the activities depends very much on the number of participating countries that are voluntarily committed to follow up the proposals of the inter-regional activities.

Given their nature and characteristics, ASEM and the FEALAC are thus member-driven forums whose institutionalization process remains informal and loose. Members of both forums prefer a "soft institutionalization" as a mode of inter-regional dialogue, emphasizing the importance of consultation, information exchange and non-binding decision making as guiding principles of the dialogue (Ruland 2002).

However, the two forums have demonstrated different degrees of institutionalization in terms of extension of the interactions. The institutionalization of ASEM remains soft, but it is to a certain degree stronger than the institutionalization of the FEALAC. ASEM activities are much more extensive and frequent than the FEALAC ones. The principle of shared and balanced responsibility is much more evident at ASEM in comparison with FEALAC.

ASEM gains benefit from many factors that make the institutionalization achieve a higher level of development. The first factor is the existence of formal regional organizations whose memberships take an active part in the informal ASEM process. ASEM enjoys full support from the European Union and ASEAN. The organizations are formally represented by the European Commission and the ASEAN Secretariat that retain the privilege to attend the Summits as well as other official and non-official meetings. This kind of existing formal nesting proves to be very contributive to the institutionalization of the ASEM process. There are strong formal commitments to become engaged in the ASEM process as both the EU and ASEAN encourage their membership to do so.

In particular, the EU's formal commitment has added value to the development of the informal ASEM institution. The European Union has included the process as one of its priorities and thus allowed the European Commission to give full support, both technically and financially. Following the first Summit in Bangkok, the European Commission issued the so-called Commission Working Document,

Table 8.2 Comparative assessment of the institutionalization of ASEM and FEALAC

No.	Elements of Institutionalization	ASEM	FEALAC
1	Channels of communication including informal and formal media/official and unofficial forums	More extensive channels for both officials and non-official representatives: Five levels of working process: Summit, FMM and Ministerial Meetings, Regional Coordinators, SOM, Working Groups and Supporting Groups	Less extensive: Three levels of working procedures: FMM, SOM, four Working Groups
2	Structure of working methods or procedures and regularized meetings	Extensive at the higher levels; intensive in Working Groups	Less extensive at the FMM; more intensive at the SOM and Working Groups
3	Active engagement and commitment by the participating members to host or to attend the meetings	Fair engagement in extensive networking	Fair engagement in less extensive networking
4	Social learning process at different levels: the multilateral, regional and sub-regional institutions, and the linkages between those institutions	Social learning proceed at both official and unofficial meetings	Social learning proceeds particularly at official meetings, but less at unofficial meetings
5	Legitimacy and political commitment by leaders to make the process endurable	Relatively strong legitimacy; Political commitment is granted at the Leaders' Summit	Lacking of strong legitimacy and top leaders' political commitment; FMM guarantees only less political commitment
6	Shared norms and principles including the inter-regionally balanced responsibility, flexibility, informality, flexibility and openness for other eligible participants	Balanced responsibility is maintained relatively well; principles of informality and flexibility are upheld; enlargement continues for eligible countries based on consensus between members	Balanced responsibility is less maintained; informality and flexibility are upheld; enlargement continues for eligible countries based on consensus between members

Source: Compiled by author.

entitled "Perspective and Priorities for the ASEM Process" in 1997 (Commission of the European Communities 1997).

Regional nesting is also contributive to the institutionalization of the ASEM process from the Asian perspective. ASEAN has initiated the regular meetings of both ASEAN and non ASEAN members. Japan, China and South Korea have taken an active part in the ASEAN+3 network. Australia and New Zealand have been very active at the Asian Regional Forum. Other Asian countries such as India have been ASEAN dialogue partners. So the meetings between Asian leaders have been quite salient. To a certain degree the meeting among Asian countries has been institutionalized in terms of regularity and frequency as well as shared norms (such as adopted in the Treaty of Amity and Cooperation). The initiative of the inter-regional cooperation between Asia and Europe has even strengthened the intra-regional interactions, and thus there is a strong incentive to institutionalize the ASEM process.

ASEM thus gains benefit from the existing intra-regional networks and the regional integration dynamics in Europe as well as a broadened Southeast Asia (such as formulated in the ASEAN+3 arrangement). This explains why leaders were able to agree on the status of the Forum at the level of Summit so quickly. Even though ASEM is an informal process, the level of Summit implies a stronger political commitment from the leaders. This level also has had a strong impact on the broadening of the process. ASEM has institutionalized various people-to-people contacts whose schedules of activities are also very tight, similar to the intergovernmental official meetings.

ASEM also enjoys political support from the leaders and thus has stronger legitimacy to adopt necessary means of institutionalization. The decision to set the Forum as Summit proves to be ASEM's strength in shaping the direction and activities, and provides a particular kind of confidence-building with a more legal basis, in addition to ensuring the longevity of the Forum.

The institutionalization of the FEALAC has encountered serious challenges since the beginning. First, FEALAC is not a leaders' summit and from the beginning it has had insufficient legitimacy or legal capacity. Second, the missing link between East Asia and Latin America is too wide and deep from a socio-historical perspective. There was no intense relationship between East Asians and Latin America prior to the establishment of the Forum. It is of course different from ASEM where the relationship between the two regions was very strong even before ASEM commenced its activities in the mid 1990s; the EU has developed a bilateral relationship with ASEAN institutionally and ASEAN members individually since 1970s; history also suggests that European countries had established a very long relationship with countries in this region during the colonial era.

Relatively matured regional nesting is still absent from the context of the FEALAC. Both the conception of East Asia and Latin America remains very loose and less institutionalized formally. No regional organization performs as an anchor for inter-regional cooperation, as the European Union and ASEAN do in the case of ASEM. East Asian countries may have developed informal intensive interactions in the ASEAN-initiated forum such as the Asian Regional Forum, yet there remains the question of whether a workable institutional commitment will develop to strengthen a sentiment of so-called *East Asianness*. East Asia shows very loose regionalism and this affects the commitment of the East Asian countries to be actively engaged in the FEALAC process. The trend in building an East Asian Community has been overshadowed by the blossoming proliferation of bilateral, trans- and sub-regional arrangements, including the preferential trade agreements (Okfen 2003). Institutionalization in this East Asian regionalism "has turned out be less exclusivist than initially anticipated" by its initiators (Acharya 2011: 12).

The intra-regional network in Latin America is similarly insufficient to strengthen the institutionalization of the FEALAC. Many Latin American countries that join the FEALAC have taken part in the Organisation of American States, Mercosur and Carricom. Yet none of these regional organizations endorses their formal commitment to strengthen the FEALAC. The FEALAC is thus a very soft institution. The foreign ministerial level of meetings is not strong enough to push forward a larger political commitment. It is thus reasonable for the FEALAC Vision Group to argue for the necessity of upgrading the Forum to the Summit level. To stimulate more commitment from the members, the Vision Group has recommended the Forum be a premier institution so that the members will give priority to being active in its activities.

Even though the degree of institutionalization is different and the ability to achieve the expectations of their members remains questionable, neither ASEM nor FEALAC have ever lost members. In fact, more nations from different regions continue to put their trust in the new mechanisms of international relations. Both forums constitute a crucial approach in bridging two different regions. Moreover, a higher expectation is developing for the forums to deliver tangible benefits for their members. This shows that the forums have a future, and the direction taken will depend on the willingness and the commitment of the participating countries as well as the legitimacy and capability of the inter-regional arrangements.

Conclusion

As inter-regional forums, ASEM and FEALAC are social constructs that involve formal and informal institutional processes. Both ASEM and FEALAC have been established to ensure that the dual trends of globalization and regionalization do not widen the gap between regions. They serve to complement regional dynamics while at the same time strengthening the existing bilateral, intra-regional and global multilateral platforms. As relatively new collaborative arrangements, they are both in search of the optimal institutional format that could sustain durable inter-regional cooperation, and simultaneously meet the expectations of the participating countries.

The preceding analysis suggests that the two inter-regional arrangements both emerge from a historical-sociological reflection, which leads to the increasing regularized interaction between nations from different regions. Informality, functionality and flexibility constitute the main features of the institutionalization process of ASEM and FEALAC. This chapter has further suggested that the degree of institutionalization of the two arrangements remains low and less matured. Both have institutionalized extensive channels of communication where top leaders, representatives of the governmental offices and other non-governmental stakeholders can exchange their views on various agendas. The exchange of views on the multidimensional issues among multi-stakeholders has proceeded extensively.

However, from a comparative perspective, the degree of institutionalization of ASEM is stronger than that of FEALAC. This shows that the institutionalization of these inter-regional arrangements can proceed better in a context where a certain degree of intra-regional institutionalization has achieved a significant level of formality. In this respect, ASEM enjoys full support from the relatively matured institutionalization of the EU, as well as the strengthening of the ASEAN's institutionalization and its existing networks of cooperation. However, this is not the case in FEALAC, where the inter-regional collaborative links between East Asia and Latin American have remained relatively loose and under-institutionalized.

Note

1 More Asian and Oceanic countries have later joined these institutions. FEALAC accepted Mongolia as full member in 2010. ASEM admitted India, Mongolia, and Pakistan in 2008, Australia, New Zealand, and Russia in 2010, Bangladesh in 2012, and Kazakhstan in 2014.

References

Acharya, Amitav. 2011. Asia is Not One: Regionalism and the Ideas of Asia. ISEAS Working Paper: Politics and Security Series No. 1.

Acharya, Amitav. 2012. Foundation of Collective Action in Asia: Theory and Practice of Regional Cooperation. ADBI Working Paper Series. No. 344, February.

Avila, John Lawrence V. 1999. Regional Cooperation in APEC and ASEM: An Institutionalist Perspective. PASCN Discussion Paper No. 99–18.

Dent, Christopher M. 2004. The Asia Europe Meeting and Inter-regionalism. Toward a Theory of Multilateral Utility. *Asian Survey* 44(2): 213–236.

Deutsch, Karl. 1953. *Nationalism and Social Communication*. Cambridge, MA: MIT Press.

Doidge, Mathew. 2007. From Developmental Regionalism to Developmental Inter-regionalism? The European Union Approach. NCRE Working Paper No. 07/01, July.

Emmerson, Donald K. 2009. East Asian Regionalism in a New Global Context: Balancing Representation and Effectiveness. A keynote speech delivered on March 19 to a conference on The Philippines and Japan in East Asia and the World: Interests, Identity and Roles, organised by The Philippines's Asian Center with support from the Japan Foundation, Manila, Philippines, March 19–20.

Gilson, Julie. 2002. Defining Inter-Regionalism: The Asia-Europe Meeting (ASEM). SEAS Electronic Working Papers. Vol. 1, No. 1, November.

Gilson, Julie. 2005. New Interregionalism? The EU and East Asia. *European Integration* 27(3): 307–326.

Gilson, Julie. 2007. Inter-Regionalism. Paper presented at the ECPR Standing Group on International Relations. University of Turin, September.

Keohane, Robert O. 1988. International Institutions: Two Approaches. *International Studies Quarterly* 32(4): 379–396.

Knops, Jonas. 2006. The EU and ASEM: Gesture Politics or Fruitful Dialogue? Policy Brief. European Policy Centre, September.

Kollner, Patrick. 2000. *Whither ASEM? Lessons from APEC and the Future of Transregional Cooperation between Asia and Europe.* Korea: FES. www.iias.nl/asem/publications/koellner_witherasem/pdf.

Okfen, Nuria. 2003. Towards an East Asian Community? What ASEM and APEC can Tell Us. The University of Warwick, CSGR Working Paper No. 117/03, June.

Olivet, Maria Cecilia. 2005. Unravelling Interregionalism Theory: A Critical Analysis of the New Interregional Relations between Latin America and East Asia. Paper presented at The 6th Conference of REDEALAP, Buenos Aires, Argentina, December 12–13.

Ruland, Jurgen. 2002. The European Union as an Inter- and Transregional Actor: Lessons for Global Governance from Europe's Relations with Asia. National Europe Centre Paper No. 13. Paper presented to conference on The European Union in International Affairs, National Europe Centre, Australian National University, July 3–4.

Smith, Steve. 2000. The Discipline of International Relations: Still an American Social Science? *British Journal of Politics and International Relations* 2(3): 374–402.

Spyros, Melitsas. 2011. Interregionalism: the Case of FEALAC. Athens: Institute of International Economic Relations.

Vidal, Lluc Lopez I. 2008. The Theoretical Contribution to the Study of Regionalism and Interregionalism in the ASEM Process. In Yeo Lay Hwee and Lluc Lopez I. Vidal, *Regionalism and Interregionalism in the ASEM Context: Current Dynamics and Theoretical Approaches.* Documentos CIDOB ASIA 23. Barcelona.

Documents

Annex I List of Participants, Chairman's statement of the Asia-Europe Meeting, Bangkok March 2, 1996.

Annex to Helsinki Declaration on the Future of ASEM, ASEM Working Method and Institutional Mechanism, 2006.

ASEM FMM Chair's Statement, 11th ASEM Foreign Ministers' Meeting, Delhi-NCR, India, November 11–12, 2013, "ASEM: Bridge to Partnership for Growth and Development."

Chairman's statement of the Asia-Europe Meeting, Bangkok, March 2, 1996.

Chairman's statement of the Asia-Europe Meeting, London, April 4, 1998.

Chairman's statements of the ASEM Summits (from 2000 to 2014).

Commission of the European Communities, *Commission Working Document, Perspective and Priorities for the ASEM Process,* Brussels, June 26, 1997.

FEALAC Foreign Ministers Meeting, FEALAC Framework Document, Framework for a Forum for Dialogue and Cooperation Between East Asia and Latin America, 2001.

FEALAC Vision Group Final Report, Evaluation and Recommendations, 2013.

Outcome documents of the FMM, FEALAC (2001–2013).

Official sites

ASEM's official website/virtual secretariat: www.aseminfoboard.org.

FEALAC's official website/cyber secretariat: www.fealac.org.

Conclusion
Themes and prospects

Alice D. Ba, Cheng-Chwee Kuik and Sueo Sudo

This volume has highlighted dynamic processes of institutionalization at work in East and Southeast Asia. It has been especially interested in the regularization of cooperative activity – how and why states come to cooperate on a more dependable basis (or not), the kinds of frameworks produced, and what these processes say about intra-regional relations and cooperation in East and Southeast Asia. In this vein, chapters illustrate some of the different ways that the region has been transformed by new and increasingly regularized cooperative activity – activity that at once reflects, and contributes to, the growing ties between the region's states and economies. Indeed, there has been an unprecedented amount of inter-state cooperative activity taking place in East and Southeast Asia.

At the same time, chapters also make clear that the activity taking place in East Asia is not always of one piece, one type, or one outcome. The chapters illustrate notable variations depending on the issue domain in question and the level of governance. Economic and security cooperation along East Asian and Southeast Asian lines have become regularized and normal; however, other areas like ethnic conflict management and disaster management remain more limited and ad hoc. Cooperative processes can also compete and cross-cut, suggesting a lack of regional consensus about regional priorities, with implications for East Asia's political geography. There are also other tensions. On the one hand, East Asian cooperation has been given institutionalized expression in a number of official frameworks and mechanisms, suggesting a degree of durability. On the other hand, the heightened intensity of exchanges is not always matched by properly developed operational mechanisms. Frameworks that look similar in form can also display different competences.

Such tensions and variations notwithstanding, chapters nevertheless collectively offer some take-aways about institutionalization processes at work in East and Southeast Asia. Below, we elaborate further on this volume's key findings with consideration for (1) the political geography of East Asia; (2) the distinguishing features of institutionalized cooperation in East and Southeast Asia; (3) East Asian institutionalization's key drivers and constraints; and (4) limitations of current frameworks and processes and their implications for what cooperation looks like. We conclude by considering future prospects and directions as regards the institutionalization of East Asia in years ahead.

Mapping and remapping regional cooperation in East Asia

The institutionalization of East Asian cooperation has been a dynamic process that has had implications for the political geography of East Asia. As this volume has shown, inter-state cooperation among regional countries in East Asia has expanded considerably over the last decades. Beginning first with the non-communist states of Southeast Asia and the creation of ASEAN in 1967, Southeast Asian regionalism was then expanded to include first Brunei, and then Vietnam, Myanmar, Laos, and Cambodia with the ending of the Cold War. In providing common frameworks for divided and internally diverse states to work together, such processes have in important ways "mapped" "Southeast Asia" onto our conceptual imaginations, with practical implications for how both states in East Asia and those outside East Asia approach regional states. Indeed, as Ba's chapter (Chapter 1) highlights, the creation of ASEAN as an institution is closely linked with the institutionalization of Southeast Asia as a meaningful political-geographic expression.

Southeast Asian regionalism then took on expanded and different significance with intensified engagements between ASEAN members and the three Northeast Asian countries of China, Japan, and South Korea especially after the 1997–98 Asian Financial Crisis. East Asian cooperation has been given particular institutional expression in the ASEAN Plus Three (APT) which has over the years evolved into the principal institutional platform for region-wide cooperation among the 13 countries. Similar to ASEAN in Southeast Asia but to a much less institutionalized extent, the APT has served to institutionalize and regularize a conception of East Asia that encompasses the entire Southeast Asia and most segments of Northeast Asia (albeit still excluding other politico-territorial entities like Mongolia, Taiwan, and North Korea).

The map of East Asian cooperation has, however, continued to evolve. In particular, the formation of the East Asia Summit (EAS) in 2005 widened the scope of regional cooperation further by including three countries (India, Australia, and New Zealand) beyond what has conventionally been considered geographic East Asia. And in so doing, the EAS also destabilizes the narrower political conception of East Asia (Southeast Asia plus Northeast Asia) as a focal point for regional cooperation. As highlighted in Chapters 2 and 3, the principle of "open regionalism," along with geographic proximity, has lent support for including the other three countries, even if they sit outside most conceptions of "East Asia." In 2010 that political-geographic expression was stretched and challenged further with the additional enlargement of the EAS and the establishment of the ASEAN Defense Ministers' Meeting Plus (ADMM+8), whose "ASEAN+8" included the United States and Russia. Both the ADMM+8 and the expanded EAS also speak to the shifting geostrategic significance of "East Asian cooperation."

The institutionalization of East Asia has now been remapped in ways that include and overlap with wider Asia-Pacific and Indo-Pacific regions. Thus, while the APT may give institutional expression to East Asia defined as Southeast Asia plus Northeast Asia, other arrangements – the EAS, the Asia Europe Meetings

202 A.D. Ba, C.C. Kuik, and S. Sudo

(ASEM), and the Regional Comprehensive Economic Partnership (RCEP) – give expression to a conception of region that is quite different and more ambiguous. These arrangements also coexist with other arrangements based on conceptions of the "Asia Pacific" – in particular, the Asia-Pacific Economic Cooperation (APEC, formed in 1989) and the ASEAN Regional Forum (ARF, created in 1993–94). Yet, these arrangements, in that they express a regularized expectation of "regional" cooperation, also form an important pillar of the emerging regional architecture in Asia – specifically, a multilateralism pillar alongside the US-led "hub-and-spokes" alliance pillar.

Key features

The institutionalization of East Asian cooperation displays a number of common features. These include: (1) leadership by small states, not large states; (2) informality and voluntarism, where institutional arrangements are characterized by decentralized, as opposed to centralized, authority; (3) multilayered cooperative processes; and (4) inclusiveness – that is, taken as a whole, East Asian institutionalization processes have tended to be broadly inclusive of different actors.

Of these features, one of the more defining has been the role played by smaller Southeast Asian states – as opposed to the larger, more materially capable Northeast Asian states – in the development of institutionalization processes. In this vein, the influence of ASEAN in driving, defining, and constraining cooperative processes has been especially notable. Clearly, as an organization of Southeast Asian states, its effect is greatest in Southeast Asia, where the creation of ASEAN facilitated the development of new regional norms of noninterference and resilience to replace the norms of interference, conflict, and division. As Ba's chapter reveals, such norms have very much defined ASEAN institutionalism – how it works, why it works, but also its constraints. Considering the questions with which this volume began, Ba's chapter highlights how such norms have been institutionalized in the structure and culture of ASEAN. On the one hand, the ethos of mutual restraint and respect for national priorities that these norms reflect has both stabilized intra-regional relations and facilitated cooperation in Southeast Asia; on the other, that same ethos has meant cooperation that is less harmonized in the sense of coordination and common operations and that consequently has fewer at the ready, developed problem-solving mechanisms.

As Kuik's chapter (Chapter 4) illustrates, ASEAN's institutional influence is evident also in East Asia's different security arrangements, with some similar tensions. While ASEAN's minimalist institutionalism has facilitated exchange and new cooperation between different states with different interests and sensitivities, it has also limited more proactive and coordinated security cooperation. As he puts it, "good progress" has been made in terms of the "frequency and regularity" of cooperative activities in the security realm, but policy harmonization and coordinated operations display a more mixed record. Kamolvej (Chapter 5) draws similar conclusions about disaster management in ASEAN and Southeast Asia.

As noted, small power leadership has been another distinguishing feature of multilateral cooperation in East Asia. As these chapters indicate, "ASEAN plus" and other cooperative frameworks have also been indicative of the external recognition ASEAN has received from non-Southeast Asian actors beyond Southeast Asia. Furthermore, such recognition has become more institutionalized itself via both institutional arrangements that give pride of place to ASEAN and a diplomatic discourse that affirms the importance of ASEAN in a larger system of institutional arrangements.

In particular, "ASEAN centrality" has become a distinguishing feature of processes at the "macro-regional" level – that is, arrangements that are inter-state and whose membership is defined more by a prior conception of political-geography than by function or issue. For example, chapters in Parts I and II of this volume illustrate ASEAN's influence in developing East Asia's most prominent "Track I" regional frameworks like the ASEAN Regional Forum (ARF), ASEAN Plus Three (APT), and the East Asia Summit (EAS), where ASEAN has dominated questions of membership and decision-making process, and, in turn, much of the agenda. Chapters by Nasrudin and Sudo and by Sudo and Tham (Chapters 2 and 3) additionally highlight how ASEAN+1 arrangements between ASEAN and other states (and also other regional groupings) have made ASEAN into an "FTA hub" for East Asian economic integration. In the area of security cooperation, Kuik (citing Jorg Friedrichs) highlights a similar phenomenon whereby ASEAN has emerged as "the main crystallization point of security regionalism" in a "most elaborate institutional fabric."

Moreover, ASEAN centrality has been "formalized" in other practices – for example, the consensus decision-making adopted by practically all East Asian institutional frameworks, the adoption of ASEAN's TAC in the ARF and EAS, ASEAN states' role in hosting meetings and agenda setting, and ASEAN's determination of membership in the EAS. Similarly, as the chapters by Sudo and Tham, and by Kuik illustrate, ASEAN's influence is also evident in other macro-regional economic and security cooperation in East Asia – for example, various FTA initiatives, RCEP, and the ADMM+. Meanwhile, Hermawan's chapter in Part III (Chapter 8) shows that ASEAN (and also the EU) and its ability to provide a focal point for organization provides the critical distinguishing difference between a more robust process of inter-regionalism (the Asia Europe Meetings (ASEM)) and a less robust one (the Forum for East Asia and Latin America Cooperation (FEALAC)).

To a lesser degree, less directly, and with more mixed effects, ASEAN also provides an institutional referent for sub-regional and sub-national processes involving smaller groups of states and sub-national localities. Its institutional role at these other levels tends also to be more challenged by normative and ideological constraints – in particular, ASEAN's still strong attachment to noninterference norms. In this volume, such constraints are most evident in na Thalang and Siraprapasiri's chapter (Chapter 6) on ASEAN's (non-)role in ethnic conflict management in Southeast Asia. Perhaps not surprisingly, ethnic conflict management is the most ad hoc and least institutionalized area of cooperation addressed by this volume. Meanwhile, other chapters emphasize the capacity limitations of ASEAN states individually and as an institution. Limitations in technical expertise and material resources are especially highlighted in chapters on disaster management and the Greater Mekong Sub-region. In those issues, the capacity constraints of ASEAN states contribute to a more limited, reactive (as opposed to proactive) ASEAN role; they also invite material assistance from larger, more capable states or entities (e.g., the Asian Development Bank in the case of the GMS; the United States, via ASEAN-US Technical Assistance and Training Facility; the United Nations, via various agencies; and the European Union in the case of disaster management).

Still, even in more challenged areas as those above, chapters show that ASEAN remains an important referent for those interested in regularizing more cooperative ties in East and Southeast Asia. Thus, as Nguyen Quoc Viet explains (Chapter 7), the Greater Mekong Sub-region is understood to be part of the process of building an ASEAN Economic Community (AEC). Similarly, the policy prescriptions made by Tavida Kamolvej in her chapter focus on the particular need for ASEAN to regularize cooperation in that particular realm and how more institutionalized mechanisms of disaster management would support the ASEAN Community's socio-cultural and/or political-security pillars. Meanwhile na Thalang and Siraprapasiri also show the influence of ASEAN – only in their case, they give empirical illustration of how ASEAN norms limit a more concerted regional response, especially by ASEAN as an institution – though individual ASEAN states have been able to play neutral third party roles in disputes (presumably in the larger interest of ASEAN resilience). Ba's chapter makes a similar observation in the case of inter-state conflict moderation/mediation efforts in ASEAN.

Given ASEAN's influence, it is also not a surprise that other features defining the institutionalization of East Asian cooperation would mirror those of ASEAN itself. In particular, as in ASEAN-Southeast Asia, the institutionalization of East Asian cooperation tends to mirror ASEAN in its institutional form. Thus, like ASEAN, East Asian institutionalization processes tend to be looser in structure, as opposed to legal-contractual and binding; they also tend to be decentralized, not centralized. Such decentralization also contributes to another feature of East Asian institutionalization – specifically, the fact that it is multilayered and at times fragmented. This is because decentralization tends to support more diverse practices. In other words, while states may agree to common cooperative objectives, their pursuit of those objectives may still exhibit variation. As chapters highlight, such decentralization and variation reflects a political concern for national autonomy, as well as an ideological disposition that tends to see mutual respect for such autonomy – in a word, noninterference – as an important foundation for regional security. However, as Kuik's chapter on security cooperation illustrates, what this means is that "cooperation" consequently may not necessarily be equated with the "harmonization" of practices.

East Asian cooperation is also multilayered because states of the region generally favor broad and inclusive engagement with a variety of actors. This is reflective of the combined effects of East Asia's (inter)dependence with extra-regional actors, persistent tensions in intra-East Asian relations, and as elaborated below, the intervening effects of geopolitics that encourage diversified, rather than exclusive, relationships. Thus, as the chapters by Sudo and Tham and by Nasrudin and Sudo illuminate, the institutionalization of East Asian cooperation is constituted by varied ASEAN+1 arrangements that interact with, and layer upon, one another. Similarly, as Kuik observes, East Asian security cooperation is distinguished by arrangements of different memberships (e.g., the APT v. the EAS), both Track 1 and Track 2 processes, as well as the coexistence of US bilateral security arrangements with region-wide cooperative security institutions. Practices and relations may vary but they also combine to form what may be considered the institutional matrix that is East Asian cooperation.

Key influences and drivers

Chapters underscore how efforts to institutionalize cooperation in East and Southeast Asia have been driven (and complicated) by a mix of functional, normative, and geopolitical factors – and are also far from automatic. Instead, they have been contingent enterprises even if they are also very path dependent. In particular, chapters point to how the perceived functional imperatives of increased and more dependable East and Southeast Asian cooperation have grown over time, accounting for the intensification of intra-regional exchanges and development of new cooperative ventures at all levels. Thus, we see at work the economic logic of maximizing trade and investment gains among regional countries – a theme evidently pertinent in Sudo and Tham's discussion on East Asian economic cooperation, and to a lesser extent, chapters on sub-regional and inter-regional cooperation. We also see functional imperatives playing out in issues involving more transnational challenges (Kuik on security; Kamolvej on disaster management; Viet on sub-regional cooperation). In contrast to the economic logics above, however, they highlight the limits of individual state actions in managing transnational security challenges. Thus, states are functionally moved to work with other states.

In addition to the functional drivers above, normative drivers are also shown to be at work. For example, in the case of intra-ASEAN cooperation, Ba highlights how a normative interest in regional resilience both grounds and defines ASEAN conceptions of security and thus cooperation. The normative drivers were especially prominent in ASEAN's first decades when the economic and geopolitical imperatives of intra-Southeast Asian cooperation were much weaker. Thus, were it not for some normative conception of "Southeast Asia" and "Southeast Asian security," the merits of regional cooperation along Southeast Asian lines would have been much less evident. Meanwhile, Hermawan gives attention to how interregional frameworks like ASEM and FEALAC have been moved by a "normative vision to promote a common understanding," political dialogue and economic cooperation so as to provide the "missing link" between regions.

As noted above, one of the more defining features associated with East Asian institutionalization processes has been the role played by ASEAN and especially the interesting feature of "ASEAN centrality." Here, as regards the drivers of East

Asian institutionalization, chapters also give attention to the facilitating role played by ASEAN and ASEAN institutionalism (the "ASEAN Way"). Chapters on Southeast Asian and East Asian cooperation and on security cooperation (Chapters 1, 2, and 4) demonstrate ASEAN's unique ability to convene East Asian states under region-wide frameworks like the APT, ARF, EAS, and ADMM+8. The unique attributes of ASEAN – its membership of smaller, less threatening powers, its consensual decision-making that assures recognition and accommodation of individual state concerns, its generally inclusive approach to regional relations – have made ASEAN a far more acceptable leading actor in the institutionalization of East Asian cooperation than others.

Moreover, the ability to convene states has also provided opportunities for states to cultivate other practices more supportive of East Asian cooperation. While these practices are also challenged by geopolitics and other factors, ASEAN centrality may nevertheless help diffuse and neutralize some of the competition for regional leadership from larger, more powerful actors. At a minimum, ASEAN's ability to convene states might be considered a necessary first step in a larger process of institutionalization. In both these respects, ASEAN has helped facilitate the institutionalization of East Asian cooperation by providing the venue and opportunity for states to develop cooperative ventures. Such a role also speaks to a kind of evolutionary process highlighted, for example, in Ba's, Kuik's, and Hermawan's chapters, especially.

Lastly, geopolitics has provided drivers for East Asian cooperation and institutionalization – though, as highlighted, it is also one of the larger obstacles. Power competition, for instance, serves as a stimulus when big powers channel more tangible and intangible resources to the process, attracting other states. While their own calculus may be competitive (to offset the influence of other larger states), the resources they bring to the process nevertheless contribute to the increased density and faster pace of the institutionalization of East Asian cooperation. The proliferation of FTAs in East Asia offers a particular illustration. Thus, China's FTA with ASEAN states had the effect of motivating Japan, South Korea, India, and the United States to also pursue FTAs and economic partnerships with ASEAN states. Furthermore, while these FTAs may not be uniform, their proliferation may also be seen as a driving factor behind more recent efforts at RCEP – that is, RCEP, as a region-wide agreement, is an effort to "regionalize" and harmonize East Asia's FTAs.

Another example is the comprehensive partnerships between ASEAN and larger powers. While larger powers clearly seek such relations in the interest of their own standing and position in East Asia vis-à-vis other larger powers, their efforts also contribute to more institutionalized ties between Northeast Asia and Southeast Asia. They also serve ASEAN states' interest in capacity building, which can also serve ASEAN's larger interest in ASEAN centrality.

Reconfiguring East Asian "cooperation"?

The final theme of the book is the relationships between institutionalization and regional cooperation. We ask: What constitutes "effective" institutions and institutionalization? What has the institutionalization process in East Asia succeeded to transform so far? What has it failed to change? To what extent does the current institutionalization trajectory promise "better" regional cooperation? Have decades of institutionalization made regional cooperation in East Asia not only more "regularized" but also more "harmonized"? To what extent has it contributed to the creation of commonly understood rules of the game, expected paths of action and behavior, and also understood constraints?

Each of these questions bear on the configuration of East Asian cooperation – that is, the parameters of East Asian cooperation (domains and levels of cooperation), the forms it takes (institutional design), the scope of political geography (institutional membership), and the formation of defining rules and norms.

As significant as the trend of East Asian institutionalization has been, it is not without challenges and limitations. The hindering factors include: the political logic of power competition among egoistic actors at various levels (all chapters), historical animosity and political distrust (Chapter 4), asymmetric stakes (Chapters 3, 4, and 6), and sensitivities about sovereignty and autonomy (Chapters 1, 4, 5, and 8). Such challenges speak to the interesting tensions that have defined the institutionalization of East Asian cooperation. While institutional development suggests important agreement in general about the need to institutionalize and expand East Asian cooperation, the process is also characterized by divergent interests and priorities, as well as ASEAN norms that have historically supported different state practices. These divergences help to sustain the informal and fragmented features of East Asian institutionalization above, challenge efforts to develop coordination mechanisms that would make collective action more regular and automatic, introduce redundancies that can diffuse cooperative efforts, and, in turn, raise questions about ASEAN centrality.

As detailed in this volume, the primary platforms for East Asian-wide cooperation have, thus far, comprised mostly the ASEAN-led regional institutions (i.e. the ARF, the APT, the EAS, and the ADMM+8), which are extensions of the ASEAN modality. ASEAN's particular role and influence in the institutionalization of East Asian cooperation make it no surprise that East Asia's institutional features would share those of ASEAN. But by the same token, it should also be no surprise that East Asia's constraints closely mirror those of ASEAN, as well.

Among the more prominent questions raised by both ASEAN and East Asian institutional developments has been the question of what constitutes "effective" cooperation. In particular the same features of ASEAN centrality – its voluntarist orientation, its consensus mechanism, and open inclusiveness – that have been shown to facilitate certain East Asian cooperative processes are also shown to complicate and challenge collective and coordinated responses to a variety of challenges facing the East Asian region.

First, ASEAN's informal orientation allows opposing countries to comfortably participate in the regional fora, but severely hinders wider and deeper integration. As the ARF amply suggests, it cannot move beyond a confidence-building stage although many member states wish it to embark upon preventive diplomacy as a second stage of institutionalization. Institutionalization has been difficult in the face of a stated commitment that the ARF would advance its agenda only at a pace comfortable to all participants. In fact, aversion to formality results in voluntarism and incrementalism. Thus while there is value to the ARF mechanism's ability to encourage member states to generate some cooperative activity, the ARF has to rely on longer-term social pressures to accomplish specific goals. In a similar vein, ASEM is said to deliver just summit-level declarations that state aspirational objectives on regional cooperation without putting in place substantive instruments to realize them.

Second, ASEAN's consensus mechanism limits the scope of cooperation and agility towards cooperative actions, especially when the institution confronts differing options. Since the need for consensus requires a non-confrontational approach and a willingness to sustain differences while crafting some minimal common understandings, many organizations tend to emphasize process and more incremental measures than actions that might have greater and more immediate effect on the common challenges facing states. In this sense, the voluntary, non-binding outcomes of ASEAN's consensual orientation can also be barriers to greater institutional change. Indeed, as demonstrated by most of the cases in this volume, the pace of cooperation is slowed by the fact that consensual processes, in effect, give individual states veto power. Similarly, cooperative objectives tend to be limited, rather than expansive.

Thus, while chapters in this volume show that while ASEAN has played a facilitative role in creating and sustaining the macro-regional processes of East Asian regional architecture, its regulative influence and normative reach at the sub-regional and inter-regional levels has been more limited. This is partly because the ideological content of ASEAN cooperation emphasizes national autonomy, for example, in the case of sub-regional issues that are more closely tied to domestic politics and arrangements; it is also partly because power asymmetries may factor larger in cases of inter-regionalism. Inter-regional cooperation may be additionally complicated by geographic distance and much more diffuse conceptions of geography.

Third, while open inclusiveness explains the co-existence of closely overlapping regional institutional arrangements, cooperation can also break down if states are working at competing or irreconcilable goals and agendas. Competitive logics also sustain questions about membership and participation. This volume has focused mostly on the institutionalization of East Asian (Southeast Asia plus Northeast Asia) cooperation; however, as chapters in Part I and II especially show, this kind of organization is not uncontested. Geopolitical concerns have motivated states to expand the EAS beyond "East Asia" as originally defined.

In sum, the role that ASEAN has played in configuring East Asian cooperation has been an interesting and critical one. As East Asia's longest standing regional organization, ASEAN's own regional agenda and programs have useful demonstration effects for APT and EAS. As already noted, it has also played a critical intermediary or facilitator role in relations between East Asian countries. On the other hand, institutional competition and relative power concerns raise questions about the ASEAN model as a governance mechanism. Thus, ASEAN centrality is not uncontentious (both practically and normatively), but its very contentiousness, as Ba's chapter illustrates, is also what heightens its importance as a principle for ASEAN itself. Such questions make the realization of the ASEAN Community's three inter-locking regional economic, security, and socio-cultural communities by 2015 all the more imperative if ASEAN's leading role is to be sustained.

Last, the contrary effects on and significance of ASEAN for the institutionalization of East Asian cooperation suggests that there may be merit in conceptualizing East Asian institutionalization in terms of stages. Thus, while ASEAN may play a critical role in driving earlier stages, its role may be more constraining at later ones. The varied effects of geopolitics may similarly support such a conceptualization. While geopolitical calculations have served East Asian institutionalization in the ways highlighted above, it is also quite clear that geopolitical competition between powerful actors also fragments efforts, introduces economic irrationalities (e.g. different economic standards and rules), and prevents regional countries from pursuing greater cooperation in military security and other domains.

All in all, the institutionalization of East Asian cooperative activities has intensified in both horizontal and vertical (multiple domains and levels) directions. Despite this progress, however, the structure of institutionalization has remained largely fragmented, with overlapping platforms, activities, and resources, all of which today define, remap, and configure what is now a decades-long process of East Asian cooperation.

Prospects

Looking ahead, what are the prospects for the ongoing institutionalization processes of East Asian cooperation? Which sectors and levels of inter-state cooperation promise greater institutionalization in the near future? What are the possible factors that might make the difference? Which enduring problems of institutionalization might persist? Are there any emerging trends that might shape the future direction of the institutionalization process? What are their potential implications for the evolving regional architecture and regional stability in the twenty-first-century Asia-Pacific? We offer the following observations.

First, the overall prospects are mixed and varied, with some issue domains and governance levels showing greater likelihood of greater institutionalization than others. If the past trajectory is any indication, economic and non-traditional security (NTS) cooperation is expected to become more greatly institutionalized than military security and conventionally defined domestic issues (e.g. ethnic conflict management). This is primarily because trade, investment, and the transboundary NTS issues are matters of shared interest and common challenge, many of which could not be handled effectively by any single country without the collaboration of others. These issues are deemed relatively less contentious than matters of high politics and domestic politics. Accordingly, greater institutionalization is seen as more feasible and desirable, especially if real world events (e.g. new rounds of economic crises or natural disasters) further deepen a sense of regional interdependence, thereby demanding regional countries to further regularize and harmonize their actions.

In terms of levels, the institutionalization of regional and sub-regional cooperation (e.g. among the APT and EAS members, and among the GMS countries) is likely to proceed faster and deeper than that of inter-regional cooperation (e.g. between East Asia and Europe, between East Asia and Latin America) in the years ahead. The reasons are that, compared to the former, inter-regional cooperation involves more member countries from geographically diverse and culturally disparate regions, where shared interests are relatively diffuse and inter-group activism relatively modest. Their institutionalization process is thus likely to be more limited in both pace and depth, than that of regional and sub-regional cooperation. The process might improve gradually, however, if and when there is an enhanced political will to push for greater two-way flows of capital, goods, people, and ideas between the two sides. The EU's enhanced diplomatic and economic engagements with the East Asian countries since 2012, if sustained, might build momentum in this direction.

Our second observation is that some of the limitations discussed above – particularly those associated with or stemming from the ASEAN Way – are likely to endure in the years to come. In particular, a habit of incrementalism, a culture of emphasizing consensus over coordinated outcomes, and a non-binding approach to dealing with difficult inter-state disputes are likely to persist as institutional features and limits of cooperation in East Asia. Such dynamics are likely to persist in part because ASEAN's institutional centrality is likely to stay for some time to come, and in part because by and large there is a lack of better alternatives to address the wide array of unresolved inter-state issues in the region.

Third and finally, there are several emerging and enduring trends that might shape the direction, extent, and pace of the institutionalization of East Asian cooperation in the decades ahead. Chief of them are: the growing great power rivalry and maritime tensions in East Asia, the increasingly salient non-traditional security challenges, and the expanding impetus for intra-regional economic integration, including regional connectivity. Each takes place in a wider geographical scope. Some foresee, for example, the emergence of a wider Indo-Pacific region that competes with East Asia for attention. Such tensions, as in earlier periods, are reflective of the continuous remapping effects of cooperative processes on East Asia's political geography.

Recent developments indicate that the future institutionalization of regional economic and functional cooperation might be increasingly driven, colored, and complicated by the growing great power competition. Already, there are signs of such competition between the United States and China. Growing tensions and realignments surrounding the maritime disputes in the South and East China Seas have, for example, resulted in the United States and China each putting forward and promoting their own regional proposals as geo-economic tools to maximize their relative influence vis-à-vis each other. As part of the Obama administration's "pivot" and "rebalancing" to Asia strategy, Washington has actively promoted the Trans-Pacific Partnership (TPP) initiative, which does not include China and several ASEAN member countries. Beijing, on the other hand, has proposed various regional integration and connectivity projects (e.g. the Asian Infrastructure Investment Bank, the new Silk Road economic belt, the maritime Silk Road) seeking to transform its geographical and economic assets into a long-term geostrategic advantage in Asia.

The major powers' moves have presented mixed implications for the institutionalization of East Asia. On the one hand, the greater attention and resources poured by both powers into the situation are likely to stimulate and expand economic exchanges among regional countries, in effect adding institutional layers that might contribute to more regularized regional cooperation over time. On the other hand, however, the greater regularization of regional cooperation – because of its power-centric nature – might not necessarily translate into greater harmonization in regional cooperation. This is due not only to the less inclusive membership of big power-driven initiatives (they include certain regional countries but not the others), but also their potentially divisive geopolitical ramifications (if intensified, great power rivalry is such that great power initiatives are equated with siding with one or the other power).

For the time being, the good news is that the major powers do not only promote their own initiatives, they also support the existing ASEAN-centered arrangements. China, for instance, out of its own interests, has actively supported the ASEAN-initiated and ASEAN-centric RCEP and various mechanisms under the ASEAN Plus Three framework (e.g. the Chiang Mai Initiative Multilateralization, CMIM). Whether and to what extent the two great powers will promote their own initiatives at the expense of the ASEAN-centered platforms will determine the future direction of institutionalization of East Asian cooperation.

Similar patterns can be observed in the institutionalization of regional cooperation in the security realm. While the United States and its regional partners have exhibited a greater tendency to use some of the existing institutional arrangements to constrain and challenge China's security position through multilateral platforms (e.g. Secretary Clinton's remarks at the Hanoi ARF in 2010, the more confrontational interactions between the two sides at the Shangri-La Dialogue in 2014), China has promoted its preferred institutionalized avenues and concepts (e.g. hosting the Conference on Interaction and Confidence-Building Measures in Asia (CICA) in 2014, and championing a new "Asian security concept") as a way to counter and reshape the discourse of regional security. As in the regional economic domains, such big power security practices might lead to greater regularization but lesser harmonization of regional cooperation. They might increase the risks of growing tension and polarization in the region, exerting pressures on regional states' external positions.

These trends, if they continue, might challenge and even undermine ASEAN's institutional centrality and ASEAN cohesion. They risk altering the nature and structure of the existing ASEAN-centered institutional framework – a framework that has helped avoid the problem of competition for regional leadership among the great powers. Moreover, trends could possibly force some ASEAN states to tilt closer to one power at the expense of other relations, thereby eroding the regional grouping's cohesion. Fortunately, alongside these potential centrifugal forces, there exist other centripetal processes that might serve to mitigate the divisive and confrontational effects of power politics. Such factors include the growing NTS challenges and the deepening intra-regional integration. While the former necessitates greater collaboration among regional countries to better tackle trans-boundary challenges that recognize no national borders, the latter demands them to further enhance and harmonize their policy coordination to maximize practical gains from deeper integration. Both require a cooperative framework that operates on a continued and strengthened ASEAN centrality (as opposed to a weakened one), in order to attain both regularization and harmonization in the ongoing institutionalization processes.

In the final analysis, the different processes at work may all contribute to "East Asian" regional cooperation. Indeed, while it may be true that processes are not all of one piece, it is also shown that few of these processes are completely discrete or independent; rather, they interact, intersect, and sometimes, layer upon one another. Path dependent processes are also at work in the sense that new proposals tend to build upon or begin with past practices. Ultimately, what makes East Asia interesting is that the normative and functional imperatives of regional cooperation appear to remain quite strong despite heightened geopolitical and competitive pressures in recent years. In this sense, growing competitive pressures – so long as they are not escalating into big power conflict – will not stop the search for mutually acceptable cooperative arrangements. Rather, they may re-map and reconfigure the parameters of cooperation by continuously expanding the domains and levels of inter-state collaboration, thereby contributing to increased regularity of interaction, increased intensity of policy coordination, and possibly increased harmonization of interests among an ever-enlarging group of "regional" countries. Future research should, among other things, further examine the interplay of centrifugal and centripetal processes and how they might affect how institutionalization manifests at different governance levels, as well as the harmonization of interests in a given region.

Appendix 1

Regional map
Lee Li Kheng

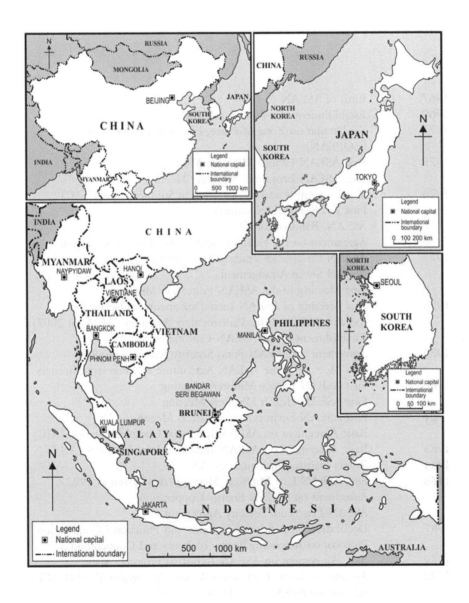

Appendix 2

Timeline of key ASEAN milestones
Azmi Mat Akhir and Alice D. Ba

1967	Birth of ASEAN
1969	Establishment of a Fund for ASEAN
1971	Declaration on Zone of Peace, Freedom and Neutrality (ZOPEAN)
1975	First ASEAN Labour Ministers Meeting
	First ASEAN Economic Ministers Meeting
1976	Treaty of Amity and Cooperation in Southeast Asia (TAC)
	First Leaders ASEAN summit
	ASEAN/Bali Concord 1
	Agreement on the Establishment of the ASEAN Secretariat
1977	ASEAN Preferential Trading Arrangements
	ASEAN Sswap Arrangements
	First Meeting of the ASEAN Education Ministers
1978	First Meeting of ASEAN Inter-Parliamentary Organization (became ASEAN Inter-Parliamentary Assembly (AIPA) in 2007)
	Establishment of the ASEAN Cultural Fund
1979	Agreement on ASEAN Food Security Reserve (AFSR)
	First Meeting of the ASEAN Agriculture and Forestry Ministers
1980	First ASEAN Energy Ministers Meeting
	First ASEAN Health Ministers Meeting
1981	First ASEAN Environment Ministers Meeting
	Basic Agreement on ASEAN Industrial Complementation (AIC)
1983	Basic Agreement on ASEAN Industrial Joint Ventures (AIJV)
1984	Brunei Darussalam joined ASEAN
1986	First ASEAN Law Ministers Meeting (regularized in 1993)
	Agreement on ASEAN Energy Cooperation
	ASEAN Petroleum Security Agreement
1987	Declaration on Political, Economic and Functional Cooperation
	Protocol on Amending Treaty of Amity and Cooperation
1989	Basic Agreement on ASEAN Industrial Projects (AIP)
1992	Agreement on the Common Effective Preferential Tariff (CEPT) Scheme for ASEAN Free Trade Area (AFTA)

	Framework Agreement on Enhancing ASEAN Economic Cooperation
1994	Establishment of Fund for ASEAN
	First ASEAN Regional Forum (ARF)
1995	Treaty on the Southeast Asia Nuclear Weapons-Free Zone (SEANWFZ)
	ASEAN Framework Agreement on Services (AFAS)
	Socialist Republic of Vietnam joined ASEAN
	First ASEAN Ministerial Meeting on Youth
1996	First ASEAN Transport Ministers Meeting
	Basic Agreement on ASEAN Industrial Cooperation (AICO)
1997	Laos and Myanmar joined ASEAN
	Memorandum of Understanding on the Establishment of the ASEAN Foundation
	First ASEAN Fnance Ministers Meeting
	Declaration on Transnational Crime
	First ASEAN Ministerial Meeting on Transnational Crime
	ASEAN Vision 2020
1998	Second Protocol on Amending Treaty of Amity and Cooperation
	First Meeting of ASEAN Tourism Ministers
	First Informal Meeting of ASEAN Ministers on Rural Development and poverty eradication
	Agreement on ASEAN Investment Area (AIA)
	Hanoi Plan of Action (HPA)
1999	Cambodia joined ASEAN
	ASEAN Surveillance Process
2000	First meeting of High Level Task Force on the AFTA-CER Free Trade Area (AFTA-CER-FTA)
	ASEAN Troika
	Declaration on Cultural Heritage
	Political Declaration in Pursuit of a Drug Free ASEAN 2015
	e-ASEAN Framework Agreement
2001	First ASEAN meeting of Telecommunications and IT Ministers
	Rules of Procedure of the High Council of TAC
2002	ASEAN Agreement on Transboundary Haze Pollution
2003	Conference of the Parties to the ASEAN Agreement on Transboundary Haze Pollution
	Declaration on Strengthening Participation in Sustainable Youth Employment
	Bali Concord II
	First ASEAN Ministerial Meeting on Disaster Management
2004	Declaration on the Elimination of Violence Against Women in the ASEAN Region
	Vientiane Action Programme (VAP) 2004–2010
	ASEAN Security Community (ASC) Plan of Action

ASEAN Economic Community (AEC) Plan of Action
ASEAN Socio-Cultural Community (ASCC) Plan of Action
ASEAN Plan of Action on Narrowing the Development Gap (NDG)
ASEAN Framework Agreement for the Integration of Priority Sectors
ASEAN Declaration against Trafficking in Persons Particularly Women and Children

2005   Statement on "One Vision, One Identity, One Community"
Kuala Lumpur Declaration on Establishment of ASEAN Charter
Agreement to Establish and Implement the ASEAN Single Window
Establishment of the ASEAN Development Fund
Coordination Agreement on Technical Assistance and Training to Combat Money Laundering and Terrorist Financing
Memorandum of Understanding on the ASEAN SWAP arrangement (by all 10 central banks)
ASEAN Agreement on Disaster Management and Emergency Response

2006   Inaugural ASEAN Defence Ministers Meeting (ADMM)
Framework Agreement on Visa Exemption

2007   Singapore Declaration on Climate Change, Energy and the Environment
Declaration towards One Caring and Sharing Community
ASEAN Committee of Permanent Representatives created
AEC Blueprint
Declaration on Protection and Promotion of Rights of Migrant Workers
Declaration on Acceleration of the Establishment of the ASEAN Community by 2015
ASEAN Charter

2008   Statement on the ASEAN Charter

2009   Declaration on [ASEAN] Intergovernmental Commission on Human Rights (AICHR)
APSC Blueprint
ASCC Blueprint
Roadmap for an ASEAN Community (2009–2015)

2010   Third Protocol on Amending Treaty of Amity and Cooperation
ASEAN Commission on the Promotion and Protection of the Rights of Women and Children created

2011   Bali Concord III (RCEP/AFEED)
Agreement on the Establishment of the ASEAN Coordinating Centre for Humanitarian Assistance on Disaster Management
Ha Noi Declaration on the Adoption of the Master Plan on ASEAN Connectivity

2012   ASEAN Comprehensive Investment Agreement enacted
        Joint Declaration of the ASEAN Defense Ministers on Enhancing
        ASEAN Unity for a Harmonized and Secure Community
        First ASEAN Ministerial Meeting on Women
        ASEAN Human Rights Declaration
2015   First Dateline for Achieving the ASEAN Community

Appendix 3

Timeline of key ASEAN+3 milestones
Azmi Mat Akhir and Alice D. Ba

1977	First ASEAN-Japan Summit
1997	First ASEAN–Republic of Korea Summit
	First ASEAN–China Summit
	First (Informal) Meeting of ASEAN+3
1999	First East Asia Cooperation/ASEAN+3 Summit (Joint Statement on East Asia Cooperation)
	First APT Finance Ministers and Central Bank Governors Meeting
2000	First Meeting of ASEAN Economic Ministers+3
	First ASEAN+3 Foreign Ministers Meeting
	Chiang Mai Initiative
2001	First ASEAN Agriculture and Forestry Ministers+3 Meeting
	First ASEAN+3 Labour Ministers Meeting
	East Asian Vision Group (EAVG) Report: "Towards an East Asian Community: Region of Peace, Prosperity and Progress"
2002	First ASEAN+3 Tourism Ministers Meeting
	First ASEAN+3 Environment Ministers Meeting
	Final report of East Asian Study Group (EASG)
	Asian Bond Market Initiative (ABMI)
2003	Establishment of ASEAN+3 Finance Cooperation
	Declaration on Revitalising Tourism for ASEAN+3
	APT meeting of Ministers of Cultures and Arts
	APT meeting of Ministers of Social Welfare and Development
	Track 1.5 East Asia Forum (EAF)
	Track 2 Network of East Asian Think Tanks (NEAT)
2004	First ASEAN+3 Ministerial Meeting on Transnational Crime (AMMTC+3)
	First ASEAN+3 Health Ministers Meeting
	First ASEAN+3 Ministerial Meeting for Social Welfare and Development
	First ASEAN+3 Telecommunications and IT Ministers Meeting (TELMIN)
	APT Ministerial Meeting on Transnational Crime
	APT Energy Ministers Meeting

2005	First East Asia summit
2007	Declaration on East Asian Energy Community
	East Asia Cooperation and the APT Cooperation Work Plan (2007–2017)
	APT Ministers Meeting on Youth
2008	Economic Research Institute for ASEAN and East Asia
	Asian Bond Market Initiative (ABMI) Roadmap
2009	Guidelines to implement the Second Joint Statement on East Asia Cooperation and the APT Cooperation Work Plan (2007–2017)
2010	Joint Declaration on APT Civil Service Cooperation
	ASEAN+3 Comprehensive Strategy on Food Security and Bioenergy Development (APTCS-FSBD) Framework and Strategic Plan of Action on Food and Energy Security (SAP-FES) 2010–2013
	Chiang Mai Initiative on Multilateralization (CMIM)
	Inclusion of United States and Russia into EAS
2011	Agreement on the ASEAN+3 Emergency Rice Reserve (APTERR)
	ASEAN+3 Macroeconomic Research Office (AMRO)
2012	Chiang Mai Initiative Multilateralisation (CMIM) Fund increased from US$120 billion to US$240 billion
	APT Plan of Action on Education: 2010–2017
	ASEAN+3 Conference on Civil Service Matters Work Plan (2012–2015)
	Work Plan on Enhancing APT Cooperation in Culture
	Work Plan on Enhancing APT Cooperation through Information and Media 2012–2017
	Work Plan to Implement the Asian Bond Market Initiative (ABMI) New Roadmap
	APT Emergency Rice Reserve Agreement
	Report of East Asia Vision Group
2013	Strengthening efforts to prevent and combat transnational crimes
	Revised East Asia Cooperation and the APT Cooperation Work Plan 2013–2017
	Asian Bond Market Initiative New Roadmap

Appendix 4

Timeline of other selected institutional developments
Alice D. Ba

1988	ASEAN Institutes of Strategic and International Studies (ASEAN-ISIS) Network formally established
1989	Asia-Pacific Economic Cooperation (APEC)
1992	Greater Mekong Subregion (GMS)
1993	Indonesia-Malaysia-Thailand Growth Triangle (IMT-GS) launched
	Council for Security Cooperation in the Asia Pacific (CSCAP)
1994	ASEAN Regional Forum (ARF)
	Brunei Darussalam-Indonesia-Malaysia-The Philippines East ASEAN Growth Area (BIMP-EAGA) launched
	Indonesia-Malaysia-Singapore Growth Triangle (IMS-GT or SIJORI) launched
1996	First Asia Europe Summit (ASEM)
	ASEAN Mekong Basin Development Cooperation (AMBDC)
1999	First Forum for East Asia-Latin America Cooperation Senior Officials Meeting
2001	First Ministerial Meeting of the Forum for East Asia-Latin America Cooperation (FEALAC)
2002	First Asia Cooperation Dialogue (ACD)
	First Shangri-La Dialogue (IISS Asia Security Summit)
	Declaration on the Conduct of Parties in the South China Sea (DOC)
	ASEAN-China Framework Agreement on Comprehensive Economic Cooperation (ACFTA) signed
	First Greater Mekong Subregion Summit
2003	Roadmap for Monetary and Financial Integration of ASEAN
2005	Trans-Pacific Strategic Economic Partnership Agreement
	ASEAN-Republic of Korea Framework Agreement on Comprehensive Economic Cooperation signed
	First East Asia Summit
	Eyes in the Sky (EiS) launched
	ASEAN Agreement on Disaster Management and Emergency Response (AADMER)

2006	Regional Cooperation Agreement on Combating Piracy and Armed Robbery (RECAAP) entered into force
2008	First China-Japan-Republic of Korea Trilateral Summit
	ASEAN-Japan Comprehensive Economic Partnership signed
2010	Trans-Pacific Partnership (TPP) negotiations launched
	ASEAN Defense Ministers Meeting Plus (ADMM +)
	ASEAN Agreement on Disaster Management and Emergency Response
2011	Establishment of Trilateral Cooperation Secretariat (TCS)
	ASEAN Coordinating Centre for Humanitarian Assistance
2012	Regional Comprehensive Economic Partnership (RCEP) negotiations launched
	ASEAN Humanitarian Centre opens
2013	First Governing Council Meeting of ASEAN Institute for Peace and Reconciliation
2015	China–Republic of Korea FTA signed
	Trans-Pacific Partnership (TPP) negotiations concluded

Appendix 5

ASEAN and Free Trade Agreements/Negotiations in East Asia

Alice D. Ba and Emmanuel Balogun

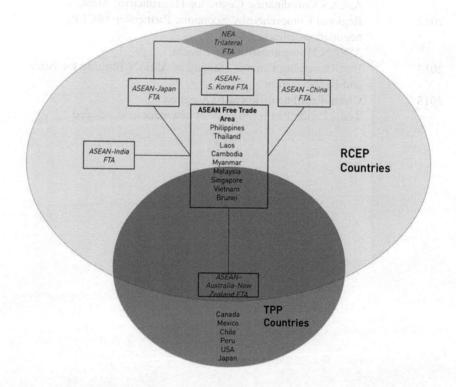

Note: The NEA Trilateral FTA refers to the China–Japan–[Republic of] Korea FTA still under negotiation.

Appendix 6

ASEAN centrality and East Asia's institutional architecture
Alice D. Ba and Emmanuel Balogun

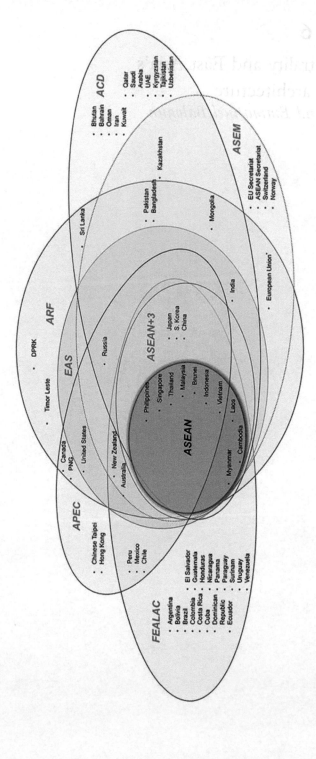

Note: EU members participate as individual states in ASEM and participate in the ARF through their EU membership

Index